# Particular Friendships.
# A Convent Memoir

# Particular Friendships: A Convent Memoir

Kathleen J. Waites

**To order additional copies of this book, contact:**
Xlibris Corporation
1-888-795-4274
www.Xlibris.com
Orders@Xlibris.com
29471

# Contents

# Acknowledgements

Writing is a decidedly solitary occupation, but that is only part of the story since the writer also revisits her writing through the eyes of others. I am fortunate to belong to a community of friends who are both readers and writers and have, at various stages of this manuscript, generously shared their feedback and expertise. My sincere thanks for his astute suggestions in the early stages of my book go to Steven Alford, as well as to Suzanne Ferriss for her splendid edits and suggestions for the title. Were it not for the unflagging enthusiasm and keen literary eye and pen of Karen Tolchin, this story would not be making its debut in public. She is a fan of one with the heart of many.

I am especially grateful to Kandis for admonishing me not to give up. Many thanks also go to NSU students Maire Cuneo, Danielle Garcia, and Liz Harbaugh for graciously agreeing to pose as nuns for the cover photo.

Lastly, thank you to my family for offering me unqualified encouragement and for setting my heart—and my story—on the right path.

The events in this story are true. However, in order to protect the privacy of certain individuals I took creative license in changing the names of some characters, creating composites of others, and dramatizing some scenes, as well as by altering the name of the religious order.

*This is my letter to the World*
*That never wrote to Me—*
*The simple News that Nature told—*
*With tender Majesty*

*Her Message is committed*
*To Hands I cannot see—*
*For love of Her-Sweet countrymen—*
*Judge tenderly—of Me*

—Emily Dickinson


*Bookends' Theme*

*Time it was and what a time it was,*
*A time of innocence a time of confidences.*

*Long ago it must be, I have a photograph*
*Preserve your memories, They're all that's left you.*

—Paul Simon, 1968

*The three shadowy figures are separated by a body of water—not a lake but a river, like the Delaware River that, at certain points, allows you to see New Jersey from the Pennsylvania shore. I wade into the water from the Pennsylvania side. I am calling out to the figure drifting downriver, strangely prostrate without a raft or flotation device in view. She needs help. She is in distress. She is surely on the verge of drowning. The river's current takes her slowly, steadily away. She appears resigned. Yet I sense her speechless cry. The pale face is placid and compliant and marks a strong contrast to the black rigid dress. At some point in the dream, I recognize the drowning figure as my convent friend Angela, fully clothed in her nun's garb. I am hesitant, uncertain. I feel unable to swim and am, therefore, helpless, even though I am certain that I can swim. Paralysis has set in. I struggle to speak, to move, to call out for help, but I am held fast, as if by an invisible steel clamp. That's when the third figure appears on the other side of the river waving and hallooing. I hear sound but no words, and I desperately want to respond and enlist her help. But Ann Rose—for I now recognize another friend from my convent days—sees only me and not my distressed friend Angela. Something else: Ann Rose can signal and shriek, but I realize that she too is immobilized by some sort of weight attached to her back, giving her the appearance of a humpback. I am electrically connected to both the drowning figure and the injured one but remain fatally separated. If only I could move. I am perspiring, breathing heavily, suffocating in inertia. I am poised to explode. Suddenly, my right arm is loosened and shoots up, removing something heavy from the upper part of my body.*

I blink my tears into the pale dawn under the loosened cover. It's the same dream always.

# Fervor (1965-1969)

Memory is a shaky agent. In recall, details blur, facts elude, and truth may escape. And yet, as I reach back into my convent past, I know that the truth of my experience sits and waits to be revealed, like a new star or planet, and memory is my only recourse.

The Roman Catholic Church is a mighty castle with many hidden doors and sacrosanct chambers, and all who gain entrance to it are required to wear the veil of secrecy and silence. As a young woman of eighteen, I earned that privilege, vowed obedience, and wore the veil. I remained faithful to the church and kept its secrets at great personal cost.

From the earliest age, I had been reared for such faithfulness. I learned the virtues of obedience, renunciation, and silence. In all matters the church was infallible, and a religious vocation for a man or a woman was considered God's highest calling. A short summer after high-school graduation, I ended my steady relationship with Denny, much to his bafflement, and, no small measure of my own, quit my job and prepared for my departure from the world.

Over my last weekend at home my mom and dad took me on a special good-bye outing to see *The Sound of Music* at a posh double-decker theater in the big city and I feasted on the special attention they gave me, minus the usual clamoring of brothers and sisters. My older brother and I had grown up watching *The Bells of St. Mary's*, *The Nun's Story*, and *Heaven Knows Mr. Allison* on late night television, so it wasn't unusual to see a motion picture about a Catholic nun. But Maria, the singing nun, was special. Pure and passionate, beautiful and happy, she embodied what I aspired to be. Swept away by the fervor of my religious vocation, I became so totally absorbed in this image that the demise of her vocation in the end was completely lost on me. How could I possibly have anticipated my own?

I went into the convent with the wide and romantic eyes of a child. Determined to give up the world and all its pleasures for the remainder of my life, I welcomed the vows of poverty, chastity, and obedience, and I looked forward to a missionary's life of serving God by loving and helping others. In my four years of living as a convent insider, I witnessed the best of what humans can accomplish when they place service to God and others above their own desires. I also saw the wreckage caused by those who abused their unchecked authority as God's representatives. My experience left me altered; my dream vanished. Such perverse and sinister things occurred in this sacred place, and I had no way to frame them. One friend was dead. Another confided that she had been molested. And one evening at midnight, I stood naked looking out the window of a darkened convent bedroom, painfully aware of my own expulsion from Eden. Yet as always, fear, repression, and silence prevailed since no one dared to question and speak openly, let alone challenge authority within the sacred walls.

I cannot provide a purely objective account of what happened in the convent, for I am not a machine that stores incontrovertible data but a person. I am equipped with integrity, born of the humble beginnings of hardworking, honest people. They got up and looked each new miserable day straight in the eye. "We know who we are, not much; we know what we have, not much; we know who we are, so we know who you are." Insight was their gift to me, and it has served me well.

I can only relate what I know, and what I, along with a few others, experienced. I trust in memory's pictures and in the images that, unsolicited, spring from the deepest part of myself. I believe in my instincts—not the ever-changing emotions but the deep-down, in-the-gut reading of people and situations. Life has taught me to rely on internal barometers. When I go wrong, it's not that they fail me, but that, for a variety of reasons, I overrule or fail to heed them. I certainly cannot claim knowledge of any grand truth. But as I reach back into the well of memory, I do believe that some truth may be found in memory's offspring—in the dream, in the image, in the gut.

With this story, which took me some thirty years to work up the courage to tell, I seek neither to damn nor to exonerate, but merely to uncover. To do this, I must reach back across the canyon of time and make the past the present. I return to the mind and spirit of an eighteen-year-old innocent who joined the hordes of other nun and priest aspirants in the 1960s and answered the church's call to be God's soldier.

This story is for all of us who lived it—and lost what we most cherished.

# No Turning Back (1965)

Denny understood me, or at least, he accepted me. I wasn't like most of the other boy-crazy, girly girls, all made up and flirty and hanging on my boyfriend's arm. My tight-knit group of high-school girlfriends sometimes came first with me, and he never begrudged my time with them. But he was my boyfriend, and I was his girlfriend, and we were lucky to be best friends as well. Denny and I had been together for two years ever since we met in the summer of '63. It was the summer after our sophomore year of high school and he was already a busboy at the Howard Johnson's restaurant when I got my first big-time job as a waitress. By the time that senior year drew to a close, I was making plans that not only excluded Denny, but they also terminated him. The end. Poor guy. He didn't get this nun thing at all. How could he? He wasn't even a Catholic and, besides, I didn't really understand it myself. A young lifetime of Catholicism and hard knocks urged me to take what appeared to be a strange and sudden turn away from the budding world of sex, drugs, and rock 'n' roll in favor of a chaste life in a Roman Catholic convent where I would serve God by helping others. When I finally decided that I wanted to be a nun, well, that was it. My mind was made up. I tried to explain my decision to Denny one evening in early July by returning the ring he had given me, a black-and-white pearl surrounded by a cluster of diamonds. I loved that ring. It was the loveliest, most expensive piece of jewelry I had ever owned, and I didn't want to give it back, but I knew I had to start giving up "things" as well as people. That was the deal in religious life and I intended to follow through on it.

We were sitting in Denny's car in the back parking lot reserved for employees at Howard Johnson's on the Pennsylvania Turnpike, where I was a waitress and my boyfriend was a busboy. I had just punched out of work. Denny had driven there to meet me because I told him that I needed to talk. I don't know why I chose this time and place to tell him. It was pretty stupid, I guess, breaking up with a guy in the same place where we had first met, but I didn't want him to come to my house and I couldn't very well put off telling him any longer. Besides, he had known for some time that something was up. The car windows were rolled down, but the air was still and moist, and our clothes were melting into the seats, baked from the brutal summer sun. My hands were sweating and I had to do something with them, so I lit up a Winston for support. My mind went kind of blank at first, as if I were in a dark tunnel and hearing things from a distance, but I heard snatches of my own prepared announcement: "love you, but," "have decided," "convent," "called by God." Beads of perspiration started bubbling on his forehead as he listened, eyes glazed and focused straight ahead. Was I making any sense at all? I couldn't really tell. The thoughts in my head made a whole lot more sense before they actually hit the air waves. "Please understand," I heard myself plead as I emerged from the tunnel. "I have to do this. It's . . . it's my vocation. It's a religious vocation. Do you see? I feel that God is calling me to a life of service and I have to respond." It's another way of saying, "It's out of my hands. God's responsible."

Denny's neck snapped backward as he turned and glared at me. "What the hell's that supposed to mean? What about me? I love you. I thought you loved me." Denny was fuming, but his firestorms, unlike mine, were always short-lived. He finally turned his tortured face away from me, as all his anger settled into the frantic hands that gripped the steering wheel of his beloved blue '56 Mercury, the thing that he loved best in the world next to me. They were crying out to be rescued. Taken aback by the force of his pain, I wavered and reconsidered: maybe I am wrong; maybe I am supposed to spend my life with Denny. He is so earnest and sweet, and he really does love me. With a sidelong glance, I surveyed the feathery wheat-colored hair, neatly combed and lying casually to the right of his forehead; the narrow face; and strong, chiseled chin. His blue gray eyes looked at me uncertainly, like a pensive sky that couldn't decide whether it would be cloudy or clear. Am I crazy? I'm the girl that never attracted boys very easily, and here I am taking a pass on this six-foot-tall hunk who loves *me*.

"I do love you." I reached over and gently laid my hand over his to reassure him, to smother the anguish that I couldn't stand to see. Wrong move. He lifted his head slowly and fixed me with a pleading look. My touch had given him hope.

"Then you won't go? You won't leave me?" Our eyes met and locked for the last time. An epiphany. Neither of us knew until that moment how fixed my decision was.

"I have to at least try this. I don't really understand it myself," I offered haltingly. "I just know it's something I have to do. I . . . I . . . I'm sorry," I whispered feebly as I slipped the ring off my finger and pressed it in his stiff palm, forcing his hand from the steering wheel. Livid once again, Denny pushed my hand away from his.

"It's Sister Bernice, isn't it? She put this idea in your head. She's turned you against me. Why? What did I do?" I wanted to collapse in tears, surrender to his need for me—for us—to be together. I longed to respond to his yearning, too fixed in my decision to feel my own. That would come later. Time was like a wave, going out and back, out and back, as we repeated the same demands, the same explanations, going back and forth and getting nowhere. I defended Sister Bernice, my mentor and high-school English teacher, but it was useless. He was adamant that my religious vocation was all her doing. Blame, I guess, is just a way of trying to make sense out of something inexplicable. Our conversation became trapped, like a fly between the windowpane and screen with nowhere to go. Defeated at last, he gave me a long, sorrowful look, fingering the symbol of our love between his forefinger and thumb before throwing it into the tall weeds bordering the deserted lot of Howard Johnson's. There was nothing more to say. I jerked the door latch, giving it a good push. It was heavy and prone to getting stuck, but this time it gave pretty easily. Dazed, I stumbled out the door and, through blurry eyes I watched a souped-up Mercury roar toward the road, kicking up a trail of dust in its wake. I had to find that ring; where had it dropped? I scanned the edge of the dusty lot, hoping it had bounced against the weeds and into the clearing. Nothing doing. The brush was too dense. I would never find it, and yet it didn't seem right to let it be thrown away like that, even though I knew I could not keep it. Maybe that's how Denny felt about me, as if I had just thrown him away. Sadness doesn't approach how I felt about losing the ring that day. About losing Denny. Forever.

Here I was, about to make a radical, permanent choice in my life. I was just eighteen. What the hell was I thinking?

Two months later, I traded in my blue jeans for the long black outfit of the Nazarene Missionary Sisters. But my story didn't start that day or the day that I said good-bye to my high-school sweetheart. Beginnings are not so clear-cut; endings are little more than beginnings; and life is not a ruler but a collection of rings—one ring inextricably bound to another, and that one to the next, and so on and so on, until all are somehow connected. So my story, from 1965 to 1969, is not a chapter but a ring in my life, and if I can train my memory like a camera, perhaps I can cast the illusion of separateness and capture the weight, the texture, the circumference of this singular ring. To do this, I have to return to an earlier ring.

*     *     *

I was never especially religious while growing up, although my working-class parents made extraordinary sacrifices to push all seven of us children through the Catholic schools, so I can certainly claim to have been *schooled* as religious. Upon high-school graduation, each of us was feted by my Irish mother's considerable bragging and the proverbial raising of the American flag. Along the way, we received the full regimen of Catholic school education which meant that besides the catechism lessons that went with reading, writing, and arithmetic every Monday through Friday came Mass on Sunday and on all the holy days of obligation throughout the liturgical year. Not permitted to eat or drink from midnight on Saturday until Communion at Mass on Sunday morning, we also had to settle for fish sticks or Campbell's tomato soup on meatless Friday nights. Such were the rituals of the old-fashioned, pre-ecumenical Roman Catholic Church of my formative years.

The watchwords were renunciation and repentance, renunciation and repentance, renunciation and repentance. This message was transmitted especially during Lent when the priest got all decked out in purple and stood in front of a cross draped in black cloth looking for all the world like a continually flashing traffic signal bearing the message: "Remember, sinner, Christ suffered and died for your sins. Now you must suffer and die in small ways in order to earn your redemption." And so I learned to deny myself simple, worldly pleasures and offer them up to God, and when Easter Sunday finally rolled around, I felt pretty good about my little sacrifices and the points I had earned toward redemption in the afterlife. For one solid month every year, I strove to be a model Catholic schoolgirl. I vowed not to fight with my brothers and sisters; I strove heartily to obey my parents; I even gave up my favorite TV show, *The Adventures of Ozzie and Harriet*, valiantly ignoring my crush on Ricky Nelson. And I filled my personal cardboard mission box with all the small change I normally saved up to buy the small bag of potato chips and bottle of Coca-Cola—snacks that my mom couldn't afford to buy for us kids. If we were lucky, the most we could expect by way of a treat during the non-Lenten season was the half gallon of Breyer's vanilla, chocolate, and strawberry ice cream that Mom got at the Acme Supermarket on payday, and seven eager kids always made short shrift of that.

I often whined about how deprived we were, particularly compared to my friend Karen, whose mom bought a case of Coca-Cola and a huge brown and gold tin of Charles potato chips every week. And they only had four kids! But my mom just waved away my selfish complaint and pointed out how much better off we were than those woeful brown and yellow faces that stared back at me from the front side of the Lenten missionary-collection box. "Hah, you think you have it tough?" she'd chide, holding the box aloft. Then she used her index finger like a pointer to complete her lesson on *real* poverty while the faces of the Indian, African, and Chinese children bobbed and waved to the rhythm of her vehement sermon on real suffering. "These children know what *tough* is, and God bless them; they're heathens to boot! Going without Coca-Cola and chips is the least of their problems."

She must have been right too because Sister Malachy, our fourth-grade teacher, showed us pamphlets with pictures of the poor, heathen children with bony limbs and gaunt faces and the missionaries who were trying to save them. The nuns looked so serene and beautiful in the pictures. They leaned affectionately toward the sad-faced multicolored foreign children, their arms clasped around them and gazing out at us, as if to say, "Do you see how lucky you are by comparison, you fortunate Catholic schoolchildren?" The kind-looking missionary sisters in the pamphlets didn't seem anything like the cranky nuns who taught us in school every day. When I dreamed about growing up and being a nun and married to God, I vowed that I would be kind and good and beautifully happy, just like the missionary sisters. I would gladly give up everything to help save God's heathen children, but I didn't want anything to do with the nuns who taught us in school.

Not all of them were harsh and ill-humored. Some were even nice. But the nice ones were fewer and far between, and they didn't leave as much of an impression as the nasty nuns did. In the fourth grade at Immaculate Conception School, I studied my Latin grammar and stumbled through *The Odyssey*. My public school friends—we called them "publics"—didn't have to learn to read in a dead language *or* obey strict nuns. For us Catholic school kids, discipline came second only to religion; and rulers, open palms, and clickers were the weapons of choice. Armed with her ruler, Sister Malachy swooped down the aisle to rap my knuckles when I turned my head during a catechism lesson to steal a glance at Cathy Hess's book because I couldn't read the page number or the lesson on the blackboard. (Later that year, following an eye exam at the school,

I discovered that I was nearsighted. I sobbed on the walk home from school that day, worried about having to tell mom and dad that I needed glasses. Even at that age, I was well aware that money was tight.) Then there was Sister Thomasine who liked to swat the back of my head with her thick palm if I left my book at home or talked in class: "There will be no talking in this room unless called upon. Is that absolutely clear, Miss Waites?" Spittle flew from her pursed lips, and her voice had this way of burrowing right through you like a drill. But it was the sound of Sister Paul Anne's clicker that I dreaded the most. When she came charging from the front of the room to pull her next suspect out of his seat by the ear, I'd wrap my trembling legs around the wrought-iron legs that anchored my wooden school desk to the floor, wishing I could transform into a swirl of energy like Mr. Clean on the TV ads and disappear into the ink-hole on my desk. Even if I wasn't the kid that was singled out and marched back to the coat closet to stand for the remainder of the school day, I was ashamed and terrified.

The school nuns didn't look very happy, and they certainly didn't seem to enjoy teaching children very much. My dream of becoming a nun when I grew up was not inspired by them. In my imagination the missionary nuns were completely different, an image born of the pictures on the side of the Lenten mission boxes, in which the nuns looked deliriously happy to be doing God's work with the heathen children in distant countries like Ethiopia and India. That's the kind of nun that I would grow up to be, I vowed, although I wasn't too sure about the faraway-places part of the plan and I figured we probably had enough poor heathens in our own country to look after. I was certain that I would be kind and beautiful and understanding and I would never be impatient or mean like the school nuns. I would treat everyone the same. One of the things that really annoyed me about the school nuns was that most of them favored the "good" kids. The "good" kids were usually the ones who came to school all sparkly and clean and made the honors' list year in and out and never ever got detention or bad marks on their report cards. My older brother was without a doubt one of the top ten "good" kids. All the nuns loved Michael. An altar boy with dark wavy hair and liquid brown eyes, he also made straight A's, even in conduct. (I usually only made a C in conduct.) My handsome, smart, and well-behaved altar-boy brother was the darling of the nice nuns and mean nuns alike, and since I wasn't particularly good or smart and I was only a girl who could never be an altar boy, I didn't have a chance of winning that game. Instead, I got the same tired question and look of astonishment as I followed him from one grade to the next, and from the very first roll call: "Kathleen Waites?" "Yes, S'ter. Present, S'ter."

"Are *you* Michael *Waites*' sister?" (In other words, "How come you aren't as smart and charming and outgoing as he is? Why is it that the other nuns haven't talked about you too in glowing terms?")

"Yes, S'ter," I'd squeak, slinking down into my seat and clenching my folded, cartridge-ink-stained fingers with my head bowed. I know, I know, I know, I'd think. There is no comparison. I'm just Michael Waites' mousy sister with average grades and a C in conduct. As far as the nuns were concerned, it didn't matter that I could lay claim to being the best player on the C.Y.O.'s (Catholic Youth Organization) girls' basketball, track, and softball teams from the fourth grade on either. Girls' sports never counted for much in Catholic school.

In my family, there was no escaping nuns, Latin, or Catholic school—no getting away from priests, Mass, or confession. And being Catholic didn't stop at the church door or the classroom for us. Catholicism was alive and well and practiced in all the traditional ways in our home, and the family rosary was a biggie because as my mother often proclaimed, "I see the changes comin' down the pike. I wasn't born yesterday. Ecumenical schmecumenical. The Roman Catholic Church can change all it wants to, but the good old-fashioned rosary will never be dead in my house!" This sacred family ritual required that we kneel together on the hardwood floor every night during the months of May and October to recite the rosary together as a family. My dad had erected a special wooden shelf in the upper corner of our living room to hold the blue and white Blessed Mother statue so that we could look up at her as we prayed. Good Catholic parents understood that the church had set aside these months to honor Mary, the queen of heaven and God's mother. I can't say that the practice strengthened my faith exactly, although I tried my hardest to look at the statue while concentrating on the words in the prayers represented by each of the beads: the Credo, the Glory Be to the Father, and the Hail Mary. But Anne Margaret, two years younger than I and the brat of our clan, would stick her tongue out and make faces at me behind my dad's back as he piously led the prayers, so of course, I had to pinch her. She was a saucy kid who deserved a good pinch now and again, but Rosemary usually rolled her eyes and "tsked" in disgust, as if to say, "Grow up, you two!" That was an odd response coming from a sister who was four years my junior. But she had always acted as though she were the firstborn. Prim, proper, and imperious, Rosemary cultivated a sense of entitlement. She was cute, smart, and well behaved and the nuns didn't hold it against her that she was only a girl, so she went around with her "nose up in the air"—as my mother would say when referring to such persons. "Oh, that one," she'd say, pointing out the stuck-up neighbor or relative. "She thinks she's the Queen of Sheba. Harrumph." So the rest of us latched on to that name for Rosemary, our very own Queen of Sheba.

Despite my parents' good intentions, the family-rosary ritual seemed to bring out the worst in us kids, especially my younger brothers. My baby sister, Reenie, was usually hanging on my mom's shoulder trying to ignore my boisterous younger brothers, Thomas and Gerry, who were busy earning points for purgatory. As my mom described it, trouble was Thomas's middle name. When he wasn't instigating fights in the schoolyard or at the neighborhood sandlot, Thomas was playing soldiers or cowboys and Indians in the house with Gerry and making my mom crazy. His cherubic blue eyes, translucent skin, and curly bronze hair rendered him disarmingly adorable and innocent, but he was a regular Dennis the Menace; that's what Mom called him when she was talking on the phone with Aunt Rose. His adorable looks were a good cover for him as he charged into adolescence. Four years his junior, baby Gerry was his adoring sidekick. Most family photos found Gerry—all angles and bones and the blonde blue-eyed baby of the family—looking inquiringly at Thomas like a midget soldier waiting for orders. When my ten-year-old cousin Gerard came to live with us after first his dad and then his mom died, he was fast enlisted in the regiment of little rascals. Our family now had eight kids and no more space or resources than we had before, but, as Mom always reminded us, we were lucky compared to Gerard who lost his parents and his siblings in a lightning strike of misfortune.

In a house with too many people and too little space, Gerard found a new home, and the three boys found a ready-made coconspirator of trouble. Throughout the rosary recitation, the boys poked and punched one another until my mother went 'round the horn giving each one of us a slap on the back of the head in between her quick jaunts to the kitchen to prepare the next day's school lunches. Her boisterous and fervent "Holy Mary, Mother of God, pray for us sinners now and at the hour of . . ." trailed away into the kitchen, only to return with a robust "Hail Mary, full of Grace, the Lord is with Thee . . ." a few minutes later. Barely five feet tall with just the right amount of maternal plumpness, my mother could, on such hallowed occasions, summon all five feet of her compact frame to loom large and threateningly in order to extort the correct behavior from her brood. All except for Michael, of course, who didn't much need disciplining because he was either kneeling at the front alongside my dad or else going away from the house to be the altar boy at the church. I, for one, liked Mom's stern look of disapproval even less than the sting of her slap. Her chin arched in the air, she'd stare at the guilty party who was pinching or making faces with a sideways glance, her flashing blue eyes darkening into pinpoints of black, as if to say, "I *know* you can't possibly be doing what it looks like you're doing." My mother had that way about her, always letting us know she was on to us and giving us an out at the same time. Usually, it left you feeling guilty rather than annoyed at being caught. Guilt was one of the church's most effective tools, and my mother learned to wield it quite skillfully.

In spite of the constant reminder of my faults at home and at school, I liked to think of myself as being on the road to holiness, especially after the rosary ritual was completed and I had the sore knees to show for it. (It took about forty minutes. I timed it. It was much more manageable, though, than the three-hour ordeal on Good Friday that found Michael, the priest aspirant, and me, his altar-boy gopher, kneeling fervently in the attic from noon until three o'clock while trying to picture Christ our Savior on the cross.)

No, I don't think my decision to join the convent turned on faith or religion exactly, although I breathed in the mystique and practices of my parents' Irish Catholic heritage and wouldn't know who I was without them. Mostly, I learned how sinful I was and how guilty to feel. It wasn't long before the liturgical prayer "mea culpa, mea culpa, mea maxima culpa" ("through my fault, through my fault, through my most grievous fault") became my unconscious mantra.

A picture of a baby appears before me, reminding me of a childhood lost well before its flowering. I don't recognize this forlorn child with sea eyes separated by a prematurely furrowed brow and clutching a squeezy toy for dear life. But her expression speaks plainly enough: "Something's missing here; I will need to make up for it somehow." That's about as close as I can come to explaining the decision to give up my young life to serve God. I guess I wanted to fill in my blank spaces with meaning and purpose. In a large family with insufficient resources, we went without a lot more than food, clothing, and material things. A mechanic by trade, my father indentured himself to a hateful factory job with a steady paycheck and tried to fend off the bill collectors. "Birth control" was a naughty word for good Catholics, so my mother produced a baby roughly every two years and my parents' dream house in the suburbs of Philadelphia promptly shrank. A veteran of World War II, my dad expected to work hard for his American dream of owning a little house in the country, so its loss came as quite a blow. Our small cluster of Bristol homes was swallowed up by Levittown, the ticky-tacky suburban development that defined the postwar landscape and, like a ravenous monster, devoured all the woods and farms in sight and, with them, my father's dream of a peaceful country life. After the sticks turned into the burbs, our small development ended up on the poor side of town.

While my mother was having babies, my brother mothered me, and together, we mothered the younger ones as well as we could. Our blue-collar father disappeared each day and many nights into the shadowy world of work to return only as the foreboding arm of discipline. From time to time, he enjoyed roughhousing with his brood after a few beers or took us on that rare family trip to the Jersey shore for crabbing, but he was largely absent by necessity. I missed him. I also missed my mother, who was too busy running a household with insufficient resources to provide any of us with the special attention that all children crave. For a long time, I fooled myself into thinking that the gaps I longed to fill existed in the lives of the poor children that I intended to love and serve through my religious vocation. As I look back, I see that they were my own. But that realization only came later. The visible, identifiable factors in my drastic choice of a religious vocation at age eighteen revealed themselves to me much sooner.

I didn't have much to give up that day, September 8, 1965. One of seven children in a poor Irish Catholic household, I also knew I would not be sorely missed. My three sisters would no doubt compete for my cubbyhole of space in the attic-turned-bedroom in which six of us slept. I cherished the solitude of the corner where my bed was positioned beneath a window. A slice of the sky was just visible between our house and the roof of the grocery store that grew up next door just a few yards from our home, much to my father's dismay. But the narrow attic space afforded me just enough of a view to study the stars in a clear summer sky or watch a winter-snow dance. I could open *my* own window too, allowing me to light up the forbidden cigarette and blow the smoke out the window. I thought I was pretty clever until my mom threw the door open and yelled up the stairs, "WHO THE HELL IS SMOKING UP THERE? YOU'D BETTER NOT BE SMOKING IN THIS HOUSE!" (Yelling was commonplace in our cramped household of disobedient and quarreling children.) She never actually climbed the stairs to discover me or my sister Anne Margaret in the forbidden act. She just wanted to let us know that she was "on" to us without actually having to *catch* us. As I've said, she was funny that way, catching us but letting us off the hook at the same time. It was a good tactic because it inspired guilt and worked more effectively than the threat of Dad's belt (which, to my knowledge, was never actually used). As products of the Catholic-school system, we were all primed to be guilt prone anyway.

Michael, my oldest brother and the jewel of my parents' marital crown, had already gone off to seminary by the time I was thinking about joining the convent. I walked feebly behind him, followed by five others who felt similarly unworthy of following in the saintlike footsteps of the brother and priest-to-be. After my departure, Anne Margaret was prepared to annex my precious bedroom territory and add it to her own. She and I quarreled constantly, mostly because of the liberties she took with *my* clothing, purchased with *my* own money, which I earned with *my* baby-sitting, ironing, and waitressing jobs. She never asked before borrowing my skirts or blouses, and when the article in question finally reappeared, it was always torn or missing a button. We nurtured a feud for as long as I can remember and for no particular reason that I can think of, except that we were so different. I was athletic and shy and didn't get into trouble outside the home. She was outgoing, boy crazy, and prone to mischief. An ordinary brunette with hazel eyes, I was considered "cute," but she was a blonde beauty with eyes the color of the Caribbean Sea. Two years my junior, Anne Margaret reached womanhood about two years before my lean body grew breasts. By the time she turned twelve, she was socially active and popular in a way that was never possible for her socially inept older sister. But her desire for acceptance and excitement introduced her to a "fast" crowd that frequently led her into trouble. My dad routinely grounded her, but to no avail. Once, after being grounded for two weeks as a result of breaking the 10:00 p.m. curfew, she jumped out of the second-story bedroom window so that she could meet her friends at the local swimming pool. When my father found her missing upon his arrival from work, he stormed down to the pool, whisked her away, and sentenced her to a month of confinement in the house. A month was an awfully long time during summer vacation in a house without an air conditioner or phone privileges. But my sister was sassy and acted as if she could not care less. In my mother's Irish vernacular, Anne Margaret was "fresh," a "corker," or a "bugger." Whatever she was, she sure had a knack for getting into trouble and infuriating me.

One school night around midnight, I dragged my weary sixteen-year-old body up the stairs after a long night of waitressing at Howard Johnson's restaurant, only to find that Anne Margaret's friend, Ann Marie, was spending the night. An hour passed after I collapsed into bed, and they were still giggling and fooling around. First, I pleaded nicely, "Would you guys please be quiet now and turn off the light? I'm really beat, and we have to get up for school tomorrow." The giggling turned into guffawing. The light stayed on. More murmuring. "Shut up!" I snapped, "I'm tired!" A moment of silence followed by escalating snickers. "Okay, that's it," I fumed. I had had it. An adrenaline rush of anger catapulted me out of my bed and across to the other side of the attic. A figure darted toward the stairway, and I found myself racing down the stairs at the heels of Anne Marie who tore open the front door and headed home through the high school football field across from our house. She ran quite fast for a chubby girl more than twice my size. I got halfway across the field myself, panting and breathless from yelling after her before I stopped, exhausted and my fury spent. I trudged back up the infamous "golden stairs" to the attic bedroom. ("Up the golden stairs" was my mother's cue for bedtime. "All right," she'd bark from her perpetual post in the kitchen, "turn that damn TV off. It's time to get up those golden stairs." There was probably some Irish myth or family tale behind the expression, but we never asked and she never explained it. Bedtime meant the reluctant climb up the golden stairs, and that was that.) When I rounded the corner into the room, I stole a look at my sister huddled under the covers that were pulled up above her mouth, hiding the snicker but not the mischievously gleeful eyes that flickered in the slant of moonlight cutting across her bed. She may have lost her friend for the night, but she had succeeded in goading me. Mission accomplished.

I didn't think she'd miss me very much after I'd gone into the convent. But my little brother Thomas was another story.

I was eight years old when my mom brought Thomas home after her week's stay at the hospital. What good luck! As soon as Mom announced that we were going to have another baby brother or sister I prayed for a boy who would grow up and play catch with me. My older brother was hopelessly disinterested in any kind of game that involved balls, and my sisters fretted about hairdos and fingernails. I looked forward to teaching my baby brother how to play baseball with the new fielder's mitt Dad gave me for taking care of the house during my mom's seven-day stay in the hospital. When baby Thomas finally arrived, I began to believe that God really did answer a kid's prayers. For my mom, the arrival of her fifth child was another matter. After four children, she thought she was done with bearing and rearing children. Thomas came unexpectedly, like a storm that appears suddenly on the horizon, and I don't think she ever forgave him for it. Here was yet another mouth to feed and more diapers to change, wash by hand, and hang on the clothesline. She came back from the hospital with that little bundle in her arms looking ragged and pale. "You wanted a baby brother so much? You take care of him," she snapped. And so I did. I cut and combed his hair. I dressed him and played with him and told him stories. He was the first thing I looked for when I got home from school, and on a summer day he tagged along with me to the softball field, a little bashful around my girlfriends and all the cooing and aahing they did over my darling blue-eyed baby brother. Determined to give my mother a few minutes of peace, I even took on the Herculean task of getting this toddler with the self-charging battery to take naps with my famed Cowboy Tom stories, which I found myself inventing as I went along. With his eyes clamped shut and his tiny trusting hands clutching my neck, he drifted off into adventure land where he was at the center of some heroic enterprise before lapsing into dreamland. Where he remained until I inadvertently moved a muscle.

Growing up, we never grew apart. As a teenager, I sometimes even took him with me on dates. He especially liked riding in my boyfriend Denny's cool blue Mercury with the roaring V-8 engine. Thomas followed me around like a faithful puppy, but he also adored Denny who spoiled him and treated him like the little brother he didn't have. Yes, my other brothers and sisters might notice that I was gone after I left for the convent, but Thomas would actually miss me. He was my fair-haired child, my sidekick, my proxy son, and I left a part of me behind with him. When my other brothers and sisters lined up to say good-bye to me the day I left home, Thomas sat slouched on the living-room sofa, "with his arms folded in front of him and a puss as long as your arm" as my mom later described it. He was in cahoots with Denny, after all. Thomas wanted me to say yes to Denny and no to religious life. How could I explain to either of them that I had a calling that compelled me to leave them both?

After two years of dating, Denny professed to love me. Certain he could overcome the objections of his Protestant mother and my Catholic parents he planned for us to marry after high school. I didn't know too many things at eighteen, but one thing I knew for certain was that I did not want to go the way of my mother. The drudgery of clamoring children and unending household tasks failed to capture my imagination. I wanted something more. I yearned for a special destiny, personal fulfillment, an exotic mission. I aspired to higher things, things of the spirit. I believed God intended for me to do—to be—something special. I had visions of ministering to the poor, of reaching out to the unwanted and abandoned, not of being homebound and tending to house, children, and husband. I nurtured a more romantic vocation. And when God called, I answered.

But I was no fool. I knew that Denny was exceptional. All my girlfriends envied me because he showered me with affection and respect and never pressured me to have sex. I guess I was afraid of sex. I didn't really know much about it. My parents acted as if we were all delivered by angels, and sex didn't exist; and our Catholic schoolyard must have lacked some basic information. In the eighth grade I palled around with my public-school friend, Karen, who was only a year older but light-years ahead of me in the ways of the world. When she bragged about how she and her eighteen-year-old boyfriend Kenny were "doing it" in his car, I had no way to picture or comprehend "it," even though I managed to behave convincingly impressed. When I was twelve and started menstruating, my mother sat me on her bed and pulled out a book called *The Catholic Girls' Guide to Sex and Marriage*. She had purchased it from the magazine rack in the vestibule of our parish church, having already acquired the corresponding book for Catholic boys for my older brother. (He never told me about it. We didn't discuss things such as that. But I came across it once while rummaging in my parents' bedroom for hidden Christmas presents.) I didn't understand "ovulation" and "procreation" and a few other words in the book, but I was too embarrassed to ask or say anything. My mom read the entire book aloud, stopped, and announced in her firmest don't-you-dare-ask-me-any-questions voice, "So remember, Kathleen, boys only want one thing from girls"—and here the word "sex" was glaringly omitted—"and then, when they get *it*, they could care less about you. Especially the EYEtalians and Porta Riccins. Remember that." That last part must have made a pretty big impression on me because I steered clear of Italian boys in high school and kept my eyes peeled for Puerto Ricans, although they seemed to be nowhere in sight. (It is with a good deal of humorous irony that I confess to having later married an Italian man, a marriage that was preceded by a brief and chaste romance with a Puerto Rican seminarian from Lorain, Ohio.) Anyway, I suppose I wasn't ready for "going all the way," as the other kids called it, and Denny never forced the issue. Maybe neither of us was. I guess I was unlike other girls in some ways, and he seemed satisfied with that. I didn't flirt or try to make him jealous the way some of my friends did with their boyfriends. And when our friends went parking to make out, we went parking and hugged tightly and kissed soulfully between long, meaningful discussions about parents, friends, jobs, and fears of the future and what it may or may not hold. I loved Denny for that, and also because he seemed oblivious to the conditions that made me fidget with shame, particularly the untidy cracker-box house swarming with children, frayed secondhand furniture and peeling wallpaper, the yard littered with junk, engine parts, and old tires. He tolerated my father's persistent, icy silence and indulged my mother's constant admonishments to "behave yourself with my daughter. You hear? Or you'll answer to ME."

But Denny was so understanding, especially when it came to my girlfriends. He wasn't possessive or jealous. During the summer of my junior year of high school, he stayed behind to work at his busboy job at Howard Johnson's while my friends and I vacationed for a week at the New Jersey seashore. Everyone knew the draw and pitfalls of Wildwood, a favorite teenage Mecca—carefree sex, ample beer, zero parental supervision—and my friends were astonished that I went without Denny but with his blessing. Although I had no desire to test his love, I needed to certify my independence, and I was surprised to find that his absence gnawed at me that month-long week of partying, beach and boardwalk bumming, and everybody on the make. When he made a surprise visit two days before our scheduled departure for home, my heart rebounded with unexpected and certain joy. We were strolling lazily back from the beach that afternoon when my best friend Nancy called my attention to his dark blue hot rod as it pulled in front of our motel. He stepped out, shading his eyes from the sun as he looked hopefully in the direction of the beach. That day, he was even more handsome than I remembered. I couldn't see his eyes or chiseled face, but his sandy hair sparkled in the sunlight. He had a cool white sport shirt tucked into his powder blue seersucker pants, and he was wearing his brown wingtips and matching leather belt. I had this thing about slender fashionably dressed guys anyway, but it wasn't the attractive packaging that roped my heart that day or the day we first met. I was felled by Denny's offhanded sweetness. After nearly a week of being separated, my heart thumped wildly anew at the sight of him strolling casually in our direction. My beach bag and towel went flying as I raced down the street and launched myself into his outstretched arms, ignoring the spectacle we made as he held me close and twirled me around in the middle of the sand-covered street.

How could I love him and give him up at the same time? I didn't even understand it myself, so how could I expect Denny to understand? My parents reacted to my *big* decision with an eerie resignation, saying little more than "Okay, Kath, if that's what you want to do," as if they had always expected me to come home one day and say, "Well, think I'll give up the world and join up with the nuns. Okay with you?"

My girlfriends, on the other hand, were as puzzled as Denny by the news that I was joining up with the nuns. Well, shocked, more like. We were little more than a band of misfits in high school: me; the twins, Donna and Diane; Nancy; Pat; Anita; Patty; Jackie. At our Catholic high school we fell into a black hole of anonymity, except for the occasional lapse into infamy owing to some infraction or other. For the most part, we were uninspired students who produced mediocre academic work while avoiding the cliques of "good" students who brownnosed the nuns and congregated in honor societies and student clubs. Our little band hated the goody-goodies, so of course, we played the role of troublemakers. Well, somebody had to do it to keep the playing field balanced. Along the way, we earned our share of detentions as well as the ire of Mother Gabriel, our imposing seven-foot-tall principal who loomed large and stiff, like Frankenstein in a habit, in her four-inch-high headgear and black veil. Always on the lookout for those of us who were known members of the outsiders' society, she glowered down ominously from her towering height. "Young ladies," she'd bark like a boot-camp sergeant, "You know you are forbidden to wear jewelry. Hand over those rings and necklaces. And what is this?" she'd demand while eyeing our sinfully exposed legs. "Your school uniforms do not appear to comply with the two-inches-below-the-knee rule. Stand up on this chair so that I can measure." So there we each stood in turn, with Mother Gabriel gauging the length of our skirts with her ruler to determine that our shortened blue uniforms did, indeed, violate the rule. Then she proceeded to hand out detentions like after-dinner mints. Good old Mother Gabriel, the nun from hell whose mission it was to make our lives miserable. Naturally, our job was to thwart her every which way we could.

I'll never forget when she personally came to class one day and ordered me and my friends to report to her office. We were sitting in our seventh-period science class when the knock came on the door. Mr. Z. didn't miss a beat in his lecture on protoplasm and ectoplasm and whatever else he was putting us to sleep with that day when he shuffled over to the side of the room, turned the door handle, and popped his head out, responding to Mother Gabriel's foreboding summons. From the half-opened door, he bellowed, "Keenan, Lutton-Diane, Lutton-Donna, Papiernik, Rolek, Waites—march yourselves down to the principal's office! Mother Gabriel herself is waiting outside to escort you." I felt as if I were under arrest and in police custody as she corralled and steered us briskly to her office on the second floor. Somehow she had discovered that the Coca-Cola at our lunch table had been laced with Jack Daniel's. She must have gotten a telephone call from Jesus or else a tip from one of the brownnosers at the next lunch table. Anyway, for once, I was innocent. I didn't even know about the alcohol until lunch period had ended, and the culprits—Jackie, Diane, and Pat—started smirking and giggling while pulling themselves up unsteadily from the stools that were, fortunately, attached to the cafeteria table. Donna walked on the safer side of the street in high school, compared to her trouble-making twin, and I think she hung out with us mostly to keep tabs on her. Anyway, Donna was aghast, and I was furious. Whether or not we participated in the deed didn't matter because we were guilty by association. We were in a serious fix too, judging by the outrage pasted on Mother Gabriel's face as she lined us up in her office. But what could I say in my defense? "Mother Gabriel, those other three passed the miniature whiskey bottles around the table and spiked their Cokes, but *I* didn't have anything to do with it. I'm innocent." There's a word for that. It's called ratting. I couldn't do that. So I just stood there dumbly under the punishing glare of Mother G. who lumped us all together in the same guilty pile and spat out fire-and-brimstone threats concerning our immortal souls. Her questions came out like successive thunderclaps: "Where did the whiskey come from? Which one of you brought it to school? Who drank it?" And our response? A series of shoulder shrugs and a very subdued plea of ignorance: "I don't know, Mother." "I don't know, either, Mother," and "I don't know anything about it, Mother."

Mother's Gabriel's office grew steadily hotter in the face of the obstinacy that met her verbal blasting. To keep my fear in check, I studied my black-and-white saddle shoes and tried to keep my clammy hands, folded respectfully in front of me, from shaking. Like a maddened pit bull, she snapped and snarled and threatened: "God sees everything you do, you know. Make no mistake. You will be punished for any violations of the codes of this Catholic school. Lying IS a sin. Alcohol IS absolutely forbidden. Bold articles. Delinquents. Every last one of you. Not fit for the privilege of attending a Catholic school. Your parents will be informed, you know." She dealt this trump card haughtily, relishing the surge of power it gave her. Aghast, I mumbled "oh, no" under my breath.

"What's that?" she demanded sharply, her head jerking from one end of the line to the other, furious at the audacious interruption and intent on locating the scoundrel. "Did one of you say something?" A chorus of "no, Mother" sounded in reply.

Resuming her stiffest pose and most severe nun-like glare, she—cop, jury, judge, and executioner—handed down our sentence: "Now, as I was about to say, you are suspended for a week as of now. Expulsion remains a possibility."

She found us reprehensible and guilty as charged without producing any evidence beyond the testimony of her all-knowing self. As we traipsed, chastened, out of Mother Gabriel's office and down the stairway to our lockers on the first floor, I lashed out at Diane and Jackie who masterminded the unthinkable crime right under the Mighty G's nose, "Are you nuts? What the HELL were you thinking? We could be expelled, for God's sake! My mother's gonna kill me when she hears about this!" My mother never did kill me, of course. But it was a figure of speech that she used quite often when she felt the need to convey the seriousness of misbehavior in any of her children, with the exception of her son, saint-to-be Michael, of course, who never needed correction.

Well, my mother did get the ever-dreaded call from the principal, who in this case also happened to be a nun and was, therefore, a stand-in for the Almighty Himself, in my Irish Catholic mother's view. In addition to being grounded for what seemed like the remainder of my junior year in high school, I got a verbal thrashing and a heated warning that "if your father finds out about this, you're REALLY gonna get it." At that point, I had to defend myself at the expense of my friends because reporting our misdeeds to my father was my mother's ultimate weapon, used only in the most extreme circumstances. I flew into a rage, protesting my innocence, and explaining how I couldn't possibly tell on my friends to get myself out of the jam. But my mother, a card-carrying Catholic, always took the word of the nuns over that of her own children. So guilty or not, I was guilty because the nun said so. The injustice of it all was complicated by the fact that I didn't know who to blame—Pat, Jackie and Diane, Mother Gabriel, or my mother. I took my unjust punishment, a week's suspension and a month of detentions, and was somewhat relieved that I was spared the two worst possible outcomes: expulsion and my strict father's ire. Months later and from a safer distance, I saw the escapade in a different light. The refusal to be coerced, manifested in our consistent "I don't know" responses, had thwarted Mother Gabriel's bullying tactics and fanned her righteous fury. Maybe we didn't win, but we did have a little fun at her expense.

Mother Gabriel just did not appreciate our gang's redeeming qualities, such as they were. My closest friend in the group was Nancy. She avoided active troublemaking because she was so busy trying to prove herself to her excessively strict parents and their consistently unfavorable comparison of Nancy to her more studious older sister. Not to be confused with Pat, a partner in many of Diane's and Jackie's crimes, Patty was the truly virtuous one of the group. She's the one that I would have pegged as convent material. Patty had good judgment and common sense. She distinguished herself by actually applying herself to her schoolwork, which she juggled with chronic family problems and a part-time job. Often, to no avail and without seeming priggish, she invested her good sense and energy into counseling and detouring the group on its road to a showdown with nun or parent law. Pat, Jackie, and Diane shared the award for "Outstanding Troublemaker," and while they managed to lure the rest of us into a guaranteed-to-get you-into-trouble scheme from time to time, their wildness was tempered by the more levelheaded among us. Dark-skinned Diane was the conniving, mischievous twin, and blonde, blue-eyed Donna foiled her twin at every turn. They were so different in appearance and looks that you would never guess they were even related. While Diane schemed, Donna pouted and threatened to tell their mother. If Diane was a troublemaker—and she was—Donna made her look worse by being goody-two-shoes. Nevertheless, Diane's twin and nemesis persisted in hanging out with her sister and our fringe group. I think she feared that if Diane strayed too far to "the bad," she might lose her forever. The genuine concern Donna felt for her sister shimmered around the edges of her frustration and disapproval.

By my sophomore year, I had strayed slightly from our group and its errant ways myself, having fallen under the influence of Sister Mary Bernice, a sweet, mild-mannered Sister of Mercy nun who re-ignited my schoolgirl dream of being a nun. Besides acquainting us with the classics in English literature, she attempted to pique our social conscience with tales of the less fortunate. While not as desperate as the orphans in a Charles Dickens's novel, the children from St. Joseph's Orphanage in Philadelphia had it pretty tough, according to Sister Bernice. The Sisters of Mercy managed the place and took care of the children, and Sister Bernice was a regular visitor. She had a special interest in a girl she knew from our high school, although how and why the girl came to be sent to an orphanage was never clear to me. I didn't recall hearing about any car crash that rendered her instantly orphaned and Sister Bernice was pretty mum on the details. But I enjoyed tagging along with her, even though I didn't really know the girl we were visiting and the place made me feel sad. What was it like to live in a cold stone building with a bunch of nuns instead of being at home with your parents? Thinking about the orphans and their problems helped me to look at my own differently. Yes, my family was poor, but at least, we had a home and parents who didn't farm us out to the nuns. Visiting the orphanage gave me a sense of purpose. I enjoyed hanging out with the younger kids, listening to their problems, and acting the part of the cool older sister. I shared the experience with my high school friends, and they got all excited about the idea of visiting the kids during the holidays and entertaining them with our minstrel show, originally developed for our high school's annual talent competition. We agreed that we would expand it and then perform it for the kids at the orphanage. A great fan of late-night TV, I was familiar with the minstrel-show routine that included Mr. Interlocutor, corny jokes, black face, song and dance numbers with tambourines, and, best of all, the Al Jolson numbers. I did a great Jolson imitation, having memorized both the words and gestures. My favorites were "Mammy" and "Swanee." My friends and I got so excited about the project that we researched minstrel shows at the public library, developed a script, rented tambourines and costumes, choreographed dance numbers, and even memorized the corny vaudeville jokes. We felt pretty good about ourselves. Diane, Patty, Pat, Donna, Jackie, and I threw ourselves wholeheartedly into the project, and for once in our life, we put our energy into an unselfish and worthwhile purpose. For weeks, we practiced every day after school in one of the classrooms under the approving eye of Sister Mary Bernice.

The antithesis of Mother Gabriel, the unwavering disciplinarian, Sister Bernice exuded kindness. She treated us all the same, as if we were all special in some way. She made no distinction between the popular and the unpopular, the smart students and the dumb ones, the well behaved and ill behaved, the insiders and the outsiders. And she reached out to the troubled teens that didn't belong to band or honor society or drama club. Sister Bernice was sensitive to the kids who were overlooked or ignored by the other nuns, which explains how I, and then the others in my group, came to her attention and fell under her influence. I don't know how much good we actually did by spending time with the orphans and performing our minstrel show. Even then I recognized that it would take a whole lot more than a single, compassionate individual or well-meaning group of teens to make a difference in their lives. They needed acceptance, support, and nurturing. They needed a loving family and even someone as giving and wonderful as Sister Bernice couldn't give them that. But the experience of donating time and talent on behalf of others certainly steered our little gang's energy in a more productive direction. Sister Bernice might have been sweet and placid, but she was no fool.

As far as I could tell, Sister Bernice was the ideal nun, and toward the end of my senior year in high school, I decided I wanted to model myself after her. I had grown up on a steady diet of Catholicism, so I was well aware of the honor that came with dedicating my life to God by being a nun. That inherited knowledge came with being Irish and Catholic and the oldest girl of seven children. Having absorbed the practices, discipline, and ideals of my religious upbringing, I developed a strong and unwavering desire to do something important and definitive with my life. Instead of getting married, I wanted to lead a virtuous life of serving God and his people, particularly the less fortunate. It was my fervent belief that with my small life I just might make some difference in the world. Not until I encountered Sister Bernice in my sophomore year of high school did I see my aspirations embodied, and over time, the mystique of religious life joined forces with her powerful influence.

I studied Sister Bernice. She was not like most other nuns. Petite and frail beneath all those layers of black cloth, she was not at all imposing or severe. Her oval brown eyes were serene pools of wisdom and compassion, and they never expressed intolerance or judgment. She loved reading the works of George Eliot and Jane Austen aloud in class, and besides stirring my religious vocation she also inspired my love of language and literature. I didn't necessarily recognize it at the time, when it seemed as if she was just assigning another long book to read with big words like "insouciant" and "perspicacious" that no one I knew ever used. But I was intrigued enough to read the entire books, unlike most of my classmates who just wanted to know what happened to George Eliot's Maggie Tulliver and whether or not Jane Austen's Emma ever got herself married. They were really only interested in passing the test, while I found myself transported to unimagined worlds and experiences that were both different and not so different than my own. After all, wasn't I just like Maggie in *The Mill on the Floss*, who yearned to fulfill her ambitions with all the freedom that her older brother enjoyed?

Sister Bernice exuded a love of books, people, and God. She was accessible and different from the other nuns who were aloof or moved easily to irritation. She was like an angel with a soft, gentle voice that made me want to listen to her more intently. I don't think I ever heard her raise it or speak crossly to anyone, no matter how rude the class was or how much a student misbehaved. In fact, on several occasions, I had to take a couple of my classmates aside for acting up and being disrespectful in Sister Bernice's class. I used a reasonable approach, of course, and I could be quite persuasive, especially with Pat or Diane there to back me up with a little muscle if needed. I had taken on a few bullies in my time, and everyone knew that I could be tough in a puny, hard-nosed Irish kind of way. One time in the third grade, I tackled a big fat bully named Annie for beating up on a frightened second grader. We wrestled and rolled around in the mud, with neither of us inflicting much damage apart from a few scratches and tears in our uniform. But I refused to let up and walk away until I received her assurance that she wouldn't pick on the scared girl again. So I made it a point to stand up for the defenseless, especially when the defenseless in this case—Sister Bernice—might be an angel or even a saint for all I knew.

Whatever she was, Sister Bernice reached out to *me*. For endless hours after school, she sat with me, patting my hand, and listening to all my schoolgirl complaints about difficult parents, harsh teachers, friend problems, boyfriend problems, and my own ever-nagging self-doubts. She made me feel special, as if everything would be all right because she loved me and God loved me, and my life had value. To be honest, I wasn't so sure how I fared with God, but Sister Bernice made me feel loved and gave me hope that one day I would amount to something. Over time, she kindled my interest in the sisterhood and a way of life that promised to bring out all that was good in me.

Denny was wrong in thinking that Sister Bernice had turned me against him, but in my senior year of high school, she did help me to figure out my direction and goal in life. She informed me about a modern religious order unlike her own more traditional teaching order, where the primary aim was to help the indigent doing something called "social work." I had never heard of the Missionary Sisters of the Nazarene before, or "social work" for that matter, but she believed that both the order and its mission suited me, my sensibility, and, I guess, my social crusader spirit. Its members wore a more modified habit to better suit them for their work with the poor. Since I aspired to lead a holy life and make a difference in the world by helping others, this religious order and its social-work mission seemed tailor-made for me.

Shortly before my high school graduation, it all came together: I wanted to be a nun, just like Sister Mary Bernice, except that instead of serving God as a teacher I would help people by doing social work. Sister Bernice was delighted by my decision, but it was another story with my friends.

Nancy, the twins, Pat, and the rest of the gang were bewildered. They had never known me to be particularly religious, so I think they suspected I'd been taken over by aliens. But they were my friends, after all—the same gang that threw me my first-ever surprise birthday party when I turned sixteen—so they were bound to be supportive even though they didn't really get it at all. Entering the convent also meant leaving behind a few of my other stray friends—Clare, an honor student at my school, and Bob, an old flame who served as a class officer at his public school. Clare couldn't envision me as a nun because I was too much of a rebel, and Bob thought it was downright abnormal for people to be celibate. Of course, Bob was a Protestant, so how could he understand? I struggled to explain my decision to them one night over french fries and vanilla cokes at the Five Points Diner where we sometimes hung out. "Well, Kathy," Bob finally offered resignedly as he threw his hands up in the air and shrugged, "it sounds pretty crazy to me, but if it makes you happy . . ." and here his voice trailed off like a road with nowhere to go. Clare, too, relented, as she grabbed my hand and gave me a squeeze of approval: "Damn, girl, of all the people in our graduating class, I never would have pegged you as the one to become a nun, but I'm okay with it, really I am." Like Bob, she seemed unconvinced that I would be happy in religious life. I understood. I was well aware that I didn't look or act the part of a typical nun, but I intended to change that.

One last matter to be resolved, though, prior to my departure from the world of boyfriend, friends, and family was my smoking habit. I would miss my Winston cigarettes, but once inside the iron gates of convent life, I had to go cold turkey from my pack-a-day habit, a habit inaugurated at age thirteen. I smoked into the wee hours that last night of freedom while out driving with Clare and Bob and his friend George. Clare and I lounged in the backseat of Bob's car and sipped some Boone's Farm Strawberry Hill wine to celebrate the occasion of my final fling. We decided to do it in style by exploring, once more, the old Pitcairn Estate that stood on several secluded acres of land on the outskirts of a neighboring town called Langhorne. According to the most reliable of rumors, the Pitcairn Estate was haunted. In a moment of alcohol-induced bravado, we decided to check it out as a good-bye gift to me on the eve of my departure from the "world." The rumors told of ghosts and intermarriages and morons and such credentials served as a neon invitation to local teenagers on the look-out for a little excitement.

The narrow roadway leading up to the estate split off in different directions. It was well after midnight, and the dense night hung around us like a black tent. For a long time, it seemed as if we were driving in circles on the sprawling property that lay shrouded under a blanket of massive ancient trees, with their spooky gnarled fingers stretched out against the dark sky. Finally, the eerie Gothic-like mansion, barely visible from the unlit asphalt road this warm and humid September evening, loomed in the distance. I wanted to get a closer look, so Clare and I crept from the car and sneaked across the manicured grass until we stood within feet of the infamous "haunted house." Circling it, with Clare close at my heels, I fingered the damp, mossy stone and tried to trace the roads of ivy climbing the building. No signs of life appeared within or without, and the absolute silence was so unsettling that I wanted to scream. The lore of the Pitcairn Estate was well-known, and I couldn't help imagining perverse captors and chained prisoners inside. But prudence held fast, and I finally made my peace with the stillness. At last, our exploration around the circumference of the house led us to a set of partially illuminated windows. Like two enormous sentries, the lead-lined windows guarded both sides of the main entry. I clambered up to get a peek inside the one to the left of the door, but couldn't see much because of the heavy drapes hanging within and parted only slightly in the center. Within seconds, though, any temptation to get a glimpse at the activities going on within that house evaporated with Clare's sudden cry, accompanied by a firm tugging of my shirt, "Kathy, Kathy, come on! Let's get the hell outta here. I saw something really spooky in there. Come on!" We shrieked and laughed nervously all the way back to the car that sat idling on a knoll and seemed a football field away. Reaching it at last, we slid into the backseat, giggling with the same strange mixture of apprehension and delight that I felt at seeing those giant ants loom over the hill in my first horror movie, *Them*. My heart was doing flip-flops and my palms were moist with sweat. What Clare had "seen," if, indeed, she had seen anything, could only be explained as a large shadow that very likely owed more to the evening and our imagination than to anything else.

By the time we scrambled into our getaway car, we were sufficiently spooked and ready for the adventure to be over. Bob and George both seconded that emotion, so we threaded our way back along the twisting tree-lined roadway trying to find our way off the grounds. The sudden appearance of an arrangement of gravestones in the car's headlamps renewed our interest though, and Bob slowed to a stop, so we could feast a bit on this fresh fear. "We're in Weirdsville, man," Bob offered. "Damn, I bet these morons kill each other off and then bury the bodies, right here on the grounds! Look out for the imbeciles and spooks, man," he half-joked, trying to play off his unmanly anxiety. We didn't get a chance to reply, though, because light beams suddenly poured into the car, at last resting on Bob who was shading his eyes from the glare. A head peered above the flashlight, and a mannequin-like man, with a waxen face, large black eyes, and protruding ears set off by what appeared to be a policeman's hat, demanded to know, in his peculiarly robotic voice, what we were doing on private property. All signs of his humorous bravado had dissipated when Bob stuttered out an answer, his voice quivering as he lied about how we had taken a wrong turn or two and then found ourselves lost on the property. A toneless voice came back, not harshly or loudly, but chillingly slow, "You . . . will . . . remove yourselves . . . immediately. You . . . will not . . . return . . . ever . . . again," he cautioned, leaving us with a long, eerie stare to punctuate the elongated warning. We felt immensely relieved when he directed us off the property. And satisfied. We had gotten what we wanted on this moonless, overcast night—a few moments of unadulterated (if fantasized) horror and another story to add to the growing Pitcairn Estate rumor mill. I thought it a shame that I wouldn't be around to scare some of the local teenagers with our story. But I had more important things to do, and besides, I knew I could trust my friends to carry on that tradition.

Bob finally pulled into the driveway of my house in the wee hours of the morning. Through the picture window, I could see my mom's bent head in the living-room chair as she sat half-asleep and waiting up for me to come home, as she always did for all her children. I kissed and hugged Bob and Clare good-bye, tossed my half-empty cigarette pack to Bob, and slipped my high school class ring off my finger and presented it to Clare. She was sick about the fact that she had lost hers, and I was well aware that I had no use for jewelry and other material things where I was going. I held my tears off long enough to slide out of the car and give my friends a final, brave good-by wave as they drove off.

The next morning, I was up early with my new trunk packed full of black and white undergarments, ready to go to 8:00 a.m. Mass with Dad for the last time. Afterward, he and Mom drove me to the convent, mingled for a while with the other entrants and their families, and then said good-bye—my mom, by clutching my hand and dabbing at her eyes, and my dad, with a stiff, stoic hug. I knew they would get to visit me periodically, at least during my first year of postulancy, but there was something awfully final about that good-bye. I felt as if I were standing at the base of an imposing mountain, eager for the challenge of the climb before me, but fearfully aware in the deep recesses of my being that there would be no turning back. My decision to leave family, home, and friends was irrevocable. But at that moment, at the dawn of my adult existence, my heart also swelled with anticipation and hope. I had determined to walk through the doors of the convent that promised an entirely new life—a *tabula rasa*. The slate would be wiped clean of social failures and personal sins and dearth of opportunity. I intended to make something of myself. I intended to offer my life up to God by joining this religious community with a profound spiritual and social charge: to love and serve God by helping the needy and the poor. From the convent doorstep, my prospects for sainthood, despite a checkered past, looked pretty good.

# Part One

## No Turning Back (1965-66)

# Winter

It is late, around midnight or so. I have no way of knowing for sure. My twenty-four classmates are sleeping soundly under coarse, woolen army blankets on unadorned wrought-iron cots that line both sides of the long dormitory room in shadows. I am crouched at the window several feet behind my cot watching the newborn snow swirling in a dance around the lamplight, the first of the winter season, 1965. The cold, bare wooden floor bites at my naked feet, and the air temperature hovers around fifty-five degrees, not including the draft factor, which is considerable given the thin walls of this aged frame structure. I hug my knees and pull my black cotton kimono up around my shoulders and face in an effort to make warm air. Tears slide down my cheeks and drip from my nose, smearing the windowpane already frosted from my breath. I am not feeling unhappy, really, but strangely romantic and nostalgic. The moon is an amber sliver pasted on a black curtain. Incandescent snowflakes fall steadily, briefly illuminating the night sky and gradually swelling the ground. Untouched. Unspoiled. Perfect. Pure. Which is what I think of this life, what I want of this life. What I want of me. I shudder to think that come morning, footprints and tire tracks will spoil the snow and turn the sparkling white earth into mush and mud.

\*    \*    \*

Unfailingly, at five thirty each morning, Sister George Ignatius strides through the two connected dormitories, twelve postulants in one and thirteen in the other. "Benedicaminus Domino! Benedicaminus Domino!" she screeches repeatedly to the obnoxious clanging of the bell that hangs at her side. My eyes still glued in sleep, I tumble out of bed on my knees and start reciting the morning prayers in Latin in unison with the others. Two minutes later, I'm standing upright next to the straight-backed wooden chair that holds my black kimono—the convent term for robe—a clean pair of white granny underwear, and my folded day garb and slip. I am becoming accustomed to dressing in the cold, still dark while half-asleep, oddly relieved that there are no mirrors by which to check my appearance. There is no time or occasion for vanity here. Straining to maintain a prayerful disposition, I pull the long black kimono over my head for maximum modesty in the open dormitory, while exchanging my white pajamas for the gray day garb. A glance sideways reveals a row of shadows, similarly fumbling in the half-morning light with the ritual change of clothing beneath a flimsy cover of black.

I wear a gray dress rather than a black one because I am in my first year of training and have not yet been accepted as a full-fledged member of the religious community. Underneath the garb, I wear a bra resembling an oversized Ace bandage that serves to flatten the breasts and desex the body as much as possible. Next comes the white cotton T-shirt, like the Fruit of the Loom kind my dad wears, followed by the black slip and, finally, the long gray garb and white plastic collar that fits around my neck. I do not wear the community cross or full habit. These will come only after I succeed in passing the major test of the novitiate in my second year of training and take my vows of poverty, chastity, and obedience. Profession and full membership seem a long way away right now. I am but a fledgling. I am being tested, and I have much to prove. I am reminded of this every day. Nothing is familiar. We live among utter strangers, separated from everyone and everything familiar. The community supplies us with our only lifeboat. If we are to be saved, we must trust in it entirely. This is our chief lesson.

After dressing, I make my way to the long line forming outside the bathroom. Four sinks and four toilets serve all twenty-five postulants. Sister George has her own bathroom attached to her private sleeping quarters. They are adjacent to our dormitory, so she can keep her radar eyes trained on us night and day. Our limited facilities prove to be one of the minor inconveniences in an austere life that is designed to determine our mettle. The dorm features no showers, but two bathtubs are located inconveniently on the first floor, as though inserted as an afterthought. Baths are permitted only on Saturday night, our "free" night, which simply means that this is the only time when we are free from prayer, cleaning, or study following supper and evening prayer. If one is unlucky enough not to be among the first seven or so in line for the Saturday night bath, she can always count on ice-cold water. As I usually do.

I actually love Saturday nights in the postulancy. I look forward to a rare evening of leisure time after all our chores and prayers are completed. I feel as young and carefree as I did when I was a kid in the summertime with no responsibilities or worries: I remember playing outside after supper and going in only after an exhausting evening of catching lightning bugs in the backyard. I felt sweaty and satisfied with my jar of throbbing light, and my bladder was like a balloon with air slowly seeping out because I didn't want to interrupt my play long enough to note the distress signal. A typical Saturday night in the postulancy usually finds me, Deirdre, Theresa, Angela, and Krista skipping off to the infirmary, a wing of the motherhouse that serves as a kind of hotel for old and sick nuns. Some of the nuns are terminally ill and bedridden, and we're not permitted to bother them, while others are just elderly and ailing from years of doing God's work among the poor and the godless. Most of the infirmed nuns are good-humored and chatty, stocked with memories about the good old pioneer days of the community. I like spending time with them and I really enjoy listening to their stories. They've arrived on the other end of this earthly life, assured of having given their life to God and resisted the seductions of the world. Their tales about patrolling the city streets armed only with the Bible and God's love and tending to the poor are fascinating, and they connect me in a personal way with the community history and its pioneers. I can tell that the older nuns enjoy the company of us younger nuns as well. Maybe it reminds them of their own youth when they were high-spirited and eager to whip the world in the service of God. Sometimes we just sit in their rooms with them and gab. Other times, Angela plays her guitar, and we sing some less-than-religious folk songs, such as "Kumbaya" and "How Many Roads Must a Man Walk Down," and they get a real kick out of that. They clap their hands and sing along. They might be old, but they're not old-fashioned, not all of them anyway. I also think they enjoy us because our youth reminds them of their own and in us they also see their beloved community's future. These Saturday-night hootenannies with the infirmary nuns are a lot of fun, but by the time I make it back to St. Gerard's—where hot water is in short supply—I can forget about a warm bath. I start to forget what it's like not to shiver while sponging my body with cold water in an unheated room.

In winter months, the dorm room is like a giant old-fashioned icebox. White circles of breath hover as we get dressed in the early-morning hours. We shiver while standing silently in line for the bathroom, each morning and night, because the Grand Silence forbids us to speak from 9:00 p.m. until after breakfast the next morning. After we are all tucked in, Sister George bounds into the room, trains her flashlight on every postulant's bed, and completes her nightly inspection of the dorm. Her final gesture finds her examining the thermostat that hangs on a wall between the two connected dorm rooms to ensure that it reads as low as possible. On unbearably cold nights, one of us boldly steals out of bed and creeps toward the small hallway that also leads to G. I.'s sleeping quarters. The bold one is usually Celia, Deirdre, or me. G. I. is our nickname for Sister George Ignatius, inherited from our postulant predecessors. On such occasions, one of us steals out of bed and over to the partially closed door to G. I.'s room. After listening for a moment to be certain that she is safely retired and asleep, the daring postulant gingerly pushes the thermostat lever upward and races back to bed in hopes that G.I. doesn't discover the switch before she has a chance to correct it in the morning. The way she studies that thermostat with her flashlight late at night and before morning prayers in the chapel, I think she must suspect something from time to time, but either she cannot believe anyone would be so cheeky or else she's biding her time.

G. I. is every postulant's nightmare, which probably explains why she was chosen for the job. She has a face like a canyon, with deep crevices and intersecting rivers running up and down her chalky skin. Her age is a mystery, although seventy sounds reasonable. Maybe even eighty. But her spry step and hawk-like eyes do not betray any hint of dotage or slowness of mind. Slender and straight as a knife, with the exception of a slight dowager's hump, she bounces forward on the balls of her sharply pigeon-toed feet with her head thrust forward as if leading a forced march. She is our master sergeant, officially titled, our "mistress." (Strange title, it occurs to me, but I dare not question it any more than her authority to cut my vocation to the quick with a wave of her liver-spotted hand.)

A stern New Englander, G. I. is a stickler for the community Rule, which is neatly and precisely set forth in a tiny black book that also outlines the order's history and mission. She has her eyes on me, I know. She thinks I'm too much of a free spirit, so she must rein me in. I guess I am. For the first time, I feel utterly intoxicated with life and this experience of living and working with a group of young people who share a common spiritual goal with no selfish interests, no personal ambitions, and no vanity. I am associated with something large and important and good, and it makes me giddy with happiness.

I love being part of a team. As a youngster, I excelled in sports, especially basketball and softball. Although I was a talented athlete, being a team member propelled and motivated me beyond the limits of my natural ability. Whether I was diving for balls, tearing into bases, stretching for hits, or passing and driving to the hoop and often finding myself on the floor, no physical cost was spared because there was something greater at stake here. The team effort held more importance than any selfish individual aim. I was the first to console, encourage, or congratulate another player. I understood that for a team to succeed, the members have to pull together, work hard, and support one another. I intuitively grasped the principle that no one team player is more or less important than another and that no one individual should accept the glory or the damnation of a team effort. As a young athlete, I was a generous team member, a solid team player, and a natural team leader.

Here, too, I am part of a team. I am also emerging as a kind of leader, but not always in the way my superiors would like. I'm usually the one who leads the singing of the musical numbers during our recreation hour after supper and while we're peeling and slicing the bushels of apples in afternoon-dessert kitchen. Or the one heading the postulants' noisy charge down the hill from the motherhouse to St. Gerard's Hall after another long day of physical labor, prayer, and study, in that order. I help write the skits for community holidays and lyrics for my classmate Angela's original music, and I'm even writing poetry in my daily meditation journal—something I didn't even know I could do. But it's true that I don't spend any extra time in chapel like some of my more pious classmates who, according to G. I., are setting a good "sisterly" example. As she puts it, I need to learn to lead not by my talents, which is self-serving, but by piety, which is self-effacing. This lesson is difficult to grasp, and after several months of training, I realize how much I have to learn about what it means to lead the life of a nun. I want to be holy—I truly do—and yet I have misgivings about this policing role we are asked to perform. How are reporting others for breaking the Grand Silence and admonishing them for singing on the stairwell connected with holiness exactly? That's what I'd like to know. Most of the others don't seem as troubled by it, though.

Eliza is a nag about this sisterly-decorum stuff because that's her job as my community-appointed "angel." Barely five feet tall with brooding brown eyes that match her dark complexion, Eliza's appearance doesn't match the images of blonde, blue-eyed angels I've seen in religious picture books. But then, I'm not much of a "cherub" either, which is the title I am given in this duo. I don't know how we were ever paired up in the first place. Anyone can see that Eliza is serious and subdued, while I'm fun-loving and boisterous. She chides me for being too loud and for reporting late to table. She gets especially annoyed at me for griping and for running—rather than walking sedately—between duties because it is so "unsisterly." It's not my fault, really. We don't have enough time to get from one chore to the next let alone complete it, and I have to let off a little steam somewhere. "This joint is gonna work us to death," I whine as I tear into the postulants' locker room for a bathroom stop between auditorium clean-up and kitchen duty. As soon as I open my mouth, Eliza arches her eyebrows and places her forefinger over her lips as a reminder that I should be observing the Grand Silence. Then she flashes me that serious you're-not-behaving-in-a-sisterly-fashion look. I hate that look, even though I know she's right.

At first, my "angel" is not very pleased with this assignment by G. I. to guide me in the history and "Rule" of the Order, given her experience of working with the nuns as a young girl in Worcester, Massachusetts. She knows all about the founders and their work with the poor in the inner cities and desolate rural areas, and I'm learning quite a lot from her. The angel-cherub arrangement makes Eliza somewhat responsible for me, and I suspect she offers this charge up as a penance of some sort, gauging from the number of "tsks" and rolling eyes I get. But I'm growing on her. I can tell by the occasional, exasperated smile and shake of her head, as if to say, "Okay, okay, I'm beginning to like you, sort of, but don't push it." Like a turtle being lured out of its shell, Eliza is more willing to join in with the storytelling and singing fests during evening recreation in the community room while we sew and write letters home. But if I'm getting Eliza to loosen up a bit, she's rubbing off on me as well. She's terribly earnest about her vocation, and her steadfast desire to achieve sisterly perfection and live out this vow of obedience is, if annoying at times, also downright inspirational. Alike in our strong-headedness, we differ in our approach to convent life: she believes in following the "rule," while I tend to be a rule challenger and bender. To me, rules are more a means than an end, and so we are learning politely to disagree. I know she is warming up to me because of the encouraging spiritual sentiments she scribbles on the back of holy cards left like little treats in my locker cubby: "Dear Cherub, May you continue to grow in God's love with the help and guidance of the Holy Spirit. Your Angel in the Blessed Trinity, Sister Eliza." It's not approval exactly, but it's a start.

So far, I cannot claim to be a leader like Eliza. I am boisterous and immature, and I realize that I have to learn to harness my energy and enthusiasm to earn my superiors' approval. There's not much place for expressing ourselves around here, not like we did on the outside anyway—no wild car rides with the radio blaring, no congregating at the late-night diner to hang out with friends, or sneaking into the drive-in theater, or hooking up at the shore. We can't get into any *real* trouble here. We don't have cars or radios and we can't leave the convent grounds except for our class's weekly visit to Riverside, the old folks' home. I'm pretty sure that I am not the only one struggling with leaving adolescence behind, along with worldly pleasures. And from time to time we do manage to find a few harmless ways of venting our frustrations. On Saturday "free" nights, for instance, while waiting in line for our weekly bath before G. I. returns from the motherhouse, our normally placid dorm room turns into a raucous teenage pajama party. Celia sits in the middle of the floor draped in her black kimono playing wild riffs on her guitar. (It doesn't help that she is just learning to play, and everybody is too nice to tell her she sounds awful.) Maria entertains us with her laughable imitation of infirmary kitchen supervisor, Sister Peter. She screws up her face, slides her glasses to the end of her nose and in a thin, squeaky soprano sings, "I've told every little star / just how wonderful you are; why haven't I told you . . ." I am usually the featured event of the Saturday-night show, when I stand atop my cot belting out the nuns' dorm rendition of "Let me entertain you; Let me make you smile" from *Gypsy Rose Lee*, as my classmates scream and clap and cheer me on. I have pretty good mimicking abilities and can recall Natalie Wood's alluring performance in great detail, although I have a lot more snaps and layers to work with, and there's no danger of any flesh ever being exposed. Miming Gypsy Rose Lee's sultry "Let me do a few tricks, some old and then some new tricks" to the delighted squeals of my classmates makes me feel terribly wicked, I admit, but on such occasions I offer up my wickedness for the sake of the common good.

I don't see these as serious lapses because I know I am growing in my spiritual life. Besides learning to discipline my mind and body through a routine of prayer and labor, I am also learning to love God and all my sisters in the community; and thanks to my weekly "charity" sessions with G. I., I am becoming more mindful of my "faults." The community's book of rules refers to our faults as impediments to our spiritual development in religious life, and poverty, chastity, and obedience are mechanisms for this growth. These private sessions with our "mistress" are intended to correct faults and weaknesses that might prevent us from stripping ourselves of worldly attachments—to things, to people, to one's will. I have no short supply of those, but it's a bit of a challenge coming up with any hard-core sins—mortal or venial—to report to the priest every Tuesday evening in the confessional, since we don't get too much of an opportunity for serious wrongdoing.

Mortal sins are the worst by far, and clear examples are lying, stealing and adultery. To die with a mortal sin on the soul is to be condemned to hell for eternity. Venial sins send the soul to purgatory for a period of time, which is like being in an uncomfortable holding cell, but eventually, the soul will get into heaven. Mortal sins are hard to come by in this place, but I finally do come up with a good one to confess: misreporting on the log we are required to maintain and submit to G. I. Each week, we must document every single activity in the column next to the appropriate time slot, from the time we meet for early morning meditation until bedtime. The infraction occurs when I take advantage of any downtime, such as when the sister in charge of the duty I am performing releases me early, and I find myself with half an hour or so between my afternoon duty and 5:00 p.m. benediction in the chapel. Instead of reporting to chapel early or studying the readings for scripture class, I sometimes join Angela who is practicing the piano in the motherhouse auditorium. One of her chores is to help the choir director plan and play the music for the liturgy, which allows her to use her talent to serve God and the community. But I have no such talent and should be elsewhere, which I am not, and worse, I fail to report it on my schedule, giving me a pretty juicy sin to tell the old priest who comes from a neighboring parish each week to hear the nuns' confessions. Not that it matters much to him anyway. He's hard of hearing and goes through the motions in the confessional box like a mechanical wind-up toy. He mumbles a prayer before he blusters toward the screen separating his head from mine: "So what are your sins, Sister?" Then he nods off until I express my sorrow and ask forgiveness, at which point he raises his right hand and offers me a blessing along with a penance of a handful of Hail Marys and Our Fathers. The ritual of confession is important, I know, so I guess Father Murphy is doing his part in my overall spiritual growth and development.

One of the sins I confess is a lack of charity toward G. I. I get angry with her when she criticizes me during our weekly charity session. I also feel shame. I realize it's her job to help me correct my faults, and I know I have to overcome these feelings of indignation. Besides, she's right. I do sometimes break the rules and I am immature and guilty of all kinds of "unsisterly" behavior: I laugh too loudly; I laugh on the stairwells; I instigate the others; I don't eat all my food; I report late for table; I talk during the Grand Silence; I'm not sufficiently prayerful, etc., etc.

"Discipline is the pathway to virtue," G. I. once again reminds me as I sit in her office for my private charity session this week, "and that, of course, is the purpose of your training in the postulancy, as it will be next year in the novitiate." I get it. I do. This formative period is like a convent boot camp where we are being broken down and built up, tried and tested to prove that we have the necessary ingredients and fortitude to live the religious life, God's highest calling.

"I'm really willing to work on these faults, Sister," I assure her, begging for more time to prove myself, which I sincerely hope to do. (Another of my Irish mother's proverbs occurs to me—"The road to hell is paved with good intentions"—and I hope it doesn't apply here.) We're having this discussion in G. I.'s large-closet-sized office, the cramped and dismal site of our weekly private sessions.

G. I. purses her lips, sucking in air as she does so, revealing her proverbial, disapproving face when delivering her "sermon from the chair" in a peremptory manner. Then she proceeds with the litany of complaints, which, at this point, I can only half hear because my heart is pounding so hard, "And the loud singing that you initiate during kitchen duty is disturbing to the sisters in the chapel," she proceeds, heedless of my galloping heart. I can feel the embarrassment heating up my neck and making its way up to my face. Even my ears are tingling. Mortified, I sit quietly and reflect.

G. I. interrupts the painful silence: "Yes, well, Sister, I am certain that you have good *intentions*"—so my mother *is* right?—"but you must realize your vocation exacts a high cost. Your superiors must decide whether or not you have been called by God to this life. Do you have the qualities? Do you have the resolve to live out the vows of poverty, chastity, and obedience? Do you fully understand what these sacred vows require?" She is sitting as stiff as a ruler in the straight-backed wooden chair, her wrinkled hands folded on the desk in front of her, as if the more composed she is, the more attentive and receptive I will be. She pauses, making certain that her meaning is being entirely absorbed (which it most assuredly is), before she continues. "It is also my duty to remind you, Sister, to be wary of forming any particular friendships during your training here because they are an impediment to the vow of chastity." Here she looks down and away from me, as if it were distasteful to her even to mention the term.

G. I. is obviously calling my attention in the dreaded "particular friendship" topic. Everyone hears about it, but no one really understands what is meant by the term, shrouded, as it is, in mystique and uncertainty. Nor do we feel comfortable talking about it among ourselves because it makes us feel guilty, as if we are "committing" it just by talking about it. The brief, vague definition provided in the order's book of rules is not much help either: "a singular attachment that violates the vow of chastity and the requirement that we love all our sisters in the community the same." This definition flashes before me as I sit in G. I.'s office, trying to listen to what she is and is not saying, and sort through my confusion.

Here G. I. proceeds cautiously, looking from the paper on her desk up to me, but not at me, really, more like over my shoulder. It's strange how obviously uncomfortable she is discussing the topic. "You understand, Sister, in religious community, all relationships must remain equal. Sisters are not to form any special bonds with one another because their hearts and minds must remain pure and belong only to God. We must pray to love one another just as Christ loves us, all the same and in the true spirit of charity. You do understand, don't you, Sister?" Here I get the full benefit of G. I.'s hawk-like gaze at point-blank range. Does she know that Eliza and I exchanged holy cards? No, that can't be what she's talking about. All the postulants and novices exchange holy cards containing personal notes and expressions of encouragement. Is she referring to Angela and Krista? It's true that I feel closer to them than I do to some of my other classmates, but that's just natural, isn't it? Does this rule mean we can't have friends at all? How can that be when it's well-known that the missioned sisters have friends? It's common to hear that Sister X and Sister Y are friends because they were recruited the same year or served together at the same mission. So the distinction must be in "particular" friends, but what does that mean exactly? Despite my quandary, I don't feel I can ask G. I. Besides, her firmness on the subject is belied by the evident distress it causes her. Somehow I stammer out an affirmative response.

"Good." She sounds relieved. The folded hands return to her lap, a sure sign that she's finished with this portion of the session. Then, out of nowhere a beam of light appears, as G.I.'s comments take a favorable turn. "It's become evident, Sister, that you perform your duties with diligence as well as cheerfulness. We are very pleased. And you don't shirk from taking on extra work to help your sisters. The community appreciates your industry and generosity, as well as your willingness to use your creative talents for the community. I'm referring to the skit that you wrote and performed with a few others for Mother General's feast day, of course. These are commendable qualities." What's this—a grudging acknowledgement that I just may have some good qualities too? "However," she chides, turning back to my "darker" side and the list before her, "you must pray for the guidance and strength to correct your faults."

Well, okay, so I've been shot back down, but she's given me a ray of hope and I determine to improve and demonstrate my worthiness to her. I do not want to fail her, the community, *or* God.

G. I. rarely praises us and she never minces words, so her compliment takes me by surprise. But by the time I utter my "thank you, Sister," and pledge to continue trying very hard, she has proceeded to the next item on the agenda.

"Well, that's fine. Now, as to your free time . . ." What free time? "Perhaps you could spend your spare time between duties and community prayers in the chapel praying"—and not with Angela at the piano?—"for God's strength and guidance in some of these matters." She glances at the clock on the wall behind my head, signaling the end of our session. "We have a few minutes before noon duties. Why not go now and pay a visit?" The interrogative phrasing is clearly at odds with her imperious tone.

Pausing for confirmation that I have been dismissed, I get up uncertainly from my chair and look inquiringly at G. I. "Yes, S'ter. I will. Thank you. Good morning, S'ter."

"Very well, Sister, until next week," and with this, she nods me out the door and in the direction of the chapel.

My head feels heavier than usual when I stand up and make my way out of G. I.'s office. The corridor leading to the chapel is deserted in the late morning when all are occupied with duties, and I am thankful for that. I want to be alone with my thoughts and my doubts. Does G. I. think I am good enough to be a nun or not? Am I? Do I have the purity, humility, and fortitude that are essential to lead a religious life? I pull open the large wooden door to God's quiet house. It's pretty empty in the chapel, except for a few older sisters spread around the pews like checkers left on a board in a game nearly over. The older nuns are either snoozing or praying intently. They don't seem to notice me as I make my way to the middle section on the left side that is reserved for postulants, and I quickly forget that I am sharing such a public space in this private state of mind. I take my place on the kneeling pad and glance up at the large cross at the back of the altar, then over to the statue of the Blessed Mother, offering my fervent prayer to her. "Dear Mary," I pray, "you are so good and pure; please help me. Give me the grace and strength to learn the lessons at hand, to grow in this community, and become worthy of my calling." When communing with Mary, I try to affix all my prayerful energy on her image, which I hope will offer me a direct line to her son, Jesus Christ. Somehow I know that appealing to her for understanding and guidance will bring me closer to God and help mold me into a good nun, despite my many human failings. I close my eyes, rest my head on cupped hands, and try to make peace with the stillness.

But even while I am praying, I am assailed by doubts. I feel guilty about my shortcomings, my homesickness and my loneliness, and I don't know what to do about these feelings. I seem unable to overcome my selfish desires and attachment to my will, the major impediment to union with God. I'm being asked to empty my head and my heart of all the things I've stored up over the past eighteen years and replace them with something else. Is this really what God wants me of me? Although such doubts make me waver in my vocation, in the deepest part of myself I feel God calling me here, to this place and to this life. I have no way of proving what I know to be true, but I am as sure of it as the fact that my grandmother loved me even though she gave few demonstrable signs of it. I read it in the way she held my hand when she marched me to church, and in the care she took preparing my bath during summertime visits at her home.

Yes, I believe that God gave me a religious vocation, but whether or not the convent authorities agree remains to be seen.

It's frightening to think that they will be the ones to judge both my vocation and me, especially when I consider that entrants to the community sometimes leave with no notice whatsoever. That's what happened to Bernadette who disappeared just two months into our postulancy. And I'm not sure that it was by her choice.

One day we were immersed in our routine of meditation, duties, Mass, breakfast, prayers, duties, prayers, lunch—and all of a sudden it occurred to us that we had not seen Bernadette the entire day. Bernadette was gone. Vanished. No one knew where or why or how, but we did know better than to ask G. I. or even talk openly about her sudden absence. We passed the news along in hushed tones and gestures at the refectory table, and mulled it over later during our walk from the motherhouse to our dormitory at Gerard's. According to our vow of obedience, the will and decisions of our superiors were not to be questioned or challenged because they represent the will of God. In less than ten months, all of us aspired to be admitted to the novitiate and, upon its completion, take our solemn vows of poverty, chastity, and obedience, with a decided emphasis on obedience. We couldn't question Bernadette's departure any more than we could question the community rule.

Even though I had known her for just a couple of months, I missed Bernadette and wished I could talk openly about her disappearance and the uneasy feelings it created in our group. The rigors of this life have thrown us together and helped us to grow close, like siblings in a strapped family or combatants on a battlefield, and so we mourned the loss of one of our own. I couldn't figure out what happened. Bernadette would not have won any awards for holiness, but she was sincere about being a nun. Okay, so she didn't spend every free minute in chapel, and she didn't walk around the motherhouse with eyes lowered and head bowed to *show her humility*. But she was unwavering in her dedication to the community's mission and ideal. She once told me that she hoped to return to her home town in upstate New York to work with wayward girls—I was impressed by that, and I also enjoyed talking with her about things because she was older and more mature than most of us who entered the convent just after high school. She had worked as a secretary for a couple of years and lived as an adult in the real world, and these were experiences that most of us would never know. But maybe that was the problem? Based on what I heard through the grapevine—Eliza told me, and she got her information from a novice friend who heard it from one of the junior sisters, this information having been passed along in whispers in front of our lockers in the hallway outside of chapel—the convent authorities asked her to leave because she was too independent. According to the convent-rumor pipeline, Bernadette was escorted from the convent in the middle of the night when all of us were assuredly sleeping. Incredible. Just gone without a trace. And G. I. said not a word to us and acted as if she had never been here in the first place. The news was disconcerting, the method terrifying, and the implications unthinkable.

Was Bernadette devastated? What was it like to face her family and friends at home? Did she feel like a failure?

I feel shame just thinking about being sent home, and I sure don't want to disappear like Bernadette did.

Aware of my wandering thoughts in the quiet of the chapel, I release my forehead from the fold of my hands, glance up at the crucifix, and determine to strengthen my commitment. In the community's hands I am but a plank of wood whose rough edges need sanding. I am prepared for that. I truly want to surrender my "self" to the community so I may more effectively be an instrument of God, but I am also finding it so hard to give up everything: family, friends, movies, pizza, romance, milkshakes, books, music, freedom, the *world*—and then to have to give up my very "self" as well. I just hope I can do it. I want to mature and have the pure heart of a nun. I want to love and serve God and do something special and important with my life; and I pray for the strength to surrender my attachment to this pesky will of mine. This blind obedience requirement troubles me, and I am still trying to figure out what a particular friendship is exactly and why it's so harmful, so I turn my doubts over to the Blessed Mother in the form of a prayer. I hope she passes it along.

Later, in my cot during the dead of night I turn my troubles and doubts over carefully, like the pages of a rare book. I miss my sister who vanished. I doubt my worthiness. And I wonder: what will happen to me? To make matters worse, my heart is swollen with homesickness for my old life, for Mom and Dad and Thomas, and even that rascal Anne Margaret. I can't allow myself even to think about Denny, although he creeps into the corners of my daydreams now and again. I have to erase my memory of him—of us—because it is a temptation that jeopardizes my vow of chastity. Each day, I will vow to work harder, to practice self-discipline, to make myself worthy. This is my new home, my new life, and a place for the person it is that I am becoming. I hold on tightly to this essential belief and it makes me feel hopeful. For God's good reason, I am in love with this life and its possibilities for me. And sleep is eluding me, so I crawl out of my bed and make my way to the frosty windowpane and look longingly at the first snow.

# Autumn

The long gray sleeves are rolled up to my elbow. With the sleeve of my upper arm, I wipe away the beads of sweat gathering across my forehead and then shade my eyes with the cup of my hand to glance at the sun suspended proudly above the horizon. I pause for a moment, to breathe in the sweet aroma of the day. It is Indian-summer warm, the kind of day that courses through the body like hot, spiced apple cider reminding me that I am alive. Kneeling on the porch of St. Gerard's Hall, I turn back to the work at hand, spreading paint thinner on four wooden chairs that are scratched and beaten with age. Next is the tedious work of peeling and scraping the layers of paint and varnish as my hands make their way down to the original wood. I labor to sand it to smooth perfection. I work alone today, despite the fact that we usually work in pairs or in groups. I reflect on the lesson that G. I. wants me to learn by isolating me in this way.

\*    \*    \*

During our early-morning trudge up the hill from St. Gerard's Hall to the motherhouse, I suck in the fall air that tastes as pungent and crisp as a Granny Smith apple. I don't even mind being awake this early-morning hour when the air bites my exposed skin and the inky sky seems much closer to night than day. We arrive about half an hour before daily Mass begins, and in that time, Eliza, Deirdre, and I storm through the second floor of the motherhouse to make up the senior sisters' beds. We do so swiftly, meticulously, and soundlessly, using the hospital-corner method, and we do not question this or any other duty we are asked to perform.

Our life during these formative years revolves around the motherhouse. The touchstone of the entire community, this is where everyone must undergo training before receiving mission assignments. Mission changes occur at regular intervals to help sisters guard against *attachment* to people and places, and they bring senior sisters to and from the motherhouse to receive their orders and, in some instances, to get a little refresher course in obedience. Like a military headquarters, the motherhouse serves as the center of policy and training. The nuns who have taken their vows and completed their training are referred to as "senior sisters." The rest of us—postulants (first year), novices (second year), and junior sisters (third and fourth year) who have taken their temporary vows—are divided by group and live in separate buildings scattered about our ample and secluded convent grounds.

Unlike the postulants'—or St. Gerard's—house, a dilapidated two-story gray frame building that looks like a forlorn army barracks, the motherhouse is an attractive modern three-story brick structure. Equipped with a chapel large enough to seat a few hundred nuns, an institutional-sized kitchen, and a fully staffed infirmary for the sick and elderly sisters, it houses up to 150 nuns. Some live at the motherhouse because they hold an important position within the convent administration, such as Mother General and her staff. Others are assigned to community missions and commute to their jobs in the city from the motherhouse. Finally, there are those who are actually missioned to the motherhouse, typically responsible for overseeing the kitchen, infirmary, or chapel. Mother Agatha is the "mother general." She is to the convent what the pope is to the church. All the nuns answer to her through their immediate superior or "mistress," as she is commonly referred to. The mission houses located away from the motherhouse may hold as few as three or as many as twenty or more sisters, and each one has its own superior. Sister Grace is the superior of the motherhouse; Sister George Ignatius is the superior of the postulants' house; Sister John is the superior of the novitiates' house; and Sister Vera Marie is the superior of the juniorate house. Being a young sister in formation, I must defer to all the senior sisters, like a private does to an officer. But my direct superiors, G. I. in the postulancy, followed by John in the novitiate, and, finally, Vera Marie in the juniorate, are directly responsible for my indoctrination in convent life, and so they control every phase of my routine and progress. I need their approval for everything: I must apply to them for my monthly supply of Kotex and toothpaste, and I need their permission to report sick to the infirmary and write a letter to my family.

In the four years of our formation, we are trained for the rigors of religious life and prepared professionally for future mission work. Confined to the motherhouse, we pray; we work; we attend scripture class, but we spend most of our time performing physical labor, including preparing and cleaning up after meals for the one hundred plus people who populate the motherhouse. We also make the beds; wash the windows; scrub the bathrooms; strip, buff, and wax the floors; and clean the chapel, as well as our own living quarters. "Cleanliness is next to godliness" is the adage by which we live every single day. This period of convent training is not a life for the lazy or the weak because the work is arduous and never ending. Our postulant leader, G. I., works just as hard along with her young charges. I often think about this, of how she is perpetually living the weary and tedious life of the postulant. At her age. Whatever it is.

*     *     *

I am busily dusting the pews, one of my easier daily chores, when I catch a glimpse of Krista gesturing to me from the left side of the chapel. "What?" I ask with raised eyebrows and shoulders and then realize she is beckoning me to join her. I take a quick inventory, but the chapel is nearly empty except for two nearly comatose elderly nuns in wheelchairs. Thinking that G. I. should still be safely ensconced in her charity sessions with the other postulants, I steal over to the doorway to the hall that leads to a side door into the sacristy. Krista abruptly opens the door, whisks me through the hallway, and ushers me in to the sacristy, closing the door behind us. I find myself standing in the sacred area where the priest dons his vestments each day and says his prayers before saying Mass and giving benediction. Krista is giggling and shushing me conspiratorially, but fear shoots through me when I realize it is nearly 4:00 p.m. and time for afternoon benediction. "Where is Sister Henrietta? What's going on?"

Instead of answering, Krista places her forefinger against her lips and points me toward Sister Henrietta herself who stands in the anteroom, across from us on the opposite side of the altar. I feel sacrilegious staring at her with the altar between us.

Though we stand unseen, I realize I am now trapped because the sisters are just beginning to file past the sacristy and into chapel for benediction, and I can't risk bumping into G. I. on my way out. But excitement soon replaces anxiety as I recognize that Henrietta—we often drop the "sister part" among ourselves—is sporting a huge grin and holding a forbidden transistor radio against her right ear. From her other hand extends two fingers, and her mouth is sounding out the words "L.A. in front." I raise a clenched fist in response, more as a signal of appreciation than celebration since I am a fan of neither team in this World Series pennant race. But I am interested; it is, after all, a link to home and my former life. The motherhouse janitor, whom we affectionately refer to as Mr. Grim because he never smiles and rarely acknowledges us, keeps a portable radio tuned into the games in his basement office. That's convenient for me since sweeping and mopping the basement floor, one of my major duties, gives me a legitimate reason for stalking his office and I can catch the score. So I am aware that the Los Angeles Dodgers and the Minnesota Twins are neck and neck, and that today's game will decide the outcome. Here I am in the sacristy of the convent chapel, excited to hear the results of the last game of the 1965 World Series, even though I have absolutely no loyalty to either team. But what is even more astonishing is seeing the friendly, if mischievous, smile on the face of demon-nun Sister Henrietta, known for inspiring terror in postulants and novices alike. After acknowledging the unexpected gift from Henrietta, I slip unobserved out the door and into my pew in chapel, just in time to see Sister Henrietta solemnly genuflect while preparing the altar for benediction. For a moment or two, I bask in the guilty pleasure of briefly touching a part of the outside world that is receding from me a little bit more each day.

*     *     *

It is a brilliant fall day, and after breakfast G. I. informs us that it's time for the twice yearly task of washing the massive seven-by-four windows spread around three sides of the rectangular-shaped refectory. Two swinging doorways lead into the kitchen on the interior wall, a short space from the main entrance to the corridor. From the second floor, the windows provide a glorious view of the wooded convent grounds on one side, and the Catholic high school that borders the west side of the motherhouse on the opposite side. The school sits so close to the main convent building that, during weekdays, our dinnertime devotional readings must contend with the general din of chatter and competing radios that accompany the daily lunch ritual of the teenagers. Such clamor intrudes on the hushed, austere atmosphere that cloaks the interior of the convent grounds. (Proust suggested that smells trigger memories, but for me, it's usually a familiar sound—a melody or the squeal of peeling car tires—that grabs me by the back of the neck, tossing me into memory's stream.) But I can no longer succumb to wistful reminders of the past. In order to practice self-discipline, I must pull myself right back to the task at hand for fear of being swayed by familiar sounds into feeling forbidden desires.

Even with twenty-four pairs of hands, given the size and number of windows, a long morning of work awaits. Gathering us around her like a vigilant mother duck, G. I. carefully instructs us, prescribing an apparently timeworn four-step process for us to follow. Windex would be too simple, I guess. Instead, we are armed with buckets, a mixture of ammonia and water, and piles of newspaper. Work is work, of course, but when everyone pitches in and does her share, it's not so bad; when it comes to working efficiently and cheerfully as a group, our class is first rate and downright inspiring, or so the novices assure us. They report that the motherhouse sisters are quite pleased by our genuinely "cheerful spirit." Imagine that. We are a crop of fine recruits. I am very proud of our reputation and the fact that we enjoy working hard and well together. G. I. is also continually reminding us that all our activities—whether we're scrubbing the bathrooms in solitude, dusting pews in the chapel, or carrying out a group project like this one—when properly carried out and offered up, become a prayer and a further entitlement to the community. When we are not praying or meditating or sitting in Scripture class, we are engaged in some sort of physical labor. I guess the idea is to keep our young bodies busy and our minds focused on a higher spiritual plane. We are ever mindful of being closely monitored and scrutinized so as to keep us on our spiritual course. What we feel most, though, is not so much spiritual as taxed, exhausted, and, when we have a few minutes to think about it, homesick.

As the "head" of the postulant class that is yearly inducted into the community, G. I. must feel enormous responsibility. Like us, she is also accountable to a higher authority, Mother General, and her awareness of this obligation is evident, especially when our activities are visible to the entire community. High-strung any way, today G. I. bounds around the refectory at a fevered pitch, inspecting equipment, barking orders, admonishing us to be careful as we stand on the three-foot tiled sills in order to reach the windowpanes. After getting the process underway and seeing to it that all hands are busily engaged, G. I. tries to steal out of the refectory. But G. I. is not the inconspicuous type and her absence is felt, if not observed, immediately. As soon as she's out of view, the chatter begins, the volume rises steadily, and everybody starts to joke and goof around.

As I stand on the windowsill, sleeves rolled up and arms stretched upward attacking the dirt with my ammonia-soaked newspaper, I can feel the sun warm my skin through the windowpane. I don't mind hard work. There's something awfully pure about abandoning yourself to a physical effort, earning your sweat, and then seeing a thing transformed before your eyes because of it. I wish the other aspects of this life were as gratifyingly simple and clear. I abandon myself to this occupation in this moment and I feel happy and carefree, and the good spirits soaring around me make me want to sing. So I do. Pretty soon, the others join in. We start harmonizing to Peter, Paul, and Mary songs: "Lemon tree very pretty and the lemon flower is sweet but the fruit of the poor lemon is impossible to eat," "a hundred miles, a hundred miles, a hundred miles, a hundred miles, Lord I'm five hundred miles away from home . . ." Then we launch into a convent favorite, "Kumbaya, my Lord, kumbaya . . ." We're in high gear now, so we start on the show tunes. I introduce the harmonizing favorite from *The Sound of Music*, "Doe a deer, a female deer . . . ," and then we are all over the musical map. Somebody else picks it up with "Raindrops on roses and whiskers on kittens," followed by *My Fair Lady's* "All I want is a room somewhere far away from the cold night air," and then on to "Dream the impossible dream" from *Man from La Mancha*. After a while, we tire of the musicals, and our energy ebbs, until I reignite the group by introducing a few pop songs from our teenage years. I don't think people ever forget the songs that got them through adolescence, and even though we are aspiring nuns, we're not that far removed from our counterparts on the outside. We launch into songs from the old days: "In the jungle, the mighty jungle, the lion sleeps tonight . . ." and "In the still of the night, darling, I held you, held you tight . . . ," "Listen to the rhythm of the falling rain telling me just what a fool I've been . . . ," "Stop in the name of love, before you break my heart, think it ooovver . . ."

By mid-morning, we're so absorbed in remembering the titles and lyrics of our favorite tunes that we don't notice G. I. slipping silently back into the room. Apparently, our singing has traveled down the refectory hallway, into the chapel and the ears of the praying senior sisters. I can't tell if she is more displeased with our choice of songs or with our unsisterly enthusiasm, but G. I. is a fuming dragon. I watch her pinched, furious face charge in my direction, gesturing for me to climb down from the windowsill. "Sister!" which is how she refers to us even though we have not yet been given our sister names, she snorts, "you are the ringleader here?" Clearly, a rhetorical question. "This unseemly behavior will simply not be tolerated. Do you realize that you are disturbing the sanctity of the chapel? You exert a rowdy influence on the others that must be checked." Scrambling down to the floor, I throw out my hands, ready to explain but then think better of it.

"Yes, Sister," I respond, chastened. "I'm sorry, Sister." The others suddenly disassociate themselves from me as well as the unpleasant scene G. I. is making. They resume attacking the dirt on the windows, while I grope mutely for more convincing words of apology in order to save myself. But it is pointless. G. I.'s in one of her sterner huffs and won't be appeased. And I am guilty, although that does not seem to be an accurate term to describe how I view the situation. Her lips are pursed and severe: "Perhaps you will benefit from some time alone?" Another rhetorical question. I do what I am expected to do, which is to accept her rebuke with humility. Then I am banished to St. Gerard's in disgrace where I am expected to reflect on my misbehavior and ways to use my "talents more prudently."

For the remainder of the day I work outside and in isolation, stripping and refinishing an antique table and matching chairs and trying to meditate on my faults and unseemly behavior. I am ashamed. I begin to understand the terms of life here and its cornerstones of docility and self-abnegation. It goes like this: G. I. is my superior; therefore, her will is an expression of God's will. Practically speaking, this means it doesn't matter that I don't think I did anything "wrong" because that is not the point. The point is that I am expected to accept the correction humbly and submit to the will of my superior in order to learn some necessary lesson or virtue (humility? obedience?). I try to accept the idea that G. I.'s will is God's will, but much as I try, my doubt keeps resurfacing. I don't honestly believe I have committed such a reprehensible act, even as I realize that my way of thinking is wrong. I wrestle with my thoughts and consider the harsh demands of religious life, alone on the porch, and in the autumn sunlight while singing out loud to myself with no one around to scold me.

# Summer

A large grassy area sprawls out behind the Victorian-looking stone structure that serves as the novitiate. We put it to good use as a makeshift ball field. Not that all of my postulant classmates want much to use it for that purpose on this muggy Philadelphia summer day, but no one asks them if they want to chase after balls and run around bases. No, as in all matters, we are told rather than polled. But for me, picking up a ball and glove is as natural as using my limbs; regardless of how long it has been, I always know just what to do. I am at home in a field surrounded by balls and bats and homemade bases.

As a little girl of eight or so, I gravitated toward the sandlot populated by neighborhood toughs, who played ball as if they were at war. Aware even then of the limitations of my gender, I eyed them with envy. I spent many solitary hours practicing my skills and improving my eye-hand coordination by throwing and catching a rubber ball against the concrete wall of the grocery store next to our house. Over time, I developed a smooth, confident delivery and sharpened my reflexes, priding myself in the ability to hook a fast-traveling ball right into my glove. I also spent hours watching the Philadelphia Phillies play on television with my dad. An excitable, passionate sports fan of hometown teams, he would storm out of the room in disgust whenever his team fell behind, a bad habit that I eventually inherited. But at that unvarnished age, I held fast, more concerned with the moves of the athletes than with the score of the game. I studied the ball players' graceful athleticism and their various offensive and defensive actions—the dips, the throws, the stretches, and, best of all, the triumphant gestures. I noted the crouched position of the infielders that fearlessly scooped the ball out of the dust and flipped it to the appropriate base without hesitation. They didn't even have to look at the ball's destination, even when they were off balance, because they knew instinctively where the ball needed to go. I admired that. In his sparse free time, Dad, a skillful athlete in his own day, would take me to the park to play catch. He always beamed when another father approached him to say, "Hey, buddy, your little girl throws just like a boy." It was the ultimate compliment for both of us.

One day at the sandlot, the kids came up short while calling sides for teams, and after much snickering and no little debate, I was invited to join and even out the sides. "Hey. You. Girl. Can you play at all?" Robbie was the tallest and cutest boy of the bunch. He wore dark, baggy blue jeans and a white T-shirt with a red Philadelphia Phillies baseball cap perched on his head. I could tell he was trying to keep those blond curls under control. He had a boyishly tough image to protect, and he didn't want to look anything like a sissy. Robbie was a pitcher, and a darn good one from what I had observed from my grassy seat. He was also the ringleader of the "sandlot league." He was obviously desperate to get on the field and get a game going, even if it meant asking a girl to play.

My heart thumped wildly when he turned from the group and addressed me. I shrugged and called back indifferently—I didn't want them to think I was *too* interested—"Yeah." I had been squatting in the grass to the left side of the field, but I sprang quickly to my feet when Robbie beckoned despite the not-so-muffled protestations that his decision incurred, "Robbieeee, SHE'S a GIRL! Oh, man, this is going to ruin everything!"

"Oh, shut up, you guys." Fortunately for me, Robbie was a leader on and off the field, and his assertiveness quickly silenced the protestors.

I don't know what made Robbie give me a chance that day. Maybe it was a hunch. Maybe he thought I was cute. (I should be so lucky.) Maybe he felt sorry for me. Maybe it had absolutely nothing to do with the fact that he knew I was always out there watching, but his choosing me was merely the chance act of a guy eager to play ball. But he did, and I reveled in the smirk of sweet satisfaction that he flashed to his teammates after seeing me field those first few balls in right field, the least desirable position reserved for the weakest player and one to which I was not banished for long. On the field, and with my trusty glove in my hand, I felt anxious rather than scared because I knew what needed to be done, and my body did as I commanded. The boys observed what I felt: I was a natural. Pretty soon, the boys replaced their complaints and derision with pats on the back and shouts of encouragement. After that day, I was one of the first kids to get picked for a side and the only girl on the field. I had something of value to offer. My life had meaning.

\*   \*   \*

I am just leaving chapel on my way to midmorning scripture class. Our instructor, Mother Michael, now retired from her position as mother general of the community, continues to wield considerable influence around the motherhouse. She is revered as one of the pioneer sisters of the community, having worked directly with the founder and original mother general. Considering her position and her characteristically severe manner, I am always a little nervous in her presence. Eager to please and make a good impression on her, I am heading to class a bit early to demonstrate my enthusiasm for the day's lesson on Genesis when G. I. intercepts me in the hallway, requesting that I accompany her to her office on the second floor. Apparently, she has been lying in wait outside the first-floor classroom. "Yes, Sister," I reply nonchalantly, while frantically searching my memory and thinking to myself, "Oh no. What did I do now?" I perform a quick mental inventory, but nothing comes up. I have been trying especially hard to monitor my behavior. I follow her meekly, relieved that she cannot read my internal whine, "Oh no! What now?"

G. I. ushers me into the metal chair in front of the well-polished desk. Then she tiptoes behind it and seats herself in the straight-backed wooden chair. A simple brown crucifix hangs alone on the wall above her, and a small bookcase filled with theological and religious texts rests against the wall to the side. While I'm waiting for her to wind up, I scan the titles: St. Augustine's *Confessions,* St. Thomas's *Summa Theologica*, and several books on saints, including St. Theresa of the Little Flower and St. John of the Cross. That's it. The office is as spartan as its primary occupant. Sidelined momentarily by apprehension concerning the reason for this little one-on-one, I miss her introduction, but my mind jumps to attention when I hear the words "use your skills to perform a service for the community." I don't have to worry about responding and revealing my distraction, because she proceeds without a pause. "You see, Sister, we are obligated to ensure that our postulants fulfill the required credits for physical education. My weekly class on folk dancing satisfies those requirements for the college only partially." I wince automatically at this, reminded of our weekly forays into square dancing and other traditional ethnic dances. Gifted with grace and balance in most athletic activities, I am, nevertheless, a total klutz when it comes to dosey-do-ing in formation on the dance floor, especially under G. I.'s impatient glare. "And," she continues breathlessly, lifting a folder from her desk and aiming it toward me, "I see that you have extensive experience in the area of sports. You competed in softball, basketball, and track, and you received the award for the 'Outstanding Athlete of the Year' when you graduated from the eighth grade. Is that correct, Sister?"

A little taken aback, I stutter, "Well, yes, yes, Sister, I did." I don't offer the fact that when my brother graduated two years before I did, he received the award for being the "outstanding student." Besides, I earned that award. It made me feel really proud of myself and special. I catch myself. Oh gosh, is this an example of pride and, therefore, a fault that I need to confess in public charity? Will I ever get the hang of this impossible virtue of humility? But if I negate my accomplishment, isn't that just another more perverse form of pride? I cannot have this debate with myself right now because G. I. is barreling along in her one-sided conversation. I catch the word "CYO." The letters stand for Catholic Youth Organization, which sponsors athletic and other activities for Catholic school kids. She's noting that I was an active member. She's holding a manila-folder file and reading to me about me and my background. It's making me a little nervous. What all is in there?

G. I. looks up. She is puzzled and wondering why I didn't continue playing sports in high school. I explain how much I regret that I didn't, but our Catholic high school did not offer competitive sports for the girls, only for the boys. I also neglect to share the part about my needing to work to help pay my own way, which left little time for sports or other recreational activities. My dad supported the idea of my attending a public school, believing I could win a scholarship to college for basketball or softball or track, but I was a Catholic school kid through and through. Besides, the money situation was tight, and I wanted to help out. On week nights, I'd drag myself home from the 5:00 to 11:00 p.m. shift at Howard Johnson's restaurant exhausted but pleased that I could dump out a pocket full of tips into my mom's lap to help meet household expenses. "You're so good," she'd coo while removing my white waitress shoes and rubbing my feet appreciatively after I collapsed, exhausted, into the living-room chair. My mom's appreciation was enough for me. It made up for the lost leisure time that I once spent having fun on a competitive athletic field. I worked for selfish reasons, too. I wanted the fashionable clothing and pocket money my friends took for granted. I wanted to buy myself a black and gray Chesterfield coat—we had always gotten my cousins' hand-me-downs—and the popular Peter Gunn shoes everyone was wearing.

My reverie is interrupted by the now-familiar guttural sound of G. I.'s voice. "Well, Sister, clearly you have ample experience and skills in the area of athletics, and I, of course, am certified as a physical-education instructor. Do you think you could work with the other postulants this semester under my supervision, promoting exercise and teaching them how to play softball?" As I have noted before, G. I. has an odd way of using the interrogative for declarative purposes. But on this occasion, I am flattered rather than put off by it. (Another example of being prideful? Is there no hope for me?)

Clearly pleased, I try not to act too excited lest she think me unworthy. "Well, sure, Sister, I would be glad to do that."

"Good," a snappy but not unfriendly reply. "Of course, you will have to grade each sister at the end of the term on the basis of her performance." My enthusiasm wanes, like the air that sputters out of a deflating balloon. Again, I stammer, "Uh, Sister, I don't really feel qualified to do that. Besides, evaluating the others would make me a little uncomfortable." It occurs to me that, maybe, this is the idea. Perhaps it isn't a compliment but a test.

Her voice is firm now, but the tone remains pleasant, almost courting, "Sister, I must be the judge in these matters," emphasizing the "I." "I am appointing you as the instructor of physical education under my supervision for this term, and I expect you will do a good job of instructing, followed by grading. Yes?" Then without a pause, "Splendid. I do thank you, Sister, for your help and cooperation." She is cueing me to leave as she has done on other occasions, but I also detect something different and more respectful in her manner toward me. I veer away from the doubt and near paranoia of a minute ago, suddenly reassured by her altered tone. Does this appointment of me as instructor mean that she is beginning to think well of me? That she trusts me? That she thinks, maybe, just maybe, I have the right stuff for this life? After promising to do my best, I back out of her office and float toward my class, vowing to visit the chapel afterward and offer a prayer of thanks.

*   *   *

Mother Agatha, the current mother general and successor to Mother Michael, has just returned from visiting some of the mission houses. Lucky for us. To celebrate her homecoming, she rings the hand bell from her presiding seat at the head table, signaling permission for us to talk during the remainder of dinner. The room immediately swells with sound. I have arrived late, so I am seated near the end of the three long postulants' tables that stretch toward the first table at the back of the refectory. Our tables, for those of us in training as well as for the senior sisters, are perpendicular to the horizontal "head table" at the front where Mother Agatha and the other community administrators oversee community meals.

The necessity for my lateness is a blessing. Were it not for my duties, I would come directly from chapel with the others and end up sitting at the first table, presided over by G. I. G. I. keeps a sharp eye on us as well as on our plates to ensure that we eat everything we are served. This is not good for me. I am a notoriously picky eater, known to eschew food simply on the basis of its appearance. Tapioca pudding, a favorite of institutional cuisine because it is economical, is a case in point. I will do everything possible to avoid placing this gray white gluey substance with holes that look like Martian eyes anywhere near my discriminating palate. One tactic of avoidance is to extend my duty or work detail well into the meal hour, thus detaining me. The result is that everyone will be nearly finished eating when I sit down, and in the melee surrounding cleanup, no one notices that I have skipped dessert. Fortunately for me, because of reporting late, I have to sit at the far end of the long rectangular table that puts me at the outer limits of G. I.'s sharp sights. The rejected tapioca in its pukey green plastic bowl lands, unobserved, on the tray of extras bound for destinations unknown, usually, our next day's dessert. Is this circular reasoning? Another more risky method which I sometimes employ, especially on "liver Tuesday," is to slide the liver (or other inedible item) on another plate concealed on my lap and then pass it, surreptitiously, under the table and over to Celia who eats just about anything. This tactic requires flawless planning and good positioning, as well as an eager Celia. The first two conditions are iffy, but I can always rely on my classmate's enthusiastic appetite.

Angela and Krista, also late because of chapel duty, are seated at the same table. I look forward to catching up with them amid the commotion of post-dinner chatter and cleanup. This thrice-daily ritual is quite an efficient process, allowing us to wash and dry all the dinnerware at the table: plastic tubs filled with boiling-hot soapy water are obtained from the kitchen, along with an empty container for leftover scraps from the plates. In this way, the sisters at each table are responsible for scraping, washing, and drying their own utensils and then resetting that same table for the next meal.

Usually, I don't get to talk with my friends until the end of the day and I am exited to share my good news. I tell them about being called to G.I.'s office and how relieved I was, not only *not* to be reprimanded but also to learn that she was actually asking for my help. "So G. I. wants me to coach you guys; you know, teach you the fundamentals of softball to satisfy our physical-education requirements. Isn't that great? Can you believe it?"

Krista picks up on my excitement and responds in her typically upbeat fashion. "Kathy"—we don't quite get the hang of calling each other "Sister"—"I think that's great! Good for you! I think it shows G. I.'s confidence in you, don't you?" Here, she mistakenly looks to Angela for support. Angela just shakes her head disgustedly and leans the heel of her hand on her forehead while saying something inaudible. In Italian, I think. It bears noting here that Angela is a gifted musician, who plays piano, guitar, and even the bongo drum, and she has a voice with near-perfect pitch. She can play almost any tune by ear, and she reads and writes music as well. I love hanging out with her at the piano. Even though I can't play an instrument, I'm learning to read notes enough to sing them, and Angela and I have fun singing and composing together because she's good at writing music, and I have a flair for writing lyrics. But Angela's talent is special. Rhythm, she definitely has, but don't ask her to do anything the least bit physical or athletic, hence, her dismayed response when I mention the softball activity that G. I. has planned for our physical-education class. You would think that I was asking her to wear a hair shirt. I don't take it personally. I'm getting to understand Angela and how she's wired. Ditto for Krista.

Angela, Krista, and I are growing closer. We are like buddies in battle who look out for one another. It's not our shared circumstances alone that connect us. Who knows why people are drawn toward one another? I sometimes think the magnetic force at work is located in our gaps, in what we are missing rather than in who we are. The three of us have such different backgrounds and personalities, and yet some invisible force pulls us toward one another.

Angela is taciturn, almost brooding, and she has a depth of feeling she herself can never quite grasp, although she expresses it in her soulful music. She is pretty in an unconventional way, with doe-like eyes encased in enviably smooth olive-toned skin. But chipmunk cheeks and a nose with a bump on the bridge combine to detract from an otherwise pretty face. Angela's nervous system is as finely tuned as her musical ear, and at first, she does not take well to my spirited personality. Two years my senior, Angela worked as a secretary in the outside world before joining the convent. Maybe that explains her sedate demeanor compared with most of the rest of us. But I don't think so. Docile and reserved by nature, Angela is, for reasons unknown, wound just a little tight. Krista and I have tacitly agreed to loosen her up a little, and so far, we are having moderate success.

The three of us connected after visiting hours ended with benediction on our first visitors' Sunday, exactly one month after entrance day. We hugged our loved ones good-bye and then watched them file to the back of chapel, while we were grouped together behind the novices, an indication of our lowly place in the religious order. Our instructions were to refrain from looking back at our families, once having taken our place in chapel. Visiting Sunday gave us a free hour or so between the end of Benediction and the bell summoning us to dinner, so I wandered outside knowing that G. I. would be preoccupied with inventorying and organizing the foodstuffs donated by the families. Krista stood at the bottom of the concrete steps outside the back door of the motherhouse, comforting a distraught Angela while sobbing disconsolately herself. Approaching cautiously, I swallowed my own rush of emotion, positioned myself between them, and placed an arm around a shoulder of each.

I decided that the situation was entirely too bleak and required a little levity. "Say," I offered cautiously, "do you two want to go on a little adventure?" It was early evening, and the sun rested languidly on the horizon, trying to decide whether to dip or rise. That's how indecisive Angela appeared at the hint of such a shady pre-dinner enterprise. But Krista perked right up. Wiping her tear-stained face with the sleeve of her gray dress and reaching behind me, she patted Angela smartly on the back. Her light brown eyebrows rose, and as her eyes caught mine they looked suddenly mischievous. "What's to lose? Whaddaya got in mind?"

We both examined Angela for signs of consent. It was risky because we had only been classmates for a month, and at this stage, we barely knew one another. How could we be sure that one of us wouldn't report our little escapade, or worse, accuse us of a "fault" in our weekly public charity? (What would the fault be exactly? I didn't know, but I knew there had to be a fault in there somewhere.)

Angela's resigned "okay, why not?" matched the shrug in her left shoulder and indicated her approval. Relief replaced my anxiety, and so I proceeded. "Well," I whispered conspiratorially, although no one else was around, "I found this spot back in the woods while walking Mother Michael's dog. It's right on the edge of the motherhouse grounds, and it's very secluded, but you can actually see into a neighboring public park. Wanna go check it out?"

Krista responded immediately by raising her finger up to her lips to signify that we should stay put because she'd be right back. With that, she flew up the stairs and disappeared inside the back door. Angela and I, left wondering what in the world she was up to, shuffled uncomfortably until she returned within minutes with several homemade chocolate chip cookies and an opened bottle of Coca-Cola, no doubt confiscated from her family's food contribution. Contraband. How did she manage to get by G. I. without being seen? She did not bother to explain. Fine by me. I won't shirk from a little danger or turn down such an uncommon treat.

"Okay. C'mon. Let's go." I grabbed both of them by the arm and led them in a brisk pace down the hill and on to the path through the woods. Dense brush and high, arching tree limbs muted the ebbing sunlight even further. Autumn's face shone everywhere. The leaves performed a lively, colorful dance on the way to the ground. Faint sounds emanated from the other side of the creek resting lazily at the bottom of a ravine about thirty feet below separating the convent grounds from the city park. The small clearing came unexpectedly and provided a clear view of life in the outside world on a fall Sunday, but the overhanging trees afforded us sufficient protection from being seen ourselves. I imagined how altered the scene would be, though, come winter, with the thinned foliage and limbs stripped bare. I came to love the solace and solitude of this place and visited it to tune my anxious heart to nature's serene rhythm whenever I could steal a free moment.

"Wow, what a neat spot," Krista cooed as she slid down and positioned herself against the ample base of an old maple tree. Immediately, she tore into the cookies and started divvying them up while scanning the view. Angela and I plunked ourselves atop a fallen and splintered tree limb at the edge of the clearing. Together, we studied the park below and watched the lovers stroll along the path, the occasional person bobbing by on horseback, and the children squealing gleefully at the bank of the creek. Krista handed us each a cookie, and took a swig of soda before she passed it to me. Then she leaned back, relaxed, and closed her eyes. I took a sip and pushed the bottle toward Angela who took a long sip.

"Tastes awfully good, huh?" I asked, biting into the soft, rich cookie.

"Yeah," Angela agreed, handing the bottle back and biting hungrily into a cookie herself.

"Maybe things always seem better when you can't have them. You think? You know, being denied something makes it that much more desirable."

Angela looked at me quizzically. "Gee, I never thought about it that way. Makes sense, I guess." I followed her eyes, which rested on a couple holding hands, their heads resting lightly against each other. They were moist with yearning. Observing the lovers after just having visited with loved ones from home reminded us what we had given up by dedicating ourselves to a religious life of prayer and missionary work.

Putting the snacks aside, I reached over and clasped her hand. "Tough visit, huh?" I offered tenderly.

"Uh huh." Angela left the cookies on her lap and placed the fingertips of her right hand against her eyes, as if to protect her fresh tears from the light.

"Miss your family and friends?"

Angela nodded.

"Me too," I added wistfully.

"Gee," whined Krista, who roused herself, scooted over to us, and crouched down in front of the limb, placing a hand atop our two. "Don't leave me out of the misery."

Despite the swell of sadness, Angela and I had to chuckle at Krista's childlike forlornness. Krista chimed in, her high-pitched giggle growing steadily more hysterical, until we were all laughing and crying simultaneously, as our pent-up emotions spilled out like apples from an upturned cart. The sound, of course, carried, and I could see the curious heads straining to locate the source through the brush and trees on the other side of the creek.

We laughed and cried at nothing and everything—at how a chocolate chip cookie tasted like pure bliss, at the absurdity that what we were doing was forbidden, at the realization that we would never have lovers or children of our own, at the discovery that bonding with one another would give us the strength to carry through with our shared resolve, which took a different shape within each of us. This moment, I decided, begged to be sealed and treasured.

"So you guys know what this means, don't you?" I prompted, firmly pressing our hands together as the hysteria waned.

"No, what?" Krista demanded, while Angela studied me quizzically.

I stood up, raised my palm to my heart, invited them to do the same, and made my proclamation: "All for one and one for all. Having found and consoled one another, we shall stick together through thick and thin, no matter the need, no matter the problem. Henceforth, we shall be there for one another always and forever just like the 'Three Musketeers,' and this spot, henceforth, shall be called 'Camelot,' our secret place of refuge and consolation." Like my mother who mixes her metaphors, I didn't mind mixing mythologies. And so the bond was formed, our pact made. We solidified it by extending our hands and piling them, one firmly on top of the other.

Now it is summer, and the bond forged that autumn day at the beginning of our postulancy has fitted us with a keen awareness, ready support, and unwavering commitment to one other, like soldiers on the battlefield.

In this moment, as in the months following the sealing of our pact, I am reminded of my commitment to look after my friend. I can see that what Angela needs right now is to be reassured, and so I attempt the optimistic-cheerleader approach. "So what are you worried about? C'mon, this is gonna be fun, I promise."

"Oh, for you, maybe," she mutters, clearly pouting now, as she scrapes food particles off her plate with a spatula before handing it over to me. "I'm a city girl. I hate physical exercise. And I don't know the first thing about sports. Besides, does this mean we're gonna be graded like we were in G. I.'s folk-dancing class?"

"Uh oh," I think to myself. With my rubber-gloved hands, I plunge her plate into the dishpan of soapy water and furiously work the miniature mop, trying to side step her unsettling question. Krista dries the plates and silverware as fast as I wash them, glancing back and forth between the two of us and waiting, no doubt, for a space to park her two cents. But I silence her with my raised right hand, the miniature dish mop punctuating the air like a conductor's baton.

"Hey, don't you think I remember how you saved me from Sister Ann Marie's sewing class?" Oh, boy did she ever save me! After the convent seamstress fitted us with our first gray "Sunday" dress to be worn on visiting days and religious holy days, we were expected to take sewing classes and learn how to sew our own work garbs. A pity for me. Besides being totally inexperienced and inept with a needle and thread, let alone with a sewing machine, I was terrified of Sister Ann Marie, dictator of the sewing room. The bespectacled, middle-aged Anne Marie wore a perpetual grimace on her yellow-hued face, as if she were constantly in pain. She obviously disdains her "mission" as community seamstress and has not taken well to being stationed at the motherhouse. I mean, who enters a domestic missionary order to be a tailor for nuns' outfits? Worse, she gets furiously impatient with inexperienced sewers. I just couldn't quite get the hang of sliding the material through the threaded machine. It came out all bunched up, or else my seam zigzagged in various unintended directions. Sister Ann Marie would stand over me, clucking her tongue in disgust and spouting directions. As in all situations where I am struggling to learn something completely new in an unsympathetic, or, as in this case, a hostile atmosphere, my anxiety paralyzes me, serving only to impede my comprehension of instructions. Incapable of processing the simplest of directions, I feel like an idiot. Anyway, Eliza came to my rescue several times in class, as she rethreaded my machine and straightened out the material, effectively warding off further reproach from Sister Anne Marie. But it was Angela, an experienced seamstress who, afterward, tore out the jagged seams to sew the drab gray dress properly, and I am deeply grateful because I have to wear it every day!

I remind Angela of how she rescued me and my garb during those first trying weeks in the community sewing room. "So whaddaya think, that I wouldn't help you out and do the same for you?"

But by now Krista has begun prattling away, her jaw flapping as fast as the dish towel in her efficient hands. "Yeah, Angela, so what's to be afraid of? I don't know the first thing about baseball either"—clearly failing to distinguish the difference between the six-inch sphere used in baseball versus the twelve-inch sphere used in softball, as well as the corresponding differences in field size and rules—"but I don't care. What's to worry about? At least, we won't have to do those dumb square dances anymore. Thank God! Besides, G. I.'s putting Kathy in charge. And Kathy'll be a lot more patient with us than G. I., won't you?" Here she looks over to me, as if passing the ball in a move toward the basket.

"Yeah, sure. Don't you think I understand that most of you have never played before? Gosh, I think Deirdre, Geraldine, and Celia are the only ones with any experience, so most of you guys will be in the same boat." Now I'm imploring her, "Angela, I'll teach you. I promise. I'll help everybody, Angela, I proomm . . . issse." I lengthen the word to achieve maximum effect, and I guess it works. Fastidious in everything, Angela meticulously slides the crumbs off the table and brushes them into the plastic pail, freeing her left hand so that she can threaten me with her raised forefinger.

"Ya know," she confides in her nasal New Yorkese, "I just don't wanna feel stupid and make a fool outta myself." Angela has this thing about looking foolish, sensitive soul that she is. Guess that's why it's so hard for her to lighten up. Krista and I will just have to keep working on that. Now, when we hook our arms through hers and skip down the hill to St. Gerard's Hall singing, "Oh, we ain't got a barrel of money / maybe we're ragged and funny / but we'll travel along / singing a song / side by side," Angela actually joins in instead of dismissing us with a peremptory shake of her head. She relaxes her finger, and her face softens, verging on the famous Angela half smile, meant to warn me it could break into a full smile at any time, but don't count on it.

"Hey," I offer, building on my encouraging tone and teasing her into a full smile now, "would I ever let you down?" Recalling our oath in Camelot, I repeat, "never ever would I let you down. Count on it." (Meant with all my heart at the time, how I wish now that I had not lived to do just that.)

"Yeah," Krista adds, hamming it up and sporting her elfin grin, "remember, we're going to see each other through this convent boot camp 'cause we're in this thing together, through thick and thin, just like 'The Three Musketeers,' right?" In chorus, just seconds shy of Mother Agatha's sharp signal for silence and prayer, we all repeat "right" and slap our palms together, mine still covered by the sudsy yellow rubber glove.

Because we reported late to dinner, we have not finished the table dishes, and that means we'll file into chapel for afternoon prayers minutes after they have started, something which is bound to rouse G. I.'s ire, no matter how justified the cause. Krista must be thinking the same thing because our eyes lock as we silently and simultaneously wave Angela away from the table, knowing that we take the heat better than she does.

Krista is an odd duck, and we probably wouldn't even be friends on the "outside." She is shrill and loud in a nervous kind of way, and because of her exceptional thinness, she looks fragile. Krista reminds me of an egret, a narrow bird with long wiry legs that skitters across the sand by the ocean. She has a sharp face with delicate features, and her pale skin has a bluish tinge to it that sometimes gives her a sickly aspect. When she expresses herself, Krista thrusts her chin upward and raises her eyebrows, and it appears as if she is "high and mighty," as my mother used to say. But she's neither. She does tend to be voluble and dramatic, and when she talks, it's not just with her mouth but with her entire face and upper body. She leans into words, and her eyebrows leap up and down in concert with her wrinkled forehead trying to keep pace with her lively eyes that do a darn good job of keeping up with her tongue.

Like me, at first, the others do not seem to take to Krista very well. Oh, of course they treat her in a polite, sisterly fashion, but I can tell they tolerate her more than they actually like her. She is high-strung and emotional, and when she lets loose with her raucous laugh, well, it sounds a little forced. Sometimes her temperament can be hard on the nervous system. But beneath the off-putting, shrill exterior lives an insecure and kind person. I am embarrassed to see my own need for approval in Krista, especially when it comes out in all the wrong ways.

Krista talks constantly of the large family she left behind in Keene, New Jersey and especially of her closeness to her "daddy." On our monthly visiting-Sunday afternoons, I get a different picture. Her parents come, but rarely do any of her brothers or sisters visit. Her father, a distinctive-looking man, cuts a dashing figure, like a suave 1940s film star. He is lean, tall, and bowed like a poplar tree in a hurricane, with a cigarette dangling perpetually from the corner of his thinly mustached mouth. Quiet and aloof, he sits cross-legged on a stool in the auditorium where we greet our families on visiting Sunday. More animated than usual, Krista flies around the room, collecting each of us to bring back and introduce to her "daddy." He nods politely, obviously flattered by Krista's attentions toward him, but that's about all. He seems oblivious to her fawning affection, and I wish she didn't need his attention so much. Like me, I suspect that Krista is also lacking something. We cry and comfort one another when we are feeling lonely; we talk about how much we love and miss our family and friends. But we never talk about what we are missing.

Angela's small family is the opposite of my own large and lively clan, and they've grown quite fond of me, to the point of treating me almost like a second daughter in their tight-knit Italian family. Angela has only one older brother, and together, they form the sun around which their parents' life revolves. Krista and I should be so lucky.

When I see Angela and Krista together, I have to laugh because they remind me of Mutt and Jeff. Krista is tall and lean with delicate features and alabaster skin, while Angela is short and compact, and her olive skin gives her a decidedly ethnic look in contrast to Krista's all-American girl look. Angela is also slow and deliberate, moving consistently at the same 35 mph speed that jars with Krista's constant overdrive. My friends in the sisterhood are both twenty years old, two years older and more experienced than I am, though age difference doesn't seem to matter much in here. Neither could pass for an intellectual giant, although Angela has a store of value-laden common sense and Krista, despite being flighty, has uncanny insight and perceptiveness when it comes to reading people. They have what my mother would call "sky hearts"—true, open, and wide. "She has a sky heart, as good as gold," my mother, the metaphor mixer, used to say. I know I am supposed to love and respect all my "sisters" equally, and yet I can't help but feel a special connection with these two. Is that wrong? Given all the warnings about "particular friendships," somehow I get the sense that it is. Anyway, I guess the others must have sky hearts too; why else would they be willing to give up their lives to serve God and his people? But for some reason, I can't read their hearts as well as Angela's and Krista's. Maybe I haven't made the effort to get to know them; maybe they haven't revealed themselves to me as yet. Maybe both.

I'm not sure about the others, but like Angela and Krista, I am constantly plagued with misgivings about being worthy of religious life. Do I have the stuff to make it through this training period? Do I have the makings of a good nun? Can I really live by the order's rules and high standards, or am I just fooling myself? And what about God? What *does* God want from me? How do I silence the cacophony and hear God in the voice of my superiors? I know that what I am expected to do is trust my superiors and give my doubts over to God. G. I. harps constantly on detachment. When I worry, it seems I am expressing attachment to my own will rather than God's, so I must work harder to surrender and purify myself. But giving up my own will seems as impossible and painful as shedding my own skin. The troubling question is: who am I without my own will? I realize that giving up my will is central to the vow of obedience, which is the bedrock of religious life, and it is much more daunting than both poverty and chastity. When G.I. pores over my laundry list of faults during weekly charity sessions—or worse, when she herds us into chapel for Wednesday's group charity, she means for me to grow in obedience and humility. What I really feel, though, is mortified. I froze in horror the first time I heard myself accused by Joanne, a fellow postulant: "I accuse Sister Kathleen of singing on the stairwell and breaking the Grand Silence." Even though I've become more accustomed to being publicly chastised since that time, I haven't quite gotten to the point where I can accuse anyone else. In group charity it is easier to accuse my self of wasting time, or being late for chapel, or nodding off in meditation, or breaking the Grand Silence, than it is to accuse one of my sisters. So I manage to check myself, to a point at least. But the inner doubts continue to plague me, like an ongoing feud that rages inside without my consent: "public charity is uncharitable and not at all Christ-like; no, public charity is an exercise in humility, which is a virtue, and it helps me to practice blind obedience."

Such are the doubts that surface, despite my best efforts, in the half-dark during morning meditation. I console myself with the knowledge that my heart's compass is straight and true, even if I can't always get the rest of me to follow. Meditation is a time to nurture interior silence in order to hear God's will instead of my own distracting thoughts. Sometimes, like this morning, I am blessed with a blissful moment in the small musty chapel at St. Gerard's Hall, and it usually happens when I am not trying so hard. But it is fleeting. Gone in a breath. In these precious moments, I wish God would take me home to Him because I fear I cannot sustain this state of grace, not even in the convent where all distractions and material things have been removed from me. I don't fear death as much as my own inability to live a pure life. But even in these breaths of oneness with God, it's not clear to me what God's will is or how I can be sure that it is God's will and not mine or someone else's. How does one know these things for certain? It remains a mystery. Perhaps this will be the chief lesson of my religious training, and so I must trust it and my superiors as the bearers of God's will for me, for all of us.

G. I.'s signal—a shifting body and the swish of her work garb as she genuflects before departing the chapel—inform me that meditation has ended. The rest of us follow suit. Sleepy-eyed postulants, just returning from various ports of silence, genuflect and bless ourselves before filing out the door of St. Gerard's Hall and up the hill to the motherhouse that looms like a castle on a hill in the early summer-morning mist. As I move in concert with the others, to duties, to Mass, to breakfast, to community prayer, and back to duties again before scripture class, I wonder: will I have a permanent place in God's castle?

Convent life seems to come more easily to some of the others. Deirdre, for instance, appears to be a natural. Cheerful most of the time, she keeps her complaints about never-ending duties and the harshness of convent life to a minimum. And yet, she is generous and likeable, and not at all self-righteous or preachy. Even the senior sisters are charmed by her uncomplicated and easy-going personality. On the outside, she'd be a candidate for the "most-popular girl," or the "nicest girl next-door." Tall and athletic with fair skin and large blue eyes, her features, like her personality, are perfectly balanced. She is the perfect child of a fairy tale family. Her mother is one of two sisters who married twin brothers, all of whom are living happily ever after in one prosperous household with their combined fifteen or so blonde, blue-eyed children. Her storybook life reminds me of the ideal American household portrayed in our first-grade Dick and Jane reader, which always made me wonder who those people were and where they lived because they didn't look like anyone I knew.

I admire Deirdre's good-natured generosity and the way she strives for holiness without being rigid or feigning piety. Neither a brownnoser nor a goody-two-shoes, she joins in the goofing around and rule-breaking, and she laughs just as uproariously as Krista and I do. When G. I. chides Deirdre for unsisterly behavior, it reassures me and makes me think that maybe it's okay to have a little spunk in here, even though we have to curb it. I like Deirdre because she is unpretentious and good-hearted. She works hard but she is also spirited, so we are quite compatible. Together, we have hit on a remedy to avoid being reprimanded for our unacceptable, boisterous laughter. We call it "going over the hill," which simply means that whenever we want to let off some steam, we go to the furthest edges of the property, well out of earshot of both the motherhouse and St. Gerard's Hall, and laugh aloud into the trees until our throats ache. And no one accuses anyone in charity about it. I like that.

Deirdre and I work hard and efficiently together during afternoon kitchen duty, but we have also gotten into a few scrapes with the nun law. Suspicious and beady-eyed Sister Maureen oversees afternoon kitchen like a warden runs his prison. Mere postulants, we are cowed by her gruff commands and the muttered string of invectives she spews our way if, for example, Deirdre should accidentally drop a clanging pot, or I should lose control of the huge electric mixer, thus, causing the mashed potatoes to spew in all directions, "You stupid dummies. Not worth a hill of beans, the lot of you. I don't know why they send these young worthless postulants to work for me. I'd be better off doing it myself." Of course, she is physically unable to do much more than sit in her chair and direct us "young, worthless dummies."

Sister Maureen appears to be in her early seventies. She has a gray square face with hairs sprouting out, and a neck that disappears in flesh folds atop her broad, stout body that ends in thick ankles crammed into her black nun's shoes. Unable to walk without the help of her silver walker, she commands her kitchen crew with a handy black cane from a stool. Her resting spot is strategically positioned in front of the stove for her periodic check or stir, and within sight of the massive double sinks, in front of which we spend the major portion of our time scraping and scrubbing. She keeps one eye constantly on us, while the other guards the dining room door at the opposite end to keep track of anyone wandering in and out of her kitchen realm. She mostly ignores the infirmary kitchen on the other side of the wall behind the stove, since that is the territory of her enemy, Sister Peter, who stands about four feet nine inches tall in her fortified nun's shoes intended, it seems, to correct a leg imbalance. Sister Maureen is the bulldog while Sister Peter is the neighborhood alley cat that irritates her from a safe distance.

No one knows the origin of their long-standing feud, but the two absolutely refuse to speak to one another. Instead, like obstinate little children, they use us to carry messages back and forth concerning any intersecting responsibilities. Maureen (bulldog) is responsible for refectory meals, while Peter (alley cat) supervises the arrangement and delivery of infirmary and special-diet meals that must be prepared in her enemy's kitchen. Hardly anyone gets along with the convent alley cat who is characteristically cranky and cantankerous most of the time. But for some inexplicable reason, she demonstrates a liking for both Deirdre and me. "Precious" she coos to us when she is in an unusual good mood, and we are out of the bulldog's earshot. "Precious" is Sister Peter's appellation for anyone she happens to like at the moment.

Whenever she summons me to her side of the kitchen, she acts as if she's including me in some sort of a conspiracy. I have to lean down and bend toward her, permitting her to whisper in my ear while her right hand remains tightly cupped around her mouth and my ear, "Psst . . . Precious, come here. I have to whisper a secret. That Sister Maureen is a pig. The way she keeps that dry closet. What a mess!" She hisses while winking mischievously at me and placing her forefinger on her lips, "Shhh." Her acid blue eyes stare at me through thick bifocals so that I feel like I'm looking at her underwater. Then she hobbles away on her platform shoes, and if she's in a really happy mood she'll suddenly burst into song, "I've told every little star just how wonderful you are / why haven't I told you . . ." while encouraging Deirdre and me to join her. The trick is to straddle the line of tension between the two rivals because we know better than to fall out of favor with either Peter or Maureen; both of whom can (and do at times) make our lives miserable.

We are Sister Maureen's hands and legs, and whenever we escape from her sight she gets particularly ornery. But sometimes she has no choice. "Hey, youse two, stop your gabbing and get over here," she calls out to us. We are stacking boxes at the head of the stairway and chatting about this and that, about Mother Michael's upcoming scripture test and how hard it's going to be, and who we're expecting to come on visiting Sunday. I tell Deirdre that I am expecting the twins, Pat, and the rest of the gang, and I am wondering how it will feel to see them. In less than a year, I have traveled so far, and I am not sure how to talk to my old friends anymore. But Sister Maureen's call to action puts an abrupt end to our activity and our conversation.

We gingerly approach her, expecting a scolding, but instead, she reaches inside her habit for the key to the much-valued dry closet where her armory of large canned and packaged foods is stored. We don't say anything aloud, of course, but I know Deirdre is thinking the same thing I am, "Yay, a few inches of freedom, and maybe we'll get lucky and find some hidden snacks to boot!"

Meanwhile, the neighborhood bulldog is barking her instructions, "I want you two good-for-nothings to go down to the dry closet and do some dusting and straightening up. Lord knows how those deliverymen left the place. And I want two of those eighty-ounce cans of tomato sauce. You got that? You dummies, you. No fooling around down there. You have thirty minutes. Now, do you think you can do that?" Not waiting for an answer, she yanks her head violently away from us as she always does after issuing an order, her face settling into a grimace of disgust while talking to herself under her breath, "I don't have enough to do around here. Cooking, cooking, cooking. Day in. Day out. Now I have to keep my eye on these rascals, too." Spinning her head back in our direction, she snaps, "What are you waiting for? Go and clean up that dry closet and get back here fast, you dummies, you." I try not to take her meanness too personally, as I sense that her persistently disgruntled state has more to do with accumulated frustrations than with us and her conviction that we're slackers sent by convent commanders to make her life more miserable. But Deirdre and I would have to be a pair of old blind dogs not to see that Sister Maureen doesn't trust us "any farther than she can throw us," as my mother would say, especially whenever we are not within close range, so she keeps a suspiciously watchful eye trained on us while we labor in "her" kitchen.

Her mistrust is not entirely unwarranted. During afternoon kitchen duty, Deirdre and I work diligently, mopping the floor and scrubbing the massive iron stove while following her gruff instructions for meal preparations. But we are ever on the lookout for an escape. Occasionally, she takes leave of her skeptical senses and rewards our hard work with a tall glass of milk from the "cow," the motherhouse's industrial-size milk machine, and milk is a luxury we are never granted at meals. But this unexpected mission outside her purview invites just a little deviance that's hard to resist.

As soon as we race down the stairs to the ground floor where the dry closet is located, we pop our heads outside the emergency-side door leading to the parking lot, barely managing not to fall over each other in our excited curiosity as we try to ascertain whether any visiting nuns are coming or going. Except for feast days and holy days when scores of missioned sisters descend on the motherhouse, ours is a monotonous routine, so we're always on the look out for stray visitors to pump some fresh blood into the place. But no such luck today.

Next, we check out the first floor to see if we can entice any stray postulants or novices to a little mischief, only to realize that everyone else is in chapel saying afternoon prayers which we've been excused from because of kitchen duty. The only one we bump into is the janitor, Mr. Grim, who looks at us quizzically, as if to say, "What are you two doing scot-free?" So we abandon our mischief hunt and make our way back to the dry closet that sits at the bottom and to the right of the stairs leading up to the kitchen on the main floor. I am gabbing away about our prospects of a vacation at the community beach house at the New Jersey shore, as Deirdre pulls out the key that hangs at the end of a long heavy piece of string to prevent it from getting lost or misplaced. Half listening to my mindless prattle, she fumbles with the key while inserting it, letting the long white string dangle in the process. Finally, the lock gives way, and Deirdre pulls the thick steel door outward, allowing me to go ahead of her as we enter the dark walk-in closet. Intrigued by my gossip, Deirdre peppers me with questions, demanding to know more details about the seashore rumors. "The novices went to the beach house for a WHOLE week last year? What was it like? Were they actually allowed to walk on the beach and go swimming? Oh my gosh, do you really think we'll get to go next summer? Does that mean we have to wear those ugly, old-fashioned bathing suits on the beach?"

I lose sight of the central question, if there was one, and squirm at the image of the old-fashioned black bloomers that nuns wear to protect their modesty. Then I flick on the lights, just as the weight of the door causes it to close behind us. Looking at each other, we both suddenly realize that neither of us has propped the door open or removed the key from the lock on the outside of the door. We are locked in the dry closet.

My mother always told me that a watched pot never boils, but it is hard not to watch and wait, watch and wait while locked in a suffocating dry closet. Especially when you know that Sister Maureen is upstairs impatiently drumming her fingers to that dreadful hum under her breath while wondering what's taking us so long. In some ways, the prospect of suffocation promised less terror than Sister Maureen's wrath.

After a shared gasp of recognition over our quandary, I proffer the first audible reaction. "Oh, my God, Maureen's gonna kill us!"

Deirdre's response is as instantaneous as an echo, "Yeah, and then she'll report us to G. I. who's gonna kill us again."

"What'll we do, Deirdre?" Recognizing that Deirdre is something akin to the favored child, I expect her to get us out of the dilemma and to come up with an escape plan as well as a plausible explanation for our stupidity. G. I. would just take one look at me and say, "You—in trouble again." But Deirdre's wide expressive blue eyes tell me she's as helpless and bewildered as a toddler who's unwittingly pulled down a tablecloth and, with it, her mother's finest china. No help here.

"Well, Deirdre," I offer feebly, "why don't we go ahead and clean up like Maureen told us to do, and maybe someone else will happen to come down to get something from the closet, and she'll never be the wiser." Fat chance. The only other one with a key is the motherhouse superior, and a timely visit by her does not seem likely.

The minutes stretch out endlessly before us like the miles on a highway as we stare at the closed door, reconsidering and questioning how both of us could be so stupid at the same time. Seeing no imminent signs of rescue, we finally decide to take action by tackling the dry closet like a couple of rookies bent on proving ourselves. I stand on a ladder hoisting the huge cans down to Deirdre from the uppermost shelf of the closet, cans that probably haven't been viewed let alone dusted by anyone in months. After a thorough wiping down of each of the floor-to-ceiling shelves lining the closet, I take the newly wiped cans from Deirdre and stack them neatly for better viewing by Sister Maureen and the rest of the dinner and supper crew. The anticipated fear of a showdown with the kitchen bulldog has quelled our adventurous spirit and stilled our tongues. We both tacitly agree that maybe, just maybe, the sight of a newly ordered, dust-free, dry closet will save our necks from the convent kitchen's chopping block.

Another twenty minutes follow before a novice flagged down and dispatched by Sister Maureen—to check on "those lazy, good-for-nothing postulants"—arrives to rescue us. Chuckling away, she attempts to smooth things over with Sister M: "Sister, you should see what a great job the postulants did down there while they were locked in. I never saw that closet looking so spiffy." (Where does she get the nerve? Isn't she terrified?) But her explanation is waved away with a bulldoggish "harrumph" and a slice of her hand through the air, and our own feeble spurts and sputters of excuse become drowned in a torrent of, by now, familiar castigations, "Dummies . . . half-wit postulants. How do they expect me to get anything done around here?" And we never even found any cookies.

*      *      *

Deirdre and I chuckle while relating our escapade to some of the other postulants on the way to our makeshift ball field the next morning even though G. I.'s private conference with us last evening was a tad less than funny. Across the dew-coated grass not yet burned dry by a mid-June sun, I drag the canvas bag filled with bleached-out wooden bats, a couple of twelve-inch softballs marred and squashed from years of use, and gloves so worn that the leather strings are stretched and frayed like old shoelaces. When we reach the edge of the field, the other dutiful postulants in tow, I spill the contents from the bag for a closer inspection, "What generous soul donated these, do you think?" I glance over at Deirdre who giggles and shrugs her shoulders in response before assuring me we can make do with this antiquated equipment. Ever-the-optimist Deirdre. Okay. Fine. I'll manage. But I made a mental note to myself to ask my dad to bring along my old glove and some new equipment next visiting day. After all, what if we were challenged by the novices or another group of postulants from a rival convent or something? We need the right equipment to have a fighting chance at least.

I grab the least squishy ball of the bunch and stride out to the pitcher's mound, which is little more than a ring of dirt amid scrubs of untended grass and weeds. Tossing the ball back and forth between my hands to get myself back into the "feel" of the game, I assign teams and positions and establish a batting order. "Okay, everybody," I yell to the reluctant group spread out around me, "now listen up. The object of the game offensively is to hit the ball with the bat into the field, allowing the runners who may already be on base to move forward, safely, of course, from one base to the next, while the batter runs to first base, and then to the other two bases positioned around the field, but only if safety permits. Got it?"

"Well, what does that mean?" Eliza, my angel, demands.

"Which part of 'that' are you talking about?" I try not to sound too flustered.

Maria shakes her head, as if to say, "Let's just get on with it and play," since she knows the game. But Eliza and Carol as well as a few of the others have about as much understanding of how this game works as I do of the stock market that, as far as I can tell, consists of funny numbers bandied about in an atmosphere of pointless hysteria. I have to find a way of explaining it that is familiar and makes sense.

"Okay. Look, you guys, do you remember how you used to play tag?" Here I get nods and looks of recognition. "Right, good, that's kind of what softball is like. When you hit the ball, you're 'it' in a way, and you have to get to the bases safely before anyone can tag you with the ball or get the ball to the player on the base before you reach it. See?" I encourage them, pointing to the respective bases arranged proportionally around the field by my assistants, Deirdre and Maria, "Run to first, then to second, then to third, and finally to home. Anytime someone gets safely home, it results in a score or a run, and whoever accumulates the most runs wins. The object of the defense is to prevent you from getting on base safely and scoring by tagging you or the base before you do safely. Get it?" What I get is replies in the form of nods, ranging from the very enthusiastic—Krista—to the least enthusiastic, Angela. It's nice to know I can always count on my friends.

After I provide a short lesson in the rudiments of the game, Deirdre, Maria, Celia, and I perform a little show-and-tell. From the pitcher's mound, Celia flips the ball to Deirdre who takes a swipe at it with the bat, launching the ball into left field where I have to scramble from shortstop to retrieve and zing it to second base and a waiting Maria, who has abandoned first base in order to cover the play. The ball reaches her beat-up mitt just a second before Deirdre's toe at the end of her long leg as she slides into the base, and Maria, Celia and I simultaneously leap into the air to celebrate the thrill of the out in a close play. The celebration ends abruptly, however, with the whine of Angela's voice, "I just hope you're not expecting *me* to run or throw like that."

"No, of course not," I shout breathlessly as I make my way back to the infield, noting that she and the other inexperienced ones are looking not at all impressed and even more miserable than when we first arrived. "Don't worry," I assure them. "Let's just get each of you into your position, and then I'll come around and work with you individually, okay?" I smile encouragingly, but to myself, I'm thinking what a long morning and longer class this is going to be and that maybe I ought to reevaluate G. I.'s motives.

I follow what I know about softball etiquette, placing those with some skill and athleticism in the infield, and those without in the outfield where they can do the least harm to their teammates and themselves. Catcher is another throwaway position because to allow stealing would be absurd under these circumstances, and once a game gets underway, I'll place myself behind the catcher both to back her up and call the plays.

As I survey the scene before me, I see images of the ridiculous, reminding me of a Laurel and Hardy comedy routine. Carol, for instance, runs away from the ball when it's hit toward her in right field. I clap my hand over my head, trying hard not to sound impatient: "No, Carol. You can't field the ball if you're not anywhere near it. You have to run *toward* the ball, not away from it. Okay, hear we go. I use my arm and toss the ball to her so that it doesn't come at her quite as hard as the previously batted ball. "Second try, you can do it. It won't hurt you if you use your glove. Right. That's right. Get under it and put the glove up. Okay, okay, you missed it; that's all right, but don't give up. Go after it; pick it up and throw it in to the shortstop. Yeah, to Deirdre, okay? That's it. Get it to Deirdre." She pushes the ball away from her the way you would toss a coin into a fountain, and it plops to the ground barely two feet in front of her. "No problem. Try it again," I offer, encouragingly. "But this time bring your arm back behind you and try to bring your left leg around and put your body weight into the throw." I turn my attention to Angela who is standing in center field sticking her glove into the air above her head as if to ward off an attacker. "All right, Angela, get ready; the ball's coming to you. No, don't cover your head with the mitt. It's not going to hit you. But you have to turn the pocket to the outside in order to catch the ball. That's it. That's right." The fly ball, of course, misses her glove by a good foot or two.

Then there's Colleen who crowds the plate and leans the bat against her shoulder, no matter how many times I show her the proper stance and boundaries of the batter's box. She swings the bat like a badminton racquet, while Krista skips from first to second like a dainty schoolgirl on a playground. "Colleen, you're going to get hurt that way. Stand back. That's it. Raise the bat, and swing. Good, fine, you hit the ball. Yay!" I watch it dribble down the first base line. "That's very good; you hit it, but don't look at *me*; hurry and run down to first. Krista, what do you think you're doing? The object is to get to the base *before* they throw the ball and tag you out, so run! Run! Run!"

I have some work ahead of me; that's for sure. But I can see that Geraldine and a few of the others have also played some before, and they help me with instructing the inexperienced ones. I use their skills to demonstrate the basics: how to eye the ball into the glove and clap the throwing hand over the mitt to secure the ball; how to run to first as soon as the ball is hit without stopping; how not to run when you're on base and the batter hits a fly ball, at least, not until you see it won't be caught; how to swing the bat and bring the body around to step into the ball; and how to stay in front of a ground ball and scoop it out of the dirt or grass. But what my classmates and I are playing is an altogether different game than the one I am accustomed to playing. This game has nothing to do with fierce competition and winning. I am quickly learning that showing off and boasting have no place in this game which doesn't offer prizes, maybe not even a pat on the back. This game is about sharing your talents with others and not seeing yourself as being better than another, and at this moment, it's about learning how to laugh good naturedly at the dropped balls, the missed grounders, the wild pitches, the erratic swings. Cardboard bases, bats, balls, nuns running around the field in long gray frocks and wearing black and white Keds—I never expected to find myself playing on a team and a field like this one.

After an hour or so, I draw away from the group to survey and take pleasure in the drama I'm directing. By midmorning, a steady stream of perspiration coats my forehead and the skin inside the long grey dress. I kneel on a carpet of bold dandelions, breathing in the sweet elixir of summer. We are like them, I muse, weeds that are beautiful in their own natural way, rather than flowers boasting of their trained beauty. We are all the same—plain and dull, yet exquisite and brilliant to the simple eye—arching toward a glorious sun and offering the gift of our short life. God sits on my left shoulder with the sun. I am happy. I am thankful. I am alive.

# Spring

I escape from the stale sickroom, haunted by the too-familiar grayish face and the rolls of pallid flesh sunk eternally into the white pillow of pain. Desperately in need of air, I find my way blindly to the side door that spills into the parking lot and the path to the outlying buildings at the edge of the motherhouse grounds. I welcome the light spring rain that falls in a diagonal line, grateful that no one is around. Racing down the path, I thrust my face upward, letting the rain mingle with the tears that I cannot stop or control. Beyond the tall trees that border the property lays our sanctuary, Camelot—the scene of my pact with Angela and Krista—a secret place that only a few of us know about and escape to during times of stress or turmoil. It is midday and I am taking a huge chance by leaving the motherhouse without permission, but I am desperate for the solace of our little sanctuary. I work my way past the trees and brush to the ravine that looks down into the neighboring park—and the life I have left. I can observe it, but it cannot see me. Only at Camelot can I be alone with my unexpected grief. Overhead, the birds are busy settling back into their northern home, and the signs of nature's call to life are everywhere: in budding trees, scurrying squirrels, and doting mothers with their children. Here, amid the seasonal tunes of renewal, I lean against an old comfortable maple tree. I let the tears flow and reflect on my experience with Sister Rita and the meaning of death.

\*　　\*　　\*

Celia, who looks and acts like an oversized, klutzy St. Bernard puppy, calls out to me and to Krista in her New England twang, "This is a blast!"

"Shh!" We both turn around at the same time, putting our fingers to our lips in warning. We are making our way quietly along the third-floor linoleum hallway to the stairwell and down to the basement of the motherhouse, clad only in our slippers, nightgowns, and black kimonos. But careful as Krista and I try to be, we cannot help but share Celia's irrepressible excitement. We are like kids in a boarding school on the loose without any policing or supervision.

We huddle together as soon as the hallway is in view. "What if we run into someone in the basement?" Krista whispers.

"I don't think that'll happen," I assure her, "not at this time of night."

It's very early in the morning, about 1:15 a.m., long after the start of the Grand Silence. Three of us have been assigned to "wake watch," which means to watch over the dead body of one of our recently deceased sisters from the missions. I did not know Sister Agnes, but I heard Sister Henrietta tell one of the junior sisters that she was only forty years old and that she died from a "female" cancer, whatever that means. But no one says anything like that officially. In fact, nothing is really said "officially," except that Sister Agnes's body will lie in a coffin in the chapel where the sisters will watch and pray with her around the clock for three days, until her funeral Mass and burial. Our shift is scheduled from 2:00 to 4:00 a.m., so G. I. has arranged for us to spend the night at the motherhouse in one of the empty third-floor rooms. We get to sleep in until a whopping 6:15 a.m., *and* we're excused from early meditation and duties. Even more exciting is the realization that we're free of the ever-vigilant G. I. for an entire night. What a treat!

Krista digs out some change from her kimono pocket, leftover from visiting day, enough to drop into the basement vending machine for one bottle of Coca-Cola. "Wow!" Celia blurts out. "I haven't had one of those since the last time my folks visited."

Coke is not to be found anywhere on our convent menu, but fortunately for us, a vending machine stands in the hallway of the basement floor where bingo is conducted for the neighborhood blue-collar locals every Tuesday night. Bingo-cleanup duty, the following morning, is not so pleasant, consisting, as it does, in attacking a roomful of stale cigarette smoke while sweeping and mopping a floor that is ankle deep in empty snack containers, cigarette butts, and millions of cardboard bingo dots. But who's complaining? Without weekly bingo, there would be no soda machine to rendezvous with surreptitiously. The loud thump of the Coke bottle being dropped by the machine startles the gloomy silence that's settled over the motherhouse, with the publicly displayed nun's dead body just a floor above us. But the disquiet only serves to fuel our giddiness. Krista yanks off the top with the machine's opener. "It's my quarter, so I get the first swig," she says, as she takes a few gulps.

"Hey," Celia orders, too loudly, "save some for us." Within seconds, the bottle is at her lips, over Krista's unheeded objections.

"Will you guys keep it down?" I plead softly. "What are you trying to do—wake the dead?" I start giggling at the realization that one of my mother's favorite sayings can be so literally applied to the situation, and the others are soon joining in. Celia starts laughing so uncontrollably that the soda spurts out of her nose, causing even more hilarity. Krista comes to her senses first. She shushes us, places her index finger over her mouth and points upstairs with the other one, reminding us of Mother Agatha's bedroom suite just a floor above us. Then we turn back to our Coca-Cola treat, polishing it off by turns in quick, hungry swallows, as we deposit ourselves on the steps leading up to the stage where we talk about death in hushed tones. I begin by recalling my grandfather's wake: "When my grandfather died, he was laid out in the front parlor of my grandparents' house. I think I was eight years old, and it was the first time I saw a dead body. I remember waiting for him to wake up, the way he always did after he nodded off on the sofa listening to the baseball game on the radio. He looked like he was smiling. But his hands, with the black rosary wrapped around them, looked as white as wax. That's when I knew he wasn't going to wake up and start teasing me. Not ever again."

"Were you spooked?" Krista wants to know. She has never attended a wake or even seen a dead body. At least not until tonight.

"Nah," I shrug. "Sad, though. After a while, I realized that the body looked like him all right, but my grandfather was long gone. I was upset because I didn't know how to understand what I was seeing. I knew he was with God and all that, but I just didn't know what that meant. You know? What does 'death' mean? What is the afterlife like? I mean, yes, of course, I believed Grandpop went to heaven after he died, but I didn't have a clear picture of it or him at all. Guess I still don't, not really."

They don't know how to respond so we all lapse into silence. Uncomfortable with my self-disclosure, I shift my body on the bottom step to avert my face from my two friends. I am vaguely aware of the ceaseless pumping of Krista's crossed leg a step above me, a sure sign of her restlessness, and, beside her, of Celia's agitation as she examines the bottom of the Coca-Cola bottle, having drained every last possible drop.

Recalling my grandfather's wake has brought on a wave of homesickness, followed by another clear memory that plays out in my mind like a home movie: I was a small child in the comforting fold of extended family: dad, his four brothers, and other male friends and family members were hanging out in Nanny's kitchen drinking beer, smoking cigarettes, and telling raucous stories peppered with laughter. As I threaded my way among the tall bodies mostly unnoticed, I got an occasional, absentminded pat on the head from an unfamiliar uncle or neighbor. How did I come to be in the land of no women or children? I felt at home, but my curiosity overtook me, leading me away from the sour smell of alcohol and high spirits of the men in the kitchen and through a swinging wooden door to a more somber room filled with grieving and prayerful women. Some were seated, while others knelt on the carpeted floor. But their collective gaze was fixed on the coffin at the room's center as they earnestly recited the rosary led by the priest and the only male in the front room. In this same room, Grandpop used to sit and listen to the Phillies play on his old radio console while puffing on his pipe, the white rings swirling contentedly above his head. Nanny absolutely forbade him from smoking *his* cigars in *her* house, but cherry pipe tobacco was legal, and its sweet scent lingered. I inched my way to the large mahogany box and, standing tiptoe while holding on to the railing that encased the coffin, I peered over the side. Inside rested a frozen figure dressed in a black suit, white shirt, and maroon-and-silver-striped necktie. Grandpop's snow-white hair was cradled in shiny cloth and black rosary beads lay coiled through his fingers. Puzzled, I turned to my usually cross aunt Elizabeth, who was standing behind me and demanded to know what had happened to Grandpop. In an uncharacteristically soft tone, she assured me, "Your grandfather's gone to heaven, honey." My fingers clutched a piece of the shiny white satin cradling Grandpop's still body until my aunt's taut fingers clasped my hand and pulled it out of the coffin.

Once again I am meeting death and I am still not sure what to make of it, not even in this holy place. Death is a divine mystery and an article of faith, or so says my weekly confessor, and that explanation will have to do. But for me, somehow, it doesn't. I crave understanding. Is that so incompatible with faith? My question darts out of the darkness in my head and punctures our short-lived silence.

"Do you think heaven's like an actual place that we go to after we die, or is it a higher level of consciousness or what?" I toss my question up in the air like a coin, not really expecting an answer in return.

Having set aside the soda bottle, Celia is now more preoccupied with the spots on her eyeglasses than my earnest speculation. She is attacking the lenses with the end of her black robe before glancing, nonchalantly, in my direction and offering an annoyingly casual response, "I think it's best just to pray and not think about it too much." After a pause punctuated by my sigh of frustration, however, she readily admits that no one close to her has died, so she hasn't given the matter serious thought. Celia's New England dialect is so thick that I often have to strain to understand her. But sometimes I think she purposefully lays it on a bit thick to ham it up. She is our self-appointed class clown, and she even looks the part. Her enormous brown eyes loom even larger behind thick horn-rimmed glasses that are always smudged, and her mouth is set in a grin that makes her appear mildly moronic. Celia thrives on the attention her looks and antics elicit, especially the ribbing she gets for gobbling her food during even the most profound of spiritual readings at table. St. John's gospel on charity being the greatest of all virtues loses some of its profundity when Celia is busy inhaling spoonfuls of overcooked peas and lumpy mashed potatoes. Hardly the graceful nun, Celia is constantly tripping over her own feet, usually on her way in and out of the chapel when all the nuns are at prayer, and she trudges around the convent hallways with the swagger of a Philadelphia Eagles linebacker. But she delivers her most comic—if unintended—performance during early-morning meditation when, still fending off sleep and blinking into the pitch-dark, we file into the unheated postulants' chapel. After a short community prayer, we are invited to enter the land of the mystics where we are expected, first, to stay awake and second, to find spiritual bliss. I have taken to jotting down my meditations in a tiny notebook in order to keep track of my journey to sainthood, but mostly to keep me vigilant. Celia does not fare so well. Her head bobs from side to side, front to back in a gallant but ill-fated effort to stem the tide of oblivion. From time to time, one of us props her up with a sharp elbow to shock her into consciousness, which it does, but usually only for the next two seconds. Even G.I.'s sharp reprimands fail. They may rouse her, but keeping her awake is another matter entirely. Only the brisk walk in the still dark up the steep hill from St. Gerard's House to the motherhouse for Mass and duties will accomplish that.

I envy Celia sometimes. She doesn't think too deeply about things. She takes things as they are. No worries. I'm more of the suffering type myself—all angst and introspection. From my Irish-Catholic parents and their ancestors, I seemed to have inherited a sense of the tragic, born of endurance, I guess, as well as poverty, starvation, loss of country and sovereignty.

"Well," Krista says, finally emerging from the fog of her thoughts and snapping me out of my own, "I think death is a mystery, and all God's mysteries have one purpose, and that's to strengthen our faith in him. That's what Father Gallagher from back home always used to say."

I do love Krista. I honestly do. But sometimes I'd just like to throttle her and her perennial optimism. "It's not easy, you know, when you want to understand things," I add, a little defensively. "It's not that I don't have blind faith, I just . . ." My sentence trails off as I struggle to find the correct words to explain my thoughts. It's not that I doubt God, or the church and faith, for goodness' sake. I just feel compelled to *think* about things, to get behind the meaning of things and to understand them, if possible. What's wrong, for example, with entertaining Father Teilhard de Chardin's notion of a transformative Christ *energy*, instead of just picturing an historical Jesus who lived and died and was resurrected a couple thousand years ago? To myself I have to admit that reading *Hymn of the Universe* and *The Divine Milieu* raises questions and encourages me to think about my faith differently and in an unconventional way. But there is something so beautiful and mystical and enticing in how de Chardin writes about offering Mass on the altar of the earth, especially since I have always found God to be just as present in nature as he is inside the church walls. And beyond the moving lyricism and the deep faith at the heart of this priest's writing lies a probing spirit that speaks to me. When I found his books on the shelf in the library, I was quite taken aback. At first, I wondered if his writing and way of thinking were heretical and I even considered asking my superior's permission to read them. Then I thought better of it. They wouldn't keep improper books on the library shelves, would they? Besides, I didn't really want to be told *not* to read them, so I gave Father Pierre de Chardin the benefit of the doubt.

Celia interrupts my reflection with a terse, if not apt, observation, "You think too much. You should try not to think so much about everything."

Hmmm, I muse, recognizing the simple truth in the simplicity of her statement. I cannot so easily dismiss the long line of coffins, though, from the short history of my past, including Uncle Joe, grandparents on both sides, Uncle Frank and Aunt Rose, Uncle Johnny and Aunt Mary—two sets of parents with ten children under nineteen left behind between them—and now this nun who is also my sister in the community.

"Hey," Krista starts as she glances at the auditorium clock, "we better think about making our way to the chapel. It's almost 2:00 a.m."

It seems strange to be headed toward the chapel in our bed clothing and slippers, but it is liberating at the same time, as if we're unmoored and on our way to a slumber party. We pad softly into the chapel, which sits practically empty except for the three novices we are relieving and Sister Agnes, a prone statue in a shiny black box in the side aisle at the front. The sleepy novices nod silently to us after they pay their last respects with a silent prayer in front of the coffin, and then they exit through the chapel door before disappearing into the upper chambers of the motherhouse. I do a quick flip to the past and the pajama parties of my youth before shaking my head at the incongruity of this lapse and returning to my life in the present. We make our way over to the senior sisters' side of chapel. I drop to the kneeling pad alongside the coffin and whisper a prayerful hello and good-bye to a woman, a sister, whom I did not know. A waxwork figure disguised in black clothing, she wears a cross on her chest and has a string of mournful beads wound around her still and awfully pale hands. Celia and Krista follow suit, and then, one by one, we settle into a pew and begin our watch.

I start thumbing the beads on my own rosary, trying to concentrate on thoughts of God and heaven and the Blessed Virgin Mary. Suddenly struck with the cold realization of death, I shiver. I glance over at Celia on my right who is kneeling upright but trying hard not to nod off, and Krista on the other side of her, who is staring at the cross behind the altar with a transfixed gaze on her face.

I gather my rosary beads together, remembering, with a slight shudder, that the pink rosary beads between my fingers once belonged to my grandmother. One by one, I roll them between my thumb and middle finger, and my prayer becomes a plea, "Faith, Lord, I beg of you, to strengthen my faith and make me your worthy servant. Remove all my doubts and fears. Help me to believe and hope and love. This, Lord, is my fervent prayer."

*   *   *

> Maahmy, my little Mammy,
> the sun shines east, the sun
> shines west, but I know where
> the sun shines best. Mammy,
> my little mammy. I'd walk
> a million miles for one of
> your smiles, my ma-haa . . . ma-haa-mee!

With the song's closing lyrics, I'm down on one knee with my hands clasped before me, giving my most earnest and mournful rendition of this Al Jolson classic. The entire refectory breaks into enthusiastic applause, and I'm gazing at a myriad of smiling and, in some cases, tearful faces. I can't believe I'm performing in front of all these visiting nuns who have come home to the motherhouse for the holy-day celebration! Following our unusually elaborate Easter Sunday noon dinner, a few of the Sisters volunteer or are invited to share their talents by playing an instrument or singing a song. I am taken off guard when my classmates coax me into doing my Al Jolson imitation, which I had learned for the minstrel show my friends and I created for our high school talent night. I hammed it up a few times during our recreation hour to squeals of delight from my classmates. Before the realization sinks in—that I am in front of the entire community, including Reverend Mother Agatha—I am up on my feet belting it out, and secretly worried that G. I. might grab me by the collar and forcibly escort me from the room. But as I complete the final, mournful lyrics to "Mammy," I look back and notice that she is clapping and wearing as close to a smile as I have ever seen on her long puritanical face.

The festivities of the day pass quickly, as leisure days do, and Monday morning and new assignments drop on us suddenly with a palpable thud. We are gathered in our meeting-recreation room, and I notice that even G. I. looks unusually strained at this start of a new workweek, as if she cannot move into second gear let alone fifth. Referring to the litany of names and duties she has just recited, she proceeds: "So, Sisters, these will be your new assignments for this three-month rotation period. Beginning today. Take a day or so with the person who has had the duty before you in order to learn the methods and schedule associated with your new assignment. Any questions?" A brief pause is followed by a peremptory "very well, you are dismissed." Her eyes take a quick tour up and down the two rectangular wooden tables, before she scrapes her chair away from the table and rises slowly, erectly, properly, with perfect sisterly decorum.

I wait until she slips out the door, of course, before I let out an audible groan: "Afternoon prayers with Sister Rita? She always looks so crabby! And dessert kitchen! I don't know anything about cooking. Especially desserts." I also silently consider the great and clever lengths I go to in order to avoid ingesting the hateful tapioca and bread puddings that are standard dessert fare at table. And now, to think that concocting the squishy bread with raisins and the gluey pudding with eyes is one of my regular duties—it's unimaginable!

Laurie, my new partner to be, offers feeble reassurance: "Aw, c'mon. We'll be fine once we get the hang of it. Besides," she adds pertly, "I like the idea of cooking much better than scrubbing bathrooms or pulling kitchen duty."

I look around for sympathy, but Krista is busy bragging about how delighted she is to have chapel duty, which I do not understand at all because Sister Henrietta is a terror to work for, according to accounts by both postulants and novices. Under the task mistress's scrutiny and supervision, the priest's vestments and altar cloths are kept spotlessly clean and ironed to perfection, and the floors and pews of the chapel are always dust free and glistening with polish. For some strange reason, though, the ever-gruff Sister Henrietta seems very fond of Krista. All that means is that, instead of growling and biting, she barks harmlessly. In her characteristically bubbly way, Krista is oblivious to Sister Henrietta's mercurial temperament, and the result is that Henrietta does not pick on her. Instead, she zeroes in on people who dread her, like me, and has done so even before that incident from several months ago in the laundry room over which Henrietta presides as autocratically as she runs the chapel.

Here my memory flushes red, as I recall the episode that nearly sent me packing my bags and heading home after little more than a month in the postulancy: I was working silently with Maria in the laundry room. Together, we were feeding newly washed sheets through the antiquated mangle machine that squeezes out the excess water. It was another Tuesday morning, which meant a long full day of laundry duty for postulants and novices alike, since we were responsible for washing, drying, folding, sorting, and delivering all the bedding and personal clothing for the entire motherhouse. On this day, as on every Tuesday, we were released from early morning meditation to get a jump on the day's work. All hands were busily engaged in sorting, loading, and folding sheets, towels, and nuns' underwear in the silence of the steamy laundry room. Sister Henrietta, her thick brows knotted and lips set in a perpetual grimace, was bustling around the dank basement like a foreman on an assembly line. Agile and strong, despite her fifty-odd years, with the swarthy looks of a pirate and a volatile temper to match, Sister Henrietta terrified me and so I worked doggedly to avoid any run-ins with her. Up to this point, I had been fairly successful. Having been lulled into a state of reverie by the constant whirr of the washing and mangle machines, I was shocked into full alert by Henrietta's fierce roar, "SISTER KATHLEEN!"

I panicked when I realized that she was yelling at me across the hushed lines of workers. My heart was a runaway drum, and my face burned with mortification when I recognized a pair of my white convent-issued underpants being waved above Henrietta's head for all to see. I felt like a helpless animal stopped short by a stun gun, only without the corresponding and blessed loss of sensation. I couldn't hear everything she said because of the noise, but her meaning was startlingly and harshly clear to me as well as to everyone in the room—something about the blood stain that should have been thoroughly washed out before putting the item in the community laundry. She continued her verbal assault by firing contemptuous and hurtful phrases at me like bullets over the whirring of the machines: "Filthy pig . . . stupid postulant . . . raised by animals . . . can't do anything right . . ." And as she did so, all the lessons about blind obedience flew out the laundry room window. I swallowed a rush of bitter tears, as I had in childhood school days at the meanness of short-tempered, cruel nuns who used humiliation as a disciplinary tool. Even though I held my tongue, inwardly I rebelled against any rule of obedience that would subject me or anyone else to such abuse, certain that if I was wrong, she was even more wrong.

I was glad that anger had taken over since tears would have betrayed weakness and served only to provoke Henrietta's ire. And for once, I cherished the Grand Silence that prevailed during laundry duty, Mass, breakfast, and morning prayers, because it wrapped me in a blanket of protective isolation. But after morning prayers, I made a bold decision to approach G. I. and request to speak to her privately. She escorted me to her small office where, between sobs, I recounted my humiliating dressing down by Sister Henrietta. Now, G. I. could never be accused of being a warm or sensitive person, so I was taken aback somewhat when, upon hearing my account, her face turned ashen and twisted in disapproval. Somehow I sensed that it was not directed at me, and so I continued my blubbering, expressing doubts about whether I was well-suited to the harsh demands of convent life until G. I., in as kind a gesture as I have seen from her, reached over and patted my hand, advising me not to fret over the incident or to question my vocation because of it. "I'm sorry this happened, Sister," she offered apologetically. "It shouldn't have. But at times certain *individuals* behave in an unacceptable and unsisterly fashion. Unfortunately, some sisters have . . . how shall I say it?" And here she paused, as if struggling to find the right words: "Well, let's just say they are not well-balanced." This seemed to be all she wanted to—or could—say on the matter, but her comments soothed and reassured me, and they sparked a realization: not *all* the sisters in my community were pure and good as I assumed they would and should be. I guess I should have known that, especially given my experience with the nuns in Catholic school, but for some reason I expected something different from the convent.

Angela's friendly tap on my shoulder brings me back to the present, where I gladly shake off the unpleasant memory of my encounter with Sister Henrietta and hasten to catch up with my classmates. As we climb the hill to the motherhouse and prepare to report for our new duties, I console myself: at least, I wasn't assigned chapel duty under Sister Henrietta, and dessert kitchen may not be as difficult as I think; and how hard can it possibly be to recite the rosary with an infirmed nun every afternoon?

*    *    *

The novice whose duty I am inheriting ushers me into the ill sister's over-heated room that immediately offends my nose with its sickly sour smell. Sister Madeline is strangely taciturn about my new charge despite my subtle prods on our way to her room. "So this is pretty easy compared to most other duties, huh?" I offer, hopefully. Her introduction of me to Sister Rita as the "postulant who will replace me to say afternoon prayers with you" is greeted with a sideways look and a disgruntled "harrumph" from the squat elderly nun seated in a wheelchair parked next to her hospital bed.

My new charge is not only old and ill, but she is also ugly and disgusting to look at. She looks like she could be a villain in a Dickens' novel: the skin sagging from her face is coarse and sallow with gray stubble shooting out from the chin, like misaligned bristles from a wire brush. The wide flabby neck seems to swallow the lower part of her jaw, and her lips protrude in a perpetual frown from an apparently toothless mouth. Add narrow black slits for eyes to the picture, and Sister Rita's face takes on an ugly, menacing aspect. I realize that these are uncharitable thoughts so I shake my head and repeat silently, "God is love," in an effort to drive them from my head. Having collected and armed myself with compassion, I finally venture, "How are you today, Sister Rita?" Meanwhile, the novice sidles wordlessly out of the room. Receiving no response and feeling both abandoned and ignored, I pull my rosary beads out of the black case in my pocket and position myself, knees down, on the cold red linoleum floor. "Would you like me to begin, Sister?" I ask, trying to be pleasant despite her rude aloofness. Receiving no response except for a slight nod of her head, I bless myself and begin the rosary with the credo, "In the name of the Father and of the Son and of the Holy Ghost, Amen. I believe in God, the Father Almighty, the Creator of heaven and earth . . ."

Sister Rita sits upright in her wheelchair, with a tattered green and white quilt covering her legs. The beads moving through her hand offer the only indication that she is even mindful of my presence. Occasionally, I am surprised when she joins in with a muffled "Holy Mary Mother of God, pray for us sinners now and at the hour of our death, amen," running the words together as if she were gobbling them. I am just beginning the third "Hail Mary" after the "Glory be to the Father" when a loud bellow, followed by a string of shocking profanity, slices through the air like a lightning strike, "JESUS, MARY, AND JOSEPH! THEY SEND ME THIS GOD-DAMNED STUPID POSTULANT! WHAT THE HELL ARE THEY THINKING?" Aiming her eyes at me like torpedoes, she inclines her head in my direction, giving the first clear sign of recognition, and then rocks back and forth, back and forth, as though keeping rhythm with the throbbing of her diseased legs before she explodes, "YOU STUPID SON OF A BITCH! WHAT THE HELL DO YOU THINK YOU'RE DOING HERE? MAKE YOURSELF USEFUL, GODDAMN IT! MOVE THAT BLANKET AWAY FROM MY LEGS. AAUW! UP! UP! MORE! AAUW!" The rosary in my left hand trembles while my right hand fumbles with the blanket. I guess I succeed in arranging it to her liking because it seems to quiet her, but now I don't know what to do. What I want to do is cry. What I want to do is run screaming from the room. How dare you, a *nun*, hurl obscenities at me! What I *really* want to do is let my fiery Irish temper fly and yell right back at her, "WHO THE HELL DO YOU THINK YOU ARE? YOU EVIL WITCH! GET YOURSELF ANOTHER LACKEY!" before slamming the door behind me as storming boldly from the room.

And I would have done just that less than a year ago in the blip of a second, let the damage fall where it may, because I didn't control my temper very well in my secular life. I didn't get mad easily as a kid, but when I did, the waves parted. My sister, Anne Margaret, went into hiding; my mother's tongue stopped clucking; and one or two cardboard walls of the upstairs attic bore the brunt of a fist carrying 110 pounds of bantamweight fury. Naturally, I controlled myself more away from home, unless someone pressed the indignant fury button, that is, at which point I morphed into an exploding bomb. Once in high school, a girl did press the button, and thereafter, my name and temper took on legendary proportions: Nancy, Anita, Jackie, Pat, the twins and I had decided to see the James Bond flick, *Goldfinger*, on that bitter Friday in February. Diane was a little wound up, which wasn't all that unusual, but when Jackie and Pat joined forces with her it usually "spelled trouble," as my mother would say. She would also often say, "Show me your company and I'll tell you what you are," but I was never sure what that said about me and my misfit friends. Anyway, there was some buildup to the brouhaha later that night, and it started when we got thrown out of the movies because Pat, Jackie, and Diane were goofing around, and the rest of us were trying to shut them up, making an even louder ruckus that got us all laughing hysterically. You could say we deserved to be forcibly "escorted" from the theater by a bald, cranky middle-aged usher who took his job quite seriously. It proved to be an inauspicious beginning to this memorable night.

Having spent our Friday-night entertainment money on a movie we didn't get to watch, we were nearly broke. We wrapped our Chesterfield coats around us to fend off the stinging chill of a winter wind, adjusted our wool berets, and made our way across the street to Bishop Egan High School where our basketball team was playing against its public-school rival, Woodrow Wilson. Owing to our lack of funds and our reluctance to go home having wasted an entire night, Jackie proposed that we sneak into the game by climbing through the first floor girls' bathroom window. So that's what we did. We put our quarters together to pay Nancy's way into the game, and then she met us at the bathroom window. I was not the smallest but I was the most nimble, so I elected to climb up and in the window first. Diane and Jackie crossed their forearms, making their hands into a type of lift on which I tentatively placed my foot. The first two tries resulted in their collapsing into giggles and me steadying my fall against Diane's ample shoulder. For the third attempt, they adopted a more sober demeanor and applied themselves to the task. With greater confidence and a little boost from them, I hoisted myself up to the window, about six feet from the ground, and grabbed the window frame with one hand and Nancy's outstretched arm with the other. The sill was narrow, but it was sufficient for me to brace my butt against before working up enough momentum to squeeze my body, head first, through the window that opened outwardly with a metal crank. With some assistance from Nancy, warm air and safety were just a short tumble from the wider inside windowsill to the floor. We pulled Anita and Pat through pretty easily. But we had to combine forces and strength to lift Diane and Jackie up and through the window, while being greeted with looks of astonishment from students who got more than they expected in their search for a less-crowded bathroom than the one on the main floor.

Halftime had already begun when we made our way to the gym on the second floor. The blue and gold Egan uniforms were running up and down the floor with renewed vigor and determination in a rhythmic seesaw joust with the black and the gold. The scoreboard registered Egan's move from two points behind to a tie, followed by a successful foul shot and a slim margin of lead that they managed to hold on to for the remainder of the game. The packed auditorium echoed with screaming, stamping fans. We trundled up the bleachers on Egan's side of the gym and joined in the frenzy. The close score kept the collective blood pressure high. There was a holy cause to defend in the ancient rivalry between the Catholics and the Publics. Like an idiot, I allowed myself to get caught up in the frenzy, to the point of following Diane to the other side of the gym, which was home to the evening's enemy. As I said, she was already primed for trouble. She stole a cowbell from someone, and pretty soon, we were in the thick of Wilson supporters—working-class, beer-swilling dads, faithful moms, sweethearts and sisters, and an assortment of aimless teenagers eager for battle with the Catholics and a win to demonstrate their superiority. We marched fearlessly and foolishly through their ranks swinging that bell and yelling "GO, Egan!" It's a wonder we escaped that auditorium without bodily injuries, but the evening was not yet over.

After the game and Egan's victory, we crossed back over the four-lane highway separating the school from the local shopping center where we could smoke out of view of the brothers and nuns who taught us and any nosy parents who might recognize us and do their parental duty by reporting us. The sidewalk and parking lot in front of Sunray's drugstore were thronged with kids from both schools, and you could just smell the fight looking for a ring, and the right moment. But I never expected to be in the center of it.

The five of us had just lit up our cigs, and we were standing around watching the tobacco smoke join forces with the frosty air when Diane whipped out five two-inch lollipops she had stashed in her purse. She proceeded to hand them out to each of us like victory cigars. I unwrapped mine, and as I was enjoying sucking on the lollipop in the one hand and the cigarette in the other, a group of six or so tough-looking Wilson girls swaggered in front of us. I stiffened a bit, sensing immediately they were the trouble Diane had been looking for all evening. Then I heard it, Diane's challenge, "Wilson's jive!" meaning, of course, uncool. It wasn't much, but it was sufficiently taunting to warrant a reaction from the Wilson girls. But instead of addressing Diane, the leader and meanest-looking one of the Wilson group, whom I later learned was a much-feared school bully, whirled around and faced me, demanding, "What did you say, girl?" (I must have looked rather menacing brandishing my raised lollipop.) A quick glance at Diane to my right assured me that she wasn't about to jump in and say, "Excuse me, but I was the one who addressed you, not her." Fat chance. Once again, I was bound by an unwritten oath not to betray her, and there could be no backing down, so I turned my head slightly, shrugged my shoulders like I didn't much care what she thought, and repeated off-handedly, "Wilson's jive." The next thing I knew was pain, her fist, equipped with the sharp stone of a large high-school ring—it must have been her boyfriend's—meeting my right eye, and then blankness. It wasn't from being knocked out, though. No, that couple of minutes was like a vacuum into which my mind had been temporarily sucked while my small frame and fists launched into a fit of uncontrollable temper in response to her unexpected attack. I didn't regain sanity until I felt myself being torn away from the girl, whom I had apparently pinned against the brick wall of Sunray's. My cigarette was long gone, but the lollipop remained stuck in my left hand, smeared with several of her black hairs and coat particles as a result of the brief, furious exchange between us. I guess my performance was most impressive because it took several of my friends to pull me away from her. Hers were stunned and had simply retreated, while a crowd of Egan fans had gathered around us to cheer me on. I had quite a shiner the next day and tried to convince my mother who "wasn't born yesterday"—as she always liked to remind me—that it happened when I walked into a door. She didn't buy it; nor did she pursue the matter, in keeping with her fashion of knowing but not knowing.

On Monday, I returned to school to find I had earned the reputation of being one fierce skinny girl who was not to be messed with. The hallway buzz was that the Wilson girl had taken quite a pounding from me, although I couldn't say that I remembered doing it, but my achievement ensured that I would never be challenged or trifled with for the duration of my otherwise-unremarkable high-school career.

But those days of exploding in anger are gone for good. Looking back at my youth, I truly regret my self-centered, hot-tempered response to conflict. In the convent I strive to temper my actions with a spirit of charity. My struggle to curb unsisterly inclinations and repress expressions or even feelings of anger is almost certainly a sign of my spiritual growth and development. Charity, as I am learning, is the true and only path to holiness.

So of course I do not give in to the anger sparked by Sister Rita's verbal abuse. I am also keenly aware that, vituperative as she is, John Rita is my charge, my "mission." Her surliness and unpredictability must be common knowledge, and my convent superiors are no doubt presenting me with another test: how will she perform? How firm is she in her faith? How obedient? How worthy? How humble? While my mind drifts back and forth between my past and present self, Sister Rita slips back into her previous uncommunicative state and I resume the rosary. Twice more she interrupts me and the rosary, as though just realizing I am there, and the miserable old woman suddenly transforms into an eager storyteller, proudly recounting her early pioneer days in the community. "Did you know," she demands in an abrupt but not unfriendly tone, "that I was one of the first members of the community to walk the streets visiting the poor with Mother Michael? Do you have any idea what I've given to this community, you young dummy?"

"No, Sister, I didn't know that." (Why does she have to ruin it by calling me a dummy?) I am still on my knees trying to decide whether I should continue the rosary. She makes the decision for me.

"Yup. It was different in those days. Not like today. All these new-fangled rules and ways. We wore our shoes out walking the streets, day and night, night and day. Now they work in offices and have fancy titles. College educated. None of that for us. I was a pioneer." Her eyes flash, "and you, young dummies, can't understand . . . can't . . . *begin* to understand how hard it was for us in those early days." Her defensive anger mixed with tears of suffering make for a strange brew, causing me to pity rather than hate her, though I still feel the sting of her scolding. When she appears quieted, I resume. "Hail Mary full of grace . . . ," and I guess it's all right for me to continue because she slumps back down in her chair as though nothing has happened.

Then the nursing sister interrupts our rosary session, as she always does, to perform the daily ritual of changing the bandages on Sister Rita's legs. A prisoner of the room until the final "amen," I am compelled to watch the excruciatingly painful ordeal. As Sister Suzanne skillfully unravels the swathes of white cloth, yanking away the final layer of gauze glued to the bloody ulcers beneath, Sister Rita shrieks, the shrill sound of her pain piercing the air. I force myself to swallow the putrid smell of rotting flesh and examine the skinless pulp that remains of her lower legs, silently vowing patience and charitable thoughts no matter how much she lambastes me.

Over the next weeks, I grow accustomed to my new charge, and in her begrudging way she grows tolerant of me. I pray and repress my uncharitable thoughts. She berates me. I pray and repress my uncharitable thoughts. She prays with me, occasionally interrupting a "Hail Mary" to recite one of her pioneer tales. I pray and repress my uncharitable thoughts. She curses me as well as the community, citing a long list of travails. Occasionally, on rare days of lesser pain, she softens slightly, nodding to me respectfully and repeating my community name, "Sister Kathleen," at times even thanking me for the service I perform in reciting afternoon prayers with her. Her gruffness and unpredictability grow strangely familiar, though it never feels good and often leaves me wounded to tears. I just pray and try to repress my uncharitable thoughts.

But I won't have to tolerate her abuse, not anymore; it is a typical day within the prayerful walls of the convent, and without, the signs of spring and budding new life perk up the air. G. I., who surprises us all by failing to appear at the breakfast table after morning Mass, corners me in the hallway on my way from refectory to chapel. "Please come with me, Sister." The others troop into chapel casting quizzical glances my way, and I shrug in response, my heart speeding up with my quickened steps as I follow G. I. through the infirmary doors, thinking, Oh, no; what now? Minutes later, I am standing in the familiar sickroom, staring at Sister Rita's mute, still body. Her labored breathing and Sister Suzanne's periodic clearing of her throat with a suction tube are the only traces of her disgruntled, pugnacious life.

I kneel down at the bedside of a dying, wretched nun, not noticing at first that G. I. has crept wordlessly from the room, no doubt to tend to the duties of the young and the living. Vaguely aware of the rosary being recited by two senior sisters at the foot of the bed, I try to join them, and though I sound the words from time to time, I find that I cannot pray. I am transfixed, staring into the mouth of the cave. I have seen the dead bodies of relatives before, but they were already dead, and there was something unreal about the experience of seeing them. I did not bear witness to the terrible, tightened grip of life in its last stage, despite the misery and the fierce pain it extorted. I did not witness the dead ones in their final, valiant struggle. Here, in this room, death is a gasping, choking breath away. What is it she is holding on to? What is it she fears? As a nun, hasn't she lived her entire life expecting this grand reunion with God? My own feelings are all tangled up like fishing line gone awry, as I recall the sting of her verbal abuse and the relief I felt during her odd moments of tolerance. We shared a forced intimacy rather than closeness, and I am not sure what I should feel: Sadness? Anger? Loss? Grief? Joy? Humiliation? All of these. And fear, of the unknown, I think, and what awaits us on the other side of this bridge.

Time numbly drives by like a slow-motion parade. Her crinkled breathing is irregular, uncertain, until at long last the awful rattle finally rises from her throat, like a shake of the fist in death's face in her final rebellious gesture. Suddenly, the priest is present, and the room is a bustle of activity as more sisters arrive to pray for Sister Rita. I touch her cold, pallid hand for the first and last time, forcing myself to think the words I must believe, "Go with God and know his peace, Sister Rita. I will miss you." Then I bolt from the room and find my way through burning tears to the hall, down the stairs, and out the back door into the rain that smells like green.

# Part II

Poverty, Chastity,
Obedience (1966-67)

# Winter

Angels We Have Heard On High
Sweetly Singing O'er the Plain
And the Mountains in Reply
Echoing their Joyous Strain
Gloria, In Excelsis Deo . . .
Gloria, In Excelsis Deo.

From a distance our procession must look like a double line of vibrating light. Candles in hand, we are harmonizing my favorite Christmas carol as we march in twos over a thinly cushioned path of snow. In a gesture reminiscent of childhood, I tilt my face upward and taste the refreshing, iced rain that continues to fall like a miracle from the ebony sky. For me, this Christmas is both white and complete. Bundled in our secondhand navy pea coats, we are repeating the custom of all the novices who have gone before us as we make our way down the roadway from the novitiate to St. Gerard's House to surprise the new first-year entrants with our wake-up call for Midnight Mass. Trundling up the dark staircase and through the two connected dormitories, my voice and spirits high, I feel a wave of nostalgia when I see the postulants rubbing their eyes in gleeful surprise. But a year older than they are, we are veterans to them. We smile back at them through our singing, still bound by the Grand Silence, and then find our way down the stairs, out the door, and up the hill to the motherhouse for the glorious yearly celebration of Midnight Mass.

With the sleepy-eyed postulants traipsing a short distance behind us, we make our way to the chapel where we join an assembly of nearly two hundred junior and senior sisters. Even the missioned sisters prefer to return home for the celebration of Midnight Mass and the beginning of the Christmas holidays. An awe-inspiring mixture of love and joy permeates the community, mingling with the aromatic scent of the enormous pine wreaths that grace the altar and chapel walls.

For several weeks, a select few of us have been assisting Mother Michael in constructing the decorative wreaths with refashioned coat hangers, pine cones, branches, and berries that we have collected from the convent property. I do arts and crafts about as well as I sew, which is to say, not well at all, but I am delighted to be working with the former mother general and contributing to this project, and I don't mind braving the frigid December weather while scouring the property for suitable wreath material.

Besides, Mother does all the creative work. My part consists of holding the metal securely as she twists the branches in place with her pliers. Mostly, I scurry around the convent grounds on my hunt-and-gather mission, grateful for the unusual opportunity to roam free on the motherhouse grounds. Being confined to a wheelchair and relegated to the position of *former* mother general have not diminished her authority. Nor do they prevent her from reprimanding us younger sisters for being boisterous in the hallways or singing too loudly during kitchen duty. On occasion, I have been among the culprits she admonishes, and so I'm especially anxious to make a more favorable impression on her, and to collect my reward of hot tea with Christmas cookies when the work is completed. We don't have many opportunities to demonstrate our good points and worthiness to her. On the other hand, whenever we conduct ourselves with less-than-sisterly decorum, Mother Michael manages to make an uncanny appearance.

I still cringe, remembering that Sunday when Mother Michael pounced on us for singing in the kitchen: Deirdre, Angela, Maria, and I were tackling the loathsome Sunday dinner pots and pans and, as usual, we started singing to distract and entertain ourselves. We started off with "Blowing in the Wind" and "If I Had a Hammer" and then settled into a medley of older tunes, better suited to our mood and task: "I've been working on the railroad, all the livelong day; I've been working on the railroad, just to pass the time away. Can't you hear the whistle blowing? Rise up so early in the morn. Can't you hear the whistle blowin'? Dinah blow your horn. Dinah won't you blow, Dinah won't you blow, Dinah won't you blow your horn . . . ." Then we moved on to one of our favorites: "Oh we ain't got a barrel of money, maybe we're ragged and funny, but we'll travel along, singing a song, side by side . . . ." We were really wound up by then and, of course, we thought we sounded pretty darn good, with Deirdre and I singing melody and Angela and Maria singing alto. Suddenly, behind us the sharp sound of "SISTERS!" sliced through the air like a jolt of electrical current. Maria dropped the cast-iron pan she was drying, sending it thudding along the linoleum floor. Deirdre and Angela, towels and pots in hand and already facing the doorway, locked eyes with the former mother general, just as my neck whiplashed in her direction and away from the double sinks where my rubber-gloved hands were wrist deep in water and grime. Seated in her wheelchair at the side door to the kitchen, Mother Michael glowered at us with hot eyes and a straight white line for lips. She was livid. She must have wheeled herself all the way from the chapel down the hallway and to the kitchen because Sister Jean, who usually pushes her wheelchair, was nowhere to be seen. She didn't say much, but her acrid tone and flushed face told a mighty tale of disapproval, and we all froze and fell silent. Finally, her thunderclap voice caught up with her face, "What's all this noise?" she boomed. "Don't you realize that the sisters are saying evening prayers in the chapel?" Then she pulled the door shut, causing it to bang against her wheelchair, as she snapped, "I don't want to hear another sound coming from this kitchen!" Her outburst that day cinched her stern, no-nonsense reputation, and while it didn't actually stop us from singing altogether during kitchen duty, it certainly encouraged us to exercise more caution.

The memory of the ferocity of Mother Michael's anger that day still makes me shudder. Nearly eighty years old, Mother Michael still shows no signs of diminished strength. She is nimble and sure-handed as she winds the prickly evergreens, which I hold in place around the wire, before attaching the pine cones and flowing red bow. Throughout Advent her handiwork decorates the chapel walls and the life-size nativity stable that sits to the left of the main altar, ironically dwarfing the tall statues of Joseph and Mary behind it. Red and white poinsettias march up and down the altar steps, and when Christmas Eve finally arrives, Sister Henrietta lights the candelabra, signaling the arrival of the priest and the start of Midnight Mass. Standing at the front of the chapel with the rest of the choir, I can hear the back doors open and close as lay Catholics from the neighborhood shuffle into the remaining pews or line up against the back wall. Only on this sacred holy day are they permitted to attend mass in the convent chapel. Most come to hear our choir, and we spend weeks rehearsing new and old Christmas hymns under Sister George's skillful direction. I feel so proud of my friend, Angela, who is playing the organ alternately with the choir conductor. I am delighted and honored to have a part in this beautiful, communal performance and prayer to God. Tonight and throughout Christmas week, our carefully prepared selections will enliven the liturgy and remind us of God's love in giving us his only begotten son to walk among us in human form. Christ's birth embodies the spirit of our own call to community, and so the celebration of Christmas has special meaning for us. As I lift my voice to the joyful, soothing strains of "Silent Night" on this, my second convent Christmas, I think I have never been happier, nor can I imagine spending Christmas or my life in any other way than with my community of sisters in the service of God.

*   *   *

"I hate her theology class, but I like Sister John okay. She's more, I don't know, real or something. And a lot more understanding." In an uncharacteristically muted tone, Krista is concluding her novitiate commentary with a comparison between Sister John, our new novice mistress, and G. I., our former postulant mistress. She is whispering because we are sitting in the novitiate chapel at night, well after bedtime and the start of the Grand Silence. For about twenty minutes of our late-night "Hardships of the Novitiate" show, Krista, Angela, and I have traded complaints about the policy of isolationism that prevails in this crucial canonical year of convent training. Unless absolutely necessary, we are not permitted to interact with the other sisters in training. We are not permitted to write or receive letters from anyone, including family members, and we can't leave the convent grounds for any reason, lest it violate a cardinal novitiate requirement. As the yaks of the motherhouse's labor force, we are also weighted down with an increased workload and greater responsibility. Where the postulancy is an introduction to religious life, the novitiate is a trial by fire. More than being monitored and scrutinized, we are being put to the final test. We are taxed and tired. We miss our families and our juniorate friends. Worst of all, we are haunted by self-doubt: Are we *really* worthy? Will we *finally* win our superiors' seal of approval? Will we pass this monumental test and be permitted to take our vows and gain official entrance to the community?

Krista's last comment hangs in the air like a trial balloon, and we let it gasp and collapse as we swim back into our own private world of doubts and worries, occasionally breaking the surface to register a complaint or pose a question. We have stolen away from our dorm rooms for this clandestine meeting in the chapel where we sit in the quiet dark, staring ahead at the oversized crucifix hanging above the small altar table. We sit on the left side of the two rows of six pews, which provide sufficient space for twenty-four novices to meet for morning meditation before departing for the motherhouse and our routine of prayer, duties, and class. In the dead of night, the miniature stained-glass windows on the wall facing the outside look ominous and reflect our own ponderous state. A single small light encased in a red lantern at the front of the chapel casts eerie shadows, assuring us that we are, indeed, in a sanctified place. But what more fitting place for three weary and anxious novices?

Our sleeping quarters, located on the two floors above our small chapel, are quite different from the aged frame structure of St. Gerard's Postulant House. The novitiate building, which was formerly a private mansion before being donated to the community, is a more aesthetically appealing stone edifice. The exterior is reminiscent of a Gothic manor, like the one in *Jane Eyre*, and inside is a spider web of rooms extending in various directions and spilling into obscure crooks and crannies. A dumb waiter, a small shaft at the back of the building that connects the uppermost floors—previously the servants' quarters—with the kitchen below, is now used as a laundry chute. An ornate winding staircase connects the third to the main floor that once served as a ballroom. The first large room to the right of the staircase and just off of the formal, high-ceilinged front room has been remodeled into a chapel. We sleep in oversized bedrooms on the upper levels, from two to four of us in each, depending on the size. It is still a dorm room after all and less than grand, but unlike St. Gerard's drafty barracks-like dormitory, it is delightfully warm and cozy.

My two dear friends and I are struggling with different issues that have raised doubts about our vocation. Krista is adapting well to the novitiate, but she suffers keen bouts of homesickness and fatigue as a result of the arduous physical labor. Angela is lethargic, in part because she has had a succession of colds that have turned into bronchitis, from which she never quite recovers. I'm managing my homesickness better than Krista, and the hard work does not leave me weakened or sick as it does them. But other things trouble me, and I am trying to figure out the whats and whys of those.

In the novitiate, I share a room with Joanne and Laurie. I always got on well with Laurie in the postulancy when she was more fun-loving and easygoing, but she has undergone a change in the novitiate. Now, like her new best friend Joanne, she is more solemn and straight-laced. Joanne takes this sisterly decorum stuff rather seriously, and she is a stickler about the convent rules. That really bugs me because my image of the ideal nun isn't at all serious and rule-bound. For instance, in the Christmas favorite *The Bells of St. Mary's* Ingrid Bergman plays Sister Benedict, a no-nonsense but good-hearted nun who doesn't let her habit or her position as principal of the school get in the way of helping a little kid out. I love the scene in which she rolls up her sleeves and pins her habit back to teach an orphan boy how to throw a jab, a hook, and a right cross so that he can defend himself against a schoolyard bully. Old Bing Crosby, the rock star of my mother's generation who plays the priest, catches her in the act with her habit all askew, and he's amused rather than scandalized by her lack of sisterly decorum. I like that.

Sister Benedict is kind as well as pretty, and she's feisty and fun and not at all like the school nuns that I remember. With one or two exceptions they were mostly staid and cranky, if not downright mean, which always made them look unattractive. But my ideal nuns must be out there somewhere because I've seen them in the movies. The Audrey Hepburn character in *The Nun's Story* is another example. Besides being pretty, Sister Luke is smart. She's also very sincere about her vocation, even though her family is not too thrilled when she decides to renounce the world and join up with a missionary order to become a nurse and serve in the African Congo. After she makes it through the rigorous convent training, she lands at her dream mission and ministers to the sick under the direction of a crusty surgeon who falls in love with her. She ends up wavering in her vocation not because of him, but because she has a problem with the vow of obedience, and that's a shame because she's a pretty darn good nun. In their attempt to test and strengthen her resolve, her superiors just end up breaking her spirit. The story takes place in the olden days when religious orders were much stricter than they are now.

I probably identify most with Maria, the frisky free-spirited nun-to-be in *The Sound of Music* who gets into trouble because she likes to go off into the hills and sing, which always makes her late for prayers. When she finally makes it back, she is greeted by a small group of nuns led by Mother Superior and her novice mistress as they sing: "How do we solve a problem like Maria?" Whether I am roaming the convent grounds or scrubbing the motherhouse floors—after making sure there is no one within earshot—I imagine that I am Maria. I sing "the hills are alive with the sound of music . . ." and "Do re mi . . ." and the rest of those wonderful tunes, although I'm pretty sure that I would never encounter a singing Mother Superior. When I consider the fact that Maria decides to leave the convent, just as the nun-nurse does in *The Nun's Story*, it makes me sad because they both would have made outstanding nuns. Sure, they're spirited and willful, but they are also sincere and loving and generous. I don't think I have to be dour to be a good nun. As I see it, charity is essential to being a good nun, and even though nuns must strive to be holy, holiness means being mindful of and receptive to God who is present in every single thing: in people, in nature, in prayer, in song, and even in work. Instead of negating life, holiness means embracing it without getting attached. That's the tricky part. A truly spiritual life grows from a fully human one, and that's the kind of nun that I want to be—both holy *and* human. I intend to combine Sister Luke's fervor with Sister Benedict's compassion and Maria's joyful spirit. At least, that's my plan, although it's pretty clear that my roommate in the novitiate, "Joanne the Proper," has a different idea about what it means to be a good nun.

Laurie isn't quite as straight-laced as Joanne. Or at least she wasn't until Joanne set out to convert her. I miss the carefree Laurie of the postulant days. Her most loveable feature is her wide plump cheeks that shake when she giggles so that I just want to pinch them. During the postulancy she was no stranger to a little mischief, and we had some fun times while working together during afternoon dessert-kitchen. We had to learn on the job, and in our first week we managed to burn twelve pans of apple strudel. Well, it wasn't entirely our fault. No one actually taught us *how* to bake. The departing postulants simply introduced us to the inventory of measuring devices, baking pans, and recipes and gave us the rundown on the daily schedule: apple strudel on Sunday, tapioca pudding on Monday, baked apple on Tuesday, and so on. Then they abandoned us to our own devices in the tiny bedroom-turned-kitchen on the third floor of the motherhouse. In addition to burning the apple strudel, we also miscalculated the amount of water in the tapioca-pudding recipe. It ended up being thin and lumpy instead of thick and gooey. Laurie and I laughed a lot during those dessert-kitchen fiascoes, at least until we were faced with the wrath of G. I. whose no-nonsense attitude had little tolerance for the public mistakes of her charges. After about two weeks of trial and error, we finally mastered the standard recipes and found that it wasn't so terribly difficult to whip out a dessert for 120 people when you became accustomed to the gargantuan proportions and baking paraphernalia and got the timing down. With time and practice, we learned to operate a trouble-free and efficient dessert kitchen, except for those occasions when we caught a scolding from one of the senior sisters for disturbing their afternoon rest with loud singing or laughing while we worked.

But Laurie is no longer her jolly, feisty self from our dessert-kitchen days. Joanne's influence and the intensity of the novitiate have made sure of that. Of course, we all seem to gravitate toward certain individuals more than others within the group because of personality or like-mindedness, or whatever. Regardless of the community's constant warning against particular friendships, closer associations with some and not others seem to be a natural occurrence, and I don't quite know how to reconcile the "rule" with the reality: I am closer to Angela, Krista and Eliza, while Deirdre, Maria, and Celia seem to have a special bond, but these friendship don't prevent us from loving all our sisters, although I am struggling to *like* Joanne. Maybe Laurie's newfound seriousness is a sign of growth. I don't know, but the change in her bothers me. I miss the easy-going and amiable Laurie, because this new version is as foreign and inflexible as her friend. It concerns me, too, that I can't seem to penetrate the veneer of Joanne's polite and grave demeanor. She doesn't smile easily or often, and she's so prim and proper that I feel the need to stand up straight and refrain from any laughing or goofing off when I am around her. Joanne is as reticent as Laurie is outgoing—or used to be—so it is an odd pairing. More and more, they seem to expect the rest of us to be as serious and rule-bound as they are. I don't agree with placing the letter over the spirit of the law. Jesus' teachings and life, as related in the New Testament, trumped the fire and brimstone of the Old Testament with charity and forgiveness. That's why he threw the hypocritical priests out of the temple. Jesus had little patience for laws and rules uninformed by love. I *get* that. I admit that I cannot always live up to it though, because being charitable toward Joanne is becoming more and more of a challenge, especially when she is so disapproving of me.

The funny thing is that I am being judged by someone whom I'm struggling *not* to judge. Maybe she simply dislikes me. Why else would she accuse me of a fault in public charity, not once or twice but several times? I don't mind so much being accused of laughing on the stairwell or even for breaking the Grand Silence, but when I heard myself accused by her for having particular friendships, well, I felt as if I had been stung by a bee. At the time I wondered: could she be right? Actually, she *is* right. Of course I have particular friends, *but most of us do*. Why does she single me out, and in this public forum? Most of my classmates accuse others of faults only sparingly, and while I muster the courage to accuse myself from time to time, I steadfastly avoid accusing any of my classmates, including Joanne. I mean, what is charitable about accusing someone of a fault in public? I just won't do it. We have been told that the practice is designed to nurture humility, but there is a world of difference between the noun (*humility*) and the verb (*humiliate*). We all hope to grow in humility, and the Blessed Virgin Mary is our model in this, but who am I, or who is Joanne, or who is any of us for that matter to judge another? Isn't this what Jesus warned against when he defended Mary Magdalene against the stone throwers? Despite what our superiors tell us, I still harbor a deep suspicion about the practice because I can't imagine that this is what Jesus would have wanted. Many of my classmates are just as critical of the practice as I am. We talk about it among ourselves—all except for Joanne who seems more than happy to practice "charity," especially towards me.

The huge differences between me and Joanne puzzle me, because we have both dedicated ourselves to a life of community in the service of God. Like me, Joanne is also a leader in our group, but she exercises her influence by modeling the convent rules, always playing the part of the well-behaved nun. My exuberance seems to irritate her. She keeps the boat steady, while I tend to rock it. She's all about convent tradition, and I'm more interested in testing its waters. On the "outside" I was not particularly outgoing or confident. Except when I was with my small band of friends, I would have been described as shy. In here, though, and for good or ill, I find that I am blossoming. I am outspoken and eager to make suggestions and take on projects. Working with others comes easily to me, probably owing to my experience of growing up in a large family with markedly different personalities, and I relish my newfound leadership role. My enthusiasm usually results in more work and responsibility, but I don't mind that. I do mind that whenever I propose an idea or initiate a project, Joanne challenges me or undermines it. Is it possible that she is jealous? But jealousy in *here*, and of what exactly? I just don't get it.

In the postulancy I proposed the idea of hosting a spaghetti dinner for family and friends to raise money for the community. Eliza, Deirdre, and the others thought it was a great idea, but Joanne objected on the basis that nothing like that had ever been done before. Who would make the spaghetti? Where would we hold it? Who could we possibly get to come? As it turned out, with Angela's mother's family recipe for the sauce and a lot of hard work, we held our dinner, had fun, and raised goodwill in our Philadelphia neighborhood as well as money for the community. Another time Deirdre, Krista, and I prevailed upon our novitiate superior, Sister John, to allow us to keep a stray miniature collie that turned up on our doorstep one night. Instead of rallying around our cause like everyone else, Joanne ticked off objections like a stern and disapproving parent: we don't have a doghouse; no one would be able to look after him during the day while we are cleaning at the motherhouse; keeping a dog in the novitiate is a silly idea that's never been done before, and blah, blah, blah. But he was so cute! He looked just like a baby Lassie with a long, pointy black nose and orange and white fur. The moment we clapped eyes on his sweet, eager face, we fell in love with him. We coaxed Sister Peter into giving us kitchen scraps and left them by the novitiate steps along with a bowl of water shortly after he appeared. Our efforts earned us his undying loyalty. After I persuaded our janitor, old Mr. Grim, to build a doghouse for our newfound pet to sleep in during the temperate months, Sister John finally agreed to let us keep the dog, much to Joanne's chagrin. She even consented to sheltering him in the enclosed part of the porch during the cold months.

In time, Sister John grew as attached to the little fellow as the rest of us, and we solved the problem of looking after him during the day by agreeing to take turns returning to the novitiate during the day between our motherhouse duties to walk him. I suppose it was a bold request that I initiated, since the idea of keeping a pet in the novitiate was certainly a novel one. But with persistence and resourcefulness, we found a way to manage the difficulties of keeping our lovable miniature collie. I suggested that we name our pet Opie, in honor of Sister John's "openness" to our appeal and her willingness to break with tradition, and my classmates agreed. Joanne, of course, managed to remain mum on the subject. Opie became a fixture at the novitiate, greeting us all with a wet muzzle and yaps of glee upon our arrival home each night, and in time he took his dutiful and rightful place at the foot of Sister John's chair in the community room. Our mistress had become Opie's master.

On another occasion in the novitiate, I came up with the idea of replacing the postulants who were assigned to switchboard and meal-preparation duties on Christmas and Easter so that they could enjoy the community festivities. I figured that it would be charitable for the novices to assume an extra burden on behalf of our younger sisters in the community. Once again, however, Joanne challenged my proposal. She hinted that G. I. and John would disapprove and see it as pampering the postulants. Krista and I decided to put the idea forth anyway, and both G.I. and Sister John consented, stipulating that it had to be done on a volunteer basis. "What a marvelous idea," Sister John cooed, "exactly in keeping with the community spirit!" See, in my view, *change* can be a very good thing, but it seems to make some people—and I think Joanne is one of those—a bit nervous.

For a short time Joanne and I worked together in infirmary kitchen under the infamous Sister Peter, and I hoped that by working side by side and contending with Peter's insanity and goofiness we would somehow grow closer. We didn't.

I don't know how to relate to her. Any interaction between us feels forced and superficial, like we are skating on the surface of one another but never quite getting to the real, underneath part. I certainly love Joanne as I love all my sisters in the community even if I don't feel connected to her in the way that I do to others, and she must feel just as disconnected from me. I realize that it's normal to find certain personalities troublesome. Trudy, for example, bugs all of us with her perpetual cheerfulness in the face of relentless work and fatigue. After slaving for nearly eight hours on laundry Tuesday, we all collapse in the break room, too tired to eat our apple butter and bread snack. Not Trudy. She bounces around the room, singing "Life is Just a Bowl of Cherries," admonishing us all to perk up and offer up our weariness to God. Needless to say, we don't respond too well. I feign her strangulation while we act out a mock-murder fantasy and imagine a headline that might read: "Shrimp-size Novice Strangled for Singing 'Life Is Just a Bowl of Cherries, Only Some Get the Pits' to Fatigued and Overworked Nuns."

Yes, sometimes Trudy can be irritating, and I could never place her in the same intimacy class as Angela or Krista or Eliza, but I still feel a kinship to her. Not so with Joanne. My struggle just to feel charitable towards her leaves me uneasy and guilty, which is why I must pray about it. And so I do in the dank dark chapel with the shadowy figure of Christ hanging on the cross behind the altar.

A muffled thump somewhere on the other side of the chapel wall on the right side short-circuits my prayer and brings my wandering mind back to the present and my late-night rendezvous with Angela and Krista. Having languished in the dim tunnel of reflection, I am startled, and it takes several moments to adjust to my surroundings. Krista's fearful squeak "what was that?" helps.

I look over at Angela who has the heel of her hand on her forehead already braced for the worst. "Oh my God!" she cries. "It's Sister John! We're going to get caught for sure now."

"Shhh," I admonish them both with my forefinger to my lips and my ear strained toward the wall and the origin of the thump. On the other side is a narrow hallway that separates the chapel from the novitiate kitchen. My voice is tense and not at all sure. "Just be quiet for a moment. It was probably just a mouse in the kitchen or dry closet. No one will have heard it upstairs. Just stay calm."

Soundless minutes—but for the chorus of our three racing hearts—pass. Nothing happens. Our novice mistress does not appear. Finally, Krista lets out a loud, anxious breath, "Phew. That sure put a scare into me." Angela and I follow suit. It feels good to breathe again.

Seated between us, Angela releases her tension by collapsing into a quiet, nervous chuckle. Then she takes hold of Krista's and my hands, holding them squarely against her forehead in place of her own sweaty palm. Calmer now, she finally lets our hands drop, and we settle back into a safe silence.

Our clandestine meeting began earlier in the evening on our way to bed following evening prayer, when Krista mouthed three words that did not surprise me, "Chapel, later tonight." So that's where the three of us sit, all for one and one for all, at midnight when we should be in bed. It is not an uncommon practice, as I have noticed others creeping out of their rooms by themselves, or sometimes with one or two of the others. On such occasions we take it upon ourselves to break the grand-silence rule because our busy days leave us no time for anything other than prayer or work. We need the time to think or to let off steam, or to commiserate with a friend, or in this case, with two friends.

On this particular night we are the only rule-breakers. Krista's most recent attack of homesickness has been fueled by the frustration of coping with the difficult reading we've been assigned in Sister John's theology class. When she feels scared and insecure, she tends to get nostalgic about what she recalls as her easier and more comfortable life in the lay world. It's easier for me to keep up with the work because I find it interesting, so I try to help her out as much as I can. But Krista's brain shuts down when we delve into such readings as St. Thomas Aquinas's *Summa Theologica*, and I sympathize with her, having suffered similar anxiety attacks myself in the community sewing room. Other factors are also wearing her down. Generally, Krista seems to be happy in the novitiate, and she definitely prefers the nervously energetic but good-humored Sister John to the more severe Sister G. I. But normally thin and frail, Krista is fatigued and rundown as a result of the excessive physical labor of recent weeks. I warned her not to volunteer for the extra duty, but Krista is generous to a fault and her goodwill often outweighs her common sense. Our regular duties are arduous enough, but there is spring cleaning or fall cleaning or feast-day celebration cleaning and the novices are always the ones to get tapped for the additional work.

One certainty about convent life is that nuns are obsessed with cleanliness. The words "spic 'n' span" take on special meaning in here where every machine, countertop, strip of floor, and piece of furniture sparkle and shine: the kitchen, refectory, laundry room, bedrooms, community rooms, chapel, and, of course, the priest's quarters. In fact, the only thing we don't have to clean is the grounds.

Recently, Deirdre, Krista, Monica and I worked alongside Sister John late into the night to scrub, mop, wax, and buff the refectory as well as the hallways on the entire first floor of the motherhouse. Outfitted with scrub brushes, mops, buckets of soapy water, scraping instruments, and waxing equipment, our task was to scrape off all traces of the old wax before applying a new coat to thousands and thousands of maroon and black linoleum squares. We took turns with the more difficult scrubbing and scraping segment of the process and then traded our stiff necks and strained backs for the easier mopping or buffing part of the process. Working the buffer machine was easier on the body, but it took a certain knack. On my first try, the buffer went all awry like a wild kid in a school yard, until both the machine and I went spinning out of control and attacked an innocent white wall. Thankfully on hand to rescue me, our experienced novice mistress righted that blue monster in a wink and set me back on course. We were the only ones fit enough to do the work at the time. Many of the others were still recovering from a bad strain of flu that had swept through the motherhouse like a hurricane, felling us all like trees in its path. Krista shouldn't have volunteered because the work was strenuous, especially when piled atop our other regular duties. Still healthy, I felt up to the task and enjoyed the chance to master "Big Blue," as the buffer machine was called. Who knows? With a little luck Reverend Mother would hear about how hard I had worked, and would bump me right up to the juniorate when the time came, no questions asked. Hah!

I wonder what time it is. I rub my eyes, which are burning from lack of sleep. I feel as if I am coming up for air as I look to my right and left in the dim light of the chapel. Unlike Angela, who is stifling a yawn with her fist, Krista is wide awake and deep in thought. Usually pale anyway, Krista is looking downright peaked, although her fatigue and homesickness seem not to have robbed her of her hearty spirit. It's Angela and her lack of reserves that have concerned both Krista and I of late. With a quick sideways glance, I catch Angela's eyelids in the act of closing. They briefly flutter and drop, flutter and drop. She looks exhausted. Next to cleanliness, health is a high priority in this place. We are clearly discouraged from having an illness of any kind, because to be sick means to be weak; and to complain about illness or pain signifies a lack of fortitude. The only time we get more than two aspirins and a suggestion that it's all in the head is when a visible contagion, such as the recent influenza, sweeps through the ranks. So it comes as quite a surprise when "they" concede that Angela, who never fully recovered from the flu, has contracted bronchitis, and that Eliza is suffering from pleurisy. Real illnesses with names—what a concept. Maybe they'll get the message that we need a little more rest and a lot less work. Maybe they'll believe that we are actually sick when we seek permission to report to the infirmary. We grumble such subversive things only among ourselves, however, and even though it does not change the situation, it makes us feel better.

Without warning, Krista resumes her earlier conversation, as if there had been no disturbing thud or protracted silence in the interim. "G. I. always seemed so cranky, you know? I'm glad that Sister John is nicer and all, but I just wonder how much more of this crap I can take. I'm sick and tired of working from the time we get up in the morning until we fall into bed at night. I would really like to go home, crash on my own bed in my own bedroom and sleep for two years. Straight." This rosy outlook is coming from Krista, the cheerful. What can I possibly hope for from myself?

Slumped back against the pew, Angela draws her knees upward and leans her chin against the heel of her hands. Then she lets out a long sigh before she, too, makes an admission. "I really miss my mom and dad more than ever. Ya think it's 'cause I've been so sick?"

It sounds more like a plea than a question, and Krista pounces on it. "Well, of course you miss them," she replies emphatically, looking over at me for support before launching into a tirade aimed against the all-powerful convent authorities. "We haven't seen our families for months, for Pete's sake, not since we entered the novitiate in August. Why does the novitiate have to be so strict? What if something happened at home and one of us needed to be there? What then? We can't even leave the motherhouse grounds. And why do they have to read our mail? Do they have to take everything away from us, even our privacy?" With each complaint her pitch rises, and I worry that someone will hear us.

Krista sounds as if she is heading for a crash. Besides being exhausted and homesick, she is still smarting from a recent confrontation with Sister John about a letter from an ex-boyfriend that she never even got to read. If she is teetering on the brink of a nervous breakdown, Angela and I are not far behind. After all, Krista is just putting words around what we feel: exhausted, homesick, and a little rebellious. I recognize my own misgivings in what she is saying, but something very deep and certain inside me refuses to be disheartened. Yes, I have moments of doubt when I question and waver, and yet I still believe in what we are doing. I believe in the fundamental goodness of my religious vocation and I believe in the mission of this community, even though I don't always have confidence in the method and the rule that govern it. We are just being tested, that's all, I tell myself. It's natural to feel taxed and overwhelmed.

I clap one reassuring arm over Angela's shoulder and the other over Krista's shoulder, pulling them into a huddle. "Listen, you guys, the junior sisters warned us that the novitiate is the most difficult year of the four years of training. It's *designed* to test us. It won't *always* be *this* way. It gets better. We . . . ," and here I look back and forth between my two friends and enunciate the words clearly and deliberately, as if there were something wrong with their hearing, "just have to make it through this year; we *are* going to make it through this year." Then I take Krista's left hand, place it on Angela's right hand, and, folding them between my two, I remind them of our pledge: "Now, listen to me. We are the Three Musketeers. Remember what that means? Through thick and thin, we are in this thing together. Novitiate only lasts a year. *One* year. We're more than halfway there, and then it'll get easier. We just need to hang in there. Help each other. Okay?" Krista nods and smiles and Angela does the same, as I release their hands but not their eyes.

I can't believe it. I have sunk to the level of a cheerleader at a pep rally. Now I'm feeling a little phony, and I hate it. My optimism and confidence ring hollow even to me. Just then Angela rescues me. Despite the fact that she comes off sounding more resigned than invigorated, her concession gives me a small victory. "Kathy's right. We're just a little down. We gotta see past these next months. They won't last forever."

"Oh, I know," Krista relents. "It just makes me feel better to tick off my gripes. You know what I mean? Plus, I don't know why Madeline seems so distant lately. We used to be so close, but since she became a junior sister she hardly ever talks to me anymore." Here her tone turns a little mournful, "I feel so . . . I don't know . . . cut off or something. And I really looked up to her like a big sister even before I entered the community." A first-year junior sister from Krista's hometown, Madeline is Krista's "big sister." She took a special interest in Krista when she first entered the community, and Krista is quite fond of her so this is a tender area for her. Angela and I nod sympathetically before we lapse back into another shared silence.

Krista's grievance has triggered one of my own concerns. I don't know where her thoughts or Angela's go, maybe to prayer, but mine center around my own friend in the juniorate, Anne Rose, a classmate of Madeline's. Only two years my senior, she seems light-years ahead of me in terms of spiritual growth, so she has become my role model. Unlike Krista, I did not know her before having entered the convent, but that did not prevent us from establishing an immediate and close connection. Although Madeline and Anne Rose are only a year ahead of us, they are eager to help us out and to share what they have learned during their three years of formation. Now that they are first-year junior sisters, they leave the motherhouse grounds each day to attend college while we remain behind, so we don't get to see much of them. Disappearing after Mass and breakfast in the morning, books and lunches in hand, they return only for supper and evening prayer before they settle into their quarters at the juniorate building. At times they do not even make it back in time for supper, so we set aside a cold plate for them in the kitchen with little notes that read: "Welcome home!" I miss finding the holy card she sometimes tucked inside my cubby in the chapel hallway, and I sure miss seeing Ann Rose on a daily basis, even though our time together is limited. We conduct our friendship from a distance—the distance that separates a postulant from a novice and a novice from a junior sister, and the distance mandated by the community rule regarding particular friendships.

Sure, I see her in the hallways on my way to or from chapel or refectory, or on the way to and from the motherhouse, and we sometimes work side by side when our duties as postulant and novice overlap in the kitchen or during choir practice. At times, and if a duty allows, we steal a couple of minutes alone just to catch up and say, "Hey, how's it going?" only to part feeling frustrated and wishing for more time to get to know one another. Whenever we are permitted to mingle with the sisters outside our group, Anne Rose and I always seek one another out. I devour these infrequent opportunities for soulful discussions about how we came to recognize our religious vocations, life before the convent, what our parents and siblings are like, and the difficulties of living out our vows. Developing a friendship in here is complicated and difficult. It requires constant vigilance and balancing so as to avoid the hazards of "particular friendships" that, as best I can determine, mean they are exclusionary and interfere with one's love of God or one's sisters. But I do not see any such danger in my relationship with Anne Rose. My affection and admiration for her motivate me to serve God and to be even more loving toward all my sisters. So I have decided that there must be a difference between particular friends and *particular friendships*, although I keep this distinction to myself.

I'm impressed with the way Ann Rose strives earnestly for holiness, but not in the affected way that some of the other nuns do. She reminds me of Sister Benedict, the principal of the orphan school in the *Bells of St. Mary's*. Like her, Anne Rose is all nun without having lost touch with her humanity. And while her compass is firmly set toward heaven, she is finely tuned to the needs of those around her, especially the sick and lonely older nuns in the motherhouse. Her special devotion to the Blessed Mother is inspiring, especially when I observe the beatific look on her face as she kneels in prayer at the altar to Mary's statue. Sister Anne Rose has quiet brown eyes that twinkle when she flashes her bashful smile, displaying a row of perfectly even white teeth. But her lowered head and downcast eyes during prayer reveal her quiet humility. Her compassionate nature is evident in the way she stops whatever she is doing to listen patiently to the elderly sisters' complaints or to help them find their way to their place in chapel. On St. Patrick's Day, this timid and unassuming young nun turns into a firecracker as she leads us all in a lively Irish jig, and her example proves to me that it is possible to be fun-loving *and* virtuous, loving *and* prayerful.

I tried to express my high regard for her by creating a rock garden alongside the walking path at the novitiate building in honor of her feast day, which is what we celebrate in place of a birthday. With Sister John's permission, Krista and I worked on it, arranging the rocks to spell out the words "Rose of Sharon" in honor of her patron saint, and then we planted flowers around the rock formation. I was sure she'd be thrilled when she saw the garden on her walk from the juniorate building to the motherhouse. With the eagerness of a little kid, I waited for her to discover our surprise gift, only to learn one long week later that what I intended as an expression of fondness and esteem caused her distress. She approached me in the small motherhouse library where I was poring over notes for my upcoming theology exam. Of course, talking was not permitted, but she caught my eye and nodded me toward the stairwell. I understood that I was to meet her in the alcove above the third-floor landing where we would not be observed. Cautiously, I climbed up the back stairway and past the third floor where the stairs come to a small and unused area that is partially obscured from view. I knew she would be waiting for me when I turned the corner, and I was sure that she wanted to thank me for our gift. My ready smile dissipated when I saw her anguished face.

"What were you thinking?" she demanded to know. "Do you have any idea how much trouble you've caused and the explaining I've had to do because of you?" Her peevish tone caught me off-guard, and her eyes were so sad that I couldn't bear to look at them. They turned away from me anyway to look out the long window framing the tops of the tall trees lined up along the edge of the novitiate and juniorate buildings, reminding me that, like those two buildings, we would also always be separated, not so much by rank but by our vows. Her angry white hands clutched the railing beneath the slanted wall.

Instinctively, I knew that she was referring to the rock garden, so I fumbled to explain while trying to make sense of the source of her displeasure. "What do you mean? What have I done? I thought you would like it. I . . . I . . . I didn't mean any harm. I thought it would make you happy. Sister John likes it. She . . . she gave me, uh . . . us—me and Krista—permission to pull the weeds and clean up the area, so I, uh we, we arranged the stones and the flowers and spelled out, you know, the name, Rose of Sharon, in honor of, you know, in honor of your feast day." Suddenly unsure of myself, I was sputtering and stammering, like an engine that couldn't get started.

She shook her head resignedly, regaining her composure before pulling a veil over her sad eyes and training them on me. I shuddered, realizing how much I had displeased her. Maybe worse. "Don't you see," she pleaded, "maybe the thought, the gesture, is innocent enough; but Vera Marie wanted to know if there was something I should tell her about us, and if there's a danger of our having a particular friendship."

Oh God, I thought, the dreaded "PF" again. Sister Vera Marie is the juniorate mistress, and she runs a tight ship, tighter even than G. I.'s. I've seen her studying me from a distance with a wry and knowing smile, as if to say, "Gonna getcha. Next year, you're mine. *I'll* tame *your* spirit." And so it will be if I ever make it through this novitiate boot-camp and the convent-tangle of unclear expectations and hidden meanings.

"But what does that mean?" I whined and then accelerated. "I can't figure out what a particular friendship is exactly. What's so wrong with it? If it means feeling a special way toward one sister that you don't feel toward the others, then I guess I'm guilty of that. But I don't understand why that's wrong. It seems natural. It's not as if I don't practice charity. It's not as if I don't love all my sisters in Christ. I work on that every single day."

The squeak of a door opening from the third floor hallway to the stairs sent Anne Rose's forefinger to her lips, cautioning me to be quiet until safety and privacy were restored. The footsteps clattered and then faded down the stairs, a door whooshed as it opened and closed, and we both breathed a sigh of relief.

My frustration gave way to an embarrassed silence. Anne Rose shook her head and whispered: "You just don't get it, do you?" And no, I guess I don't, I thought to myself but didn't dare say so and tempt her disapproval more than I already had.

She looked downward while she leaned, as if exhausted, against the wall. "Look," she pleaded, suddenly meeting my eyes and grabbing both my hands, "We just have to be careful what we do with it, this friendship. We can't violate the spirit of our vows, and we can't give our superiors any reason to suspect us of doing so. I know you mean well." Noting the distress in my face, she returned my gaze with soft, familiar eyes, trying to reassure me. "But we, *you*, have to be careful. You can't be so free and expressive with your feelings," she prodded as she tugged on my hands. "Do you understand?"

I nodded yes, but I didn't understand anything. I started trembling, and I knew it wasn't from fear. A strange feeling seemed to come from my hands, which were wound firmly through hers, and it matched a sweet, flashing pain in my stomach that I did not recognize. I felt my eyes melting.

"Fine, yes, whatever you say," I muttered. "I'm so, so sorry. It was just a gift. I had no idea . . . I didn't mean . . . I . . . I . . . only wanted to please you. Are you really in trouble?" She released my hands, and I managed to hold myself up by gripping the wall.

"I confided to Sister Vera that we are friends, and I assured her that you just got a little carried away because you wanted to give me something special for my feast day, which is true, isn't it?" I nodded. She continued, "But I assured her there was no danger, and that both you and I are praying for direction to keep our friendship in Christ's love." For a moment, we fell silent, dipping more intimately into each other's eyes. "Look," she declared firmly, breaking the trance. "I have to get back. We've stayed away too long already, and someone might notice and report us. I'll go first, okay?" Again, I nodded. She turned to go, suddenly returned, and embraced me briefly, warmly. Then she disappeared around the corner and through the heavy doors leading to the third-floor hallway. I felt confused and afraid to put words to the feelings traveling through me like an alien visitor, but I commanded myself to descend the stairs on rubbery legs and return to my studies in the library.

Another louder thump this time shakes me from the memory of this unsettling episode in my friendship with Ann Rose, returning me to Angela and Krista in the cold, shadowy chapel. Krista is kneeling now with her arms propped up and chin cupped in her hands, and Angela is sitting back with her arm draped over the pew. I am leaning forward with my head down and my elbows resting on my knees. The sound of the second thump startles and scoops us out of the dungeon of our private reveries. We look questioningly from one to the other. "What in the world can *that* noise be?" Angela demands to know.

So do we all, but we won't find out this contemplative night. The revelation of that mystery will come later, on another mischief-prone night which finds Celia, Deirdre, Krista, and I descending the "servants'" or back staircase from our dorm rooms and making our way, not to chapel to reflect, but to the pantry on the first floor to forage for food. Famished, we are rummaging for snacks to compensate for our earlier unappetizing, unsatisfying, inedible meal.

I blame Sister John for the fact that we are so famished. Despite her own lack of experience in the knowledge and practice of culinary skills, our sweet but antic novice mistress insists on teaching us how to cook—supposedly, to prepare us for life in the missions—by requiring that we make our own supper in the novitiate every Saturday. A bonus—in her view—is that our group gets to spend quality time together in a shared project. I do not know where she gets her recipes or ingredients but they appear magically in our small ill-equipped kitchen. Eager to play her part, our mistress hustles into the kitchen wearing a large chef's hat and an oversized white apron over her garb. She scurries from the small wooden table to the stove, issuing directions and brandishing cooking utensils. On this particular Saturday, she has red cabbage, lots of it. She is intent on making some kind of nutritious casserole comprised of cabbage and not much else from what I can tell, but thankfully, it's my turn for cleaning duty so I can avoid the up-close and personal preparation and cooking part of the meal. I can hardly stand the urine-like stench of the cooking cabbage, let alone the prospect of ingesting red-colored leaves. Why not just eat them raw? Even Celia is making woeful faces at me behind John's back, and she will devour pretty much anything, no questions asked. I occupy myself with setting the table and looking after Opie, anything to keep me out of the kitchen, but I cannot avoid sitting down with the others at table, where a giddy Sister John encourages us to dig in because we made such a large amount, and we do not have much room in the freezer to store leftovers.

When the bowl is passed around, I help myself to the tiniest possible portion. A cursory glance across the table at Sister John, who is flanked by Joanne and Laurie, assures me that she is too absorbed in reciting the nutritional benefits of cabbage to her rapt audience to notice how much, or how little, I am eating. Fortunately, too, Sister John is not gifted with G. I.'s radar vision, so I don't worry too much about what is or isn't on my plate. What I do worry about is the amount of cabbage remaining in the kitchen. I force myself to swallow, without tasting, a few bites of the festive-looking but stinky dish. Then I get up and return to the kitchen for second and third helpings, along with several others. But instead of returning directly to table, Celia and I conspire to duck into the first-floor half bathroom where we dump and flush the better part of the poisonous cabbage that we have heaped onto our plates down the toilet. We are very pleased with our clever plan to eliminate the enemy-dish, and we are carrying out our self-appointed mission for the third time when something tells me to look up just as Celia is pushing down the lever. Standing outside the bathroom doorway with folded arms and a shocked expression is Sister John.

Well, as my mother would say, she "wasn't born yesterday," or better still, we should have known that John is "too old of a cat to be scratched by a kitten." Whatever the cliché, the result is still the same: Sister John has caught us *red*-handed. Fully expecting the iron hand of judgment to fall on our heads, Celia and I are stumbling over each other verbally in a fruitless effort to explain what we are doing, when John steps inside, leans down, and takes a long look at the vestiges of red that disappear down the gurgling bowl. She raises her hand to silence us and shrieks halfheartedly, "What are you doing? Is that our good cabbage? Owww, how awful. All that cabbage. What an awful waste." And then I see something so unexpected it almost fails to register: Sister John is holding her hand to her mouth and suppressing a giggle like a conspiratorial schoolgirl. After we withdraw from the scene of the crime, our superior recovers her business-as-usual face, giving no hint that she acknowledges either our wrongdoing or her own unorthodox response. Is she letting us off the hook because she cannot believe what she has seen? Or does she recognize how truly awful the cabbage casserole is? I guess it doesn't matter, because sometimes life is just good and we get an unexpected and welcome break. But being pardoned does not appease our hunger.

Now it's after 11:00 p.m., and we can't sleep, so we are hoping to satisfy our grumbling stomachs. Deirdre assures us there are cookies in the pantry. She knows because her mother sent a care package recently, and John had her store the goodies away "for a special occasion." Well, the four of us have decided that this is the occasion. We are scanning the pantry shelves in the dark, and that's when we hear the same thump that Angela, Krista and I heard the other night in the chapel, only louder. It sounds like it is directly overhead, which it is, because it just thumped against the ceiling.

Suddenly, Krista lets out a sudden piercing scream and then screeches, "Oh my God, it's a bat . . . ahhh, eoww . . . It's caught in my hair . . . Help . . . get me out of here!" We wave it away from her head and then scramble into the kitchen and head back up the narrow "servants" stairway at the back of the house, but the bat precedes us, flapping into walls right and left. We duck and stumble in the dark. Krista is in the lead, and I am bringing up the rear behind Deirdre and Celia. We finally tumble on to the second-floor hallway where the bat continues its aimlessly frantic flight. Dipping and grazing our heads, the bat makes its way to the main staircase leading to the uppermost floor amid our escalating squeaks and squeals, as sleepy-eyed novices, stirred from sleep, venture out of their rooms. Just then I realize that Krista is around the corner tapping on the door to John's private chamber and calling out an alarm, "Sister, there's a problem out here, a bat . . ." Within moments, the door flies open revealing our bedraggled commander, her black kimono half-drawn around her pajamas, obviously awakened from a deep sleep but prepared, nevertheless, for action.

"Did you say a bat, Sister?" She disappears for a moment to step back into her room, returning with her silver-rimmed spectacles in place, "Show me where. And get a broom from the closet. Quickly."

By this time the bat is on the third floor seeing to it that no one will rest this night of our Lord. Armed with her broom, Sister John leads our small squad up the stairs in pursuit of the nocturnal intruder, ordering us to close all the doors and open the window off the staircase between the second and third floors. In the meantime, the fearful bat is still swooping back and forth over our heads, and even John ducks and swerves while swatting at it with her broom, urging it toward the open window. We direct her, first this way and then that, until the bat disappears into the ceiling shadows. After she finally succeeds in guiding it through the opening, she leans with relief against the wall. Nervous laughter follows, first hers, and then ours. The Grand Silence has been temporarily dismissed, I guess. "Well," she finally observes, "that's a first for the record book; we've never had that happen in the novitiate before. I wonder where it came from and how it got in here." It is on the tip of my tongue to satisfy part of her curiosity when Krista silences me with glaring eyes, and I realize that the bat has both exposed and saved us, and the less said, the better. While securing the window, she answers her own question anyway. "It must have gotten in through the attic somehow. Don't you think, Sisters?"

A chorus of "yesses" and "uh-huhs" reassures her before she reminds us of the Grand Silence and waves us back to bed, to which Krista, Deirdre, Celia, and I return with growling and unhappy stomachs.

*     *     *

"Well, Sister, the group has asked me to bring it up." The "group" is assembled in the second-floor sitting room where we hold regular meetings to discuss housekeeping matters, to share concerns, or just to bounce around ideas for upcoming feast-day celebrations. My bold words work like a wand, suddenly silencing the room. Many did not expect that I would go through with it. But why not? Unlike G. I., Sister John seems genuinely open to discussing matters such as this one with us, and unlike the other superiors, she gives serious consideration to our views on community issues. This forum is her idea, after all, and most of us have expressed similarly strong, negative feelings about public charity among ourselves. I'm just making our concerns public. Besides, the policy changes resulting from Pope John XXIII's Vatican Council II a few years earlier are reverberating throughout the Catholic world, from the parishes to the monasteries and convents such as our own. As a result, the Mass is now being said in English instead of Latin, and folk music is replacing traditional hymns during the liturgy, making it an opportune time to reconsider another outmoded practice in the convent: public charity.

Sister John examines me with her light green eyes, wisps of graying hair straying onto her forehead. She's a very slight and wiry woman, full of energy and gusto in carrying out her responsibilities and happy, I think, to be working closely with young people. Less strict and austere than G. I., she takes us aside privately if we need to be reprimanded. Because of her softer approach, I want to please her so I work especially hard by volunteering for extra duties and making it a point not to be late for prayers or meals if I can help it. Nor does she seem to be as troubled by my minor infractions, such as the red cabbage fiasco. Her intense look reminds me, however, that she takes her job and the community rule seriously, and our discussion is not a trifling affair.

"Why don't you tell me your thoughts, Sister, and then I'd like to hear what some of the others think as well." With this, she nods at the group assembled around the room on assorted chairs. All are alert with anticipation. I follow her eyes, noting the various signs of nervousness in my classmates. Laurie, Joanne's new ally, is chewing her thumbnail. My former kitchen partner, Deirdre, is sitting erectly at full alert, as if anticipating an emergency call to action. Celia is twisting and folding her bottom lip and Eliza is seated with her small body pitched forward, her eyes downcast and her hands folded as if in prayer. The others are all terribly still and attentive.

Despite a sudden rush of doubt like a wave that comes out of nowhere, I forge ahead. "Many of us feel very uncomfortable accusing others of a fault in public because it seems so . . . so uncharitable. I understand that the purpose is to teach us humility, but it seems unkind to accuse and to, well, to humiliate another. The way it works now, the group charity encourages us to look at others judgmentally and to focus on their faults, not so much on our own except in a negative or defensive way." I pause, needing some indication that I have not strayed out of bounds. Lines of sweat are traveling down my side and curving back, finally gathering in what feels like tiny puddles at the small of my back.

Sister John's elbow leans on the black folds of garb covering her locked knees. Her chin resting on the palms of her hands, she appears not to be blinking, although it's hard to tell from the way the lamplight glances off her silver-rimmed spectacles. "Hmmm," she ventures, "hmmm." She does a quick study of the attentive group, deciding to target Maria, "And you, Sister, what are your thoughts?"

Interesting choice. Maria is my unacknowledged rival for most popular class leader. Congenial and round with a flat face like a lovable pug-nosed dog, her soft-spoken demeanor belies her intelligence and forcefulness. The others often look to one or the other of us to take charge of class projects, and she and I sometimes disagree on matters ranging from the inconsequential to the significant. She is a bit more traditional than I, but she is a good egg overall. She can be a bit stubborn and opinionated, but so can I. I don't begrudge her the views she expresses, and I don't believe she holds mine against me. We actually share a good deal in common: we work unstintingly; we sing alto together in choir; we don't mind spending time with the older nuns; we create skits and help Angela with her songwriting; we participate in the small folk-singing group that performs for the community; and we enjoy having the others look to us for leadership in matters small and large. Maria knows where I stand on this public charity issue, but her views are not clear to me, and I have no idea how she will reply to the question put to her. But in inviting Maria to express her views on the matter, I realize that Sister John is one fully aware and smart nun. Maria clears her throat and begins speaking in her breathy voice, oddly coupled with her nasal Philadelphia twang: "Well, Sister, I think there is a value to group charity. It's a good opportunity to reflect on our faults and weaknesses in a communal way. But I agree that it's not the best way for us to learn humility. It does seem uncharitable to accuse someone else of a fault in front of the entire group, although I wouldn't want to do away with the practice entirely."

"Pheww," I think. At least on this issue we agree, and I can withdraw my head from the chopping block.

As if on cue following Maria's comment, some of the others chime in, with Deirdre proposing that we accuse only ourselves in charity. Eliza thinks that we should practice charity by negating ourselves and going out of our way to do for others, suggesting that we abandon the practice entirely, and pretty soon, we have a free-wheeling dialogue going. Whichever way it turns out, I am immensely relieved that some of the others have shared the risk and joined in the discussion.

But thus far, our novice mistress has not responded with anything more than "hmmm," a nod of the head, and a quizzical look. Finally, our bemused novice mistress scrunches up her brow and taps her cheek with her forefinger, as if the gesture enables her to absorb our concerns and suggestions. I fully expect her to bring our little forum to a close with a promise to pray about the matter before broaching it with Mother General. Instead, she adjusts her glasses, pushing them back up the bridge of her slight nose, and offhandedly delivers an unexpected and stunning victory to us. "Sisters, I think we can treat this as an internal matter. Since charity is practiced within the privacy of each of the groups, we may take the liberty of experimenting with the practice. I will discuss this with Mother Agatha, of course, but in the meantime, we'll agree to continue meeting for charity but not to accuse others, and to accuse yourselves publicly only when it is warranted and as determined by your own conscience. Well, then?" She looks at us blandly, as if the roof of our novitiate world had not just collapsed.

What can we say? Murmurs of appreciation like "great," "sure, Sister," and "gosh, thank you, Sister," trickle out, as Deirdre's broad infectious smile sweeps through the group like wildfire in a forest. I am so lighthearted that I think I might defy gravity and float up to my bed on the third floor when Sister John's raised voice interrupts my fanciful flight. "Don't forget, Sisters, next Sunday I will be leaving for my weeklong retreat, and I want to be certain everything is in order for my departure. Sister Gabriel will be staying with you in my absence. See to it that everything goes smoothly for her, please. Good night, Sisters, God bless." At any other time, I might have thought, "When the cat's away the mice will play," but not tonight. Our ability to effect a change, to modify a tradition that has prevailed unchallenged for years, sobers me and reinforces my optimism about convent life as well as my respect for our novice mistress. Far from looking forward to her being away and the measure of "freedom" it will bring, I realize that I may even miss her.

How prophetic. Not only would I miss her, but the events that occur in her absence would instigate a dizzying, downward spiral and raise the first of many red flags about the danger and the damage to come.

\*     \*     \*

It's Wednesday, three days after our good-byes to Sister John following our glorious victory over public charity. Filling in for Angela who is sick yet again, I am in the kitchen helping Maria with the pots and pans following noon dinner. Of late, Angela is sick more than she is well, and it troubles me. Except for the banging of the pots against the stainless-steel sink and the periodic rush of water from the faucet, all is silent since Mother Agatha has not yet dispensed us from the Grand Silence following the meal. That's not unusual. We frequently eat our meals and perform our duties in utter silence. But it is odd when Mother General, just back from the missions, does not celebrate her homecoming with us by permitting us to talk at least during cleanup.

I am tossing the dishtowels in the laundry and removing my apron, wondering how Angela's visit to the infirmary is going and whether the nursing nun will finally take her continuous illnesses more seriously, when Sister Gabriel, Sister John's temporary replacement, startles me with a tap on my shoulder. "Sister Kathleen, Mother Agatha wants you to report to her office at 2:00 p.m." I look at her as if to say, "Well, why not just zap me with a bolt of lightning?" She reads the terror in my face but shrugs her shoulders and whispers, "That's all I am permitted to tell you."

Five minutes later, I am kneeling at the altar railing in the empty chapel. I don't remember actually making my way from the kitchen to the chapel, but I can tell that the shock of Sister Gabriel's message is wearing off because I suddenly feel my heart making short, loud raps against the wall of my chest. My mind is racing forward and backward, and fear parches my mouth. I am staring at the oversized blue and white statue of the Blessed Mother perched in the center of the side altar, an understanding look on her face and her arms stretched out as if they were prepared to gather me up, and I try to focus and pray but the eye of my memory fixes on something else.

I return to February, nearly a year ago. Still a postulant, I had driving duty at the time because I was an experienced driver with a Pennsylvania license unlike most of my classmates. One of the more desirable of the duties, it gave me the opportunity to escape the motherhouse and breathe the free air of the real world in short spurts. I was mostly charged with picking up and dropping off visiting nuns at the Philadelphia airport and, occasionally, with delivering a package to the downtown Catholic Charities office. But on this night I was instructed by G. I. to report to Sister John at the novitiate at 11:00 p.m. How odd, I thought. I was also told not to speak to anyone about the assignment, and to slip out of the dormitory when everyone else was sleeping. I couldn't help but wonder: what gives?

I climbed the hill to the motherhouse in the dark brutal cold and found the 1963 Plymouth Valiant parked at the end of the line of cars, as if waiting for duty. My fingers were very nearly frozen after only about ten minutes of exposure, and I kept rubbing them inside my mittens so that I could control them enough to get the key in the ignition. I was relieved when it started up on the second try, and while it warmed up, I scraped the thin layer of ice plastered against the windshield. I eased the car down the hill and into the covered circular driveway in front of the novitiate building. Unsure of what I should do next, I finally stepped from the car, leaving the engine running to keep it warm, and made my way up the stairs to the large wooden double doors. It opened before I even knocked, as Sister John was evidently lying in wait for me. She pulled me through the doorway by the lapels of my pea coat, and whispered, "Come inside so you don't get a chill, Sister."

"Ah, yes, Sister. Thanks," I whispered back.

She examined me quizzically. "Sister George Ignatius gave you clear instructions?"

"Well, yes, Sister, but not exactly. I mean, I don't know where I'm going. I know I am not to speak to anyone."

Then peremptorily, "Yes, right. That's fine. Now here's the address, together with directions." She handed me a scrap of white paper with a downtown address for a place called The Lucy Eaton Home for Single Women. I was thoroughly perplexed but I had no way of processing my confusion and uncertainty about my mission. Somehow I sensed that I was not to ask more questions than were necessary, so I reminded myself silently: blind obedience, blind obedience, *blind* obedience.

Sister John interrupted my silent drama by giving me firm directives in oddly hushed tones. "You are to deliver Sister Helen to this address. Your job is simply to deliver her there and to see to it that she enters the building safely. Then come back straightaway. Do you understand?"

"Yes, Sister," I muttered, not understanding at all. Alarms were going off in my head, but I remained focused and dutiful, like a robot following orders.

"Here," she pointed to a corner of the room where a black steamer trunk, much like the one I packed and brought with me into the convent, sat waiting. "Help me to lift this into the car, Sister." I nodded, and we each picked up an end, carrying all that Sister Helen owned in the world down the long stone steps to the portico where the car was parked with the engine still running. Together we lifted it into the trunk of the Valiant and slammed it shut. "Now wait in the car, Sister. And do not engage in any conversation with Sister Helen under any circumstances. Remember your vow of obedience." She looked at me intently to be sure that I understood, and then she winced a little, as if realizing that the "sister" part was better left out, and I was beginning to get a clearer picture of my surreptitious and odious "duty."

As I pulled the car out on to the roadway, Sister Helen, who was evidently no longer a sister, sobbed uncontrollably in the backseat of the car. I could see her through the rearview mirror huddled in the corner, her cloak wrapped around her unfamiliar, ill-fitting civilian clothes as she dabbed her eyes with a man-sized handkerchief. I started trembling, negotiating my way through the unfamiliar city streets at night, and wished I had never been granted this "favored" duty. So this is how it's done, I thought, remembering Bernadette and a few others who also disappeared from our ranks in the dead of night. Suddenly, Sister Helen started wailing and talking simultaneously, not so much to me—she too had been given instructions—but out loud to herself.

"I can't believe this. I can't believe it. I have nowhere to go, no family to go home to, and they know it. Why are they doing this to me? Why do I have to leave? I don't want to go. I don't know what I am going to do . . . ohhh, ohhhh, ohhh. I just can't bear it. God, please, please help me."

I did not utter a single compassionate word. I felt trapped in speechlessness, not only by my superior's orders but also by virtue of my own combustion of feelings: pity mixed with fear and helplessness. I was only a postulant, and even if I were at liberty to console her, what could I possibly do or say to relieve her pain? And there was something else I felt too—relief. I am not her. I am safe. I am not an outcast. I am not banished. I am not her.

In the face of this shameful recollection, the tall statue of Mary now offers little more than a hard blank stare and no solace. My mind focuses on the dilemma before me. Mother Agatha has summoned me to her office. I don't know where to turn. Sister Gabriel will not speak to me. Our beloved Sister John is away on her retreat. How I wish she were here now. I turn and examine the clock at the back of the chapel. It reads 1:45 p.m. I'm supposed to be somewhere. Where? Oh, yes, I have to scrub the ground-floor locker rooms and mop the first-floor hallway. But I can't. Not now. I am expected in Mother General's office in fifteen minutes. Oh, dear Lord, I pray. Give me your strength and consolation. Help me. This can't be happening. Please don't let this be happening. I awaken from my short stupor to clammy skin and uncertain limbs. I give myself orders as if I were someone outside my body. "Get hold of yourself. Calm down. Maybe it's nothing. Get up, that's it; now bless yourself, genuflect, and walk out of chapel."

Mother Agatha's office is part of a suite of rooms tucked into a corner of the third floor of the motherhouse. Her stately secretary, Sister Regina, is seated behind a desk in the anteroom when I walk through the open doorway. Although I do not know her personally, she recognizes my purpose instantly because she points me to one of three metal chairs lined up against the wall opposite her desk. The door to Mother General's office is secure. I try to study the bare tree limbs drifting outside the window on the far wall when I see a reflection of two figures entering the room through the hall. I look up and recognize Krista and Angela, who are also being ushered into the waiting chairs. We do not speak. We know better. Krista arches her eyebrows ever so slightly when she sits down beside me, looking momentarily in my direction to catch my eyes, but Angela avoids me altogether. Her face is ashen, and I sense the tremor in her hands two chairs away. I am almost certain my own heart has stopped beating because of the numbness that has set in.

A short, harsh jangle sounds from the phone on the desk. Sister Regina speaks softly into the mouthpiece. "Yes, Mother. Right away, Mother." She rises and walks erectly to the door, beckoning us to her as she knocks and turns the handle, "Mother General will see you now, Sisters." Not yet twenty, I am certain that my life is over.

The room feels dark and heavy, like the oversized mahogany desk that guards the heavy-set woman behind it. I don't much care for her face, which is quite wide and pasty white. Full lips and too many tarnished teeth for the size of her mouth are crammed together and make her talk strangely, as if she has a lisp, but it's not really a lisp. It's more like slurred speech. But there is nothing lazy or weak in the baritone voice that makes her sound like a tough guy in a gangster movie.

Her craning neck stretches from one end of our short line to the next as she examines the three of us standing at attention. We are like prisoners just delivered to a Gestapo officer. I think I might stand here all day waiting for orders and inspecting her face when her booming voice breaks my spell. "DO YOU KNOW WHY YOU'RE HERE? DO YOU HAVE ANY IDEAR"—and here there are clear traces of her Brooklyn accent—"WHY I'VE SENT FOR YOU?" I can't seem to speak. I guess my friends can't either, so I try to shake my head, but my body seems to be incapable of carrying out any of the commands from my brain. Besides, I don't think it matters. She's a steamroller just getting started and my words would only be flattened.

"SO YOU WANT TO BE A PART OF THIS COMMUNITY? YOU THINK YOU HAVE A RELIGIOUS VOCATION? ARE YOU CERTAIN ABOUT THAT?" Two beats go by. Her head is bobbing up and down to the beat of her shrill, rapid-fire words. "IT HAS BEEN REPORTED TO ME THAT YOU HAVE BROKEN THE GRAND SILENCE ON NUMEROUS OCCASIONS. GETTING OUT OF BED IN THE MIDDLE OF THE NIGHT TO CONSORT WITH ONE ANOTHER, DOING . . . GOD KNOWS WHAT. HAVEN'T YOU LEARNED THE DANGERS OF PARTICULAR FRIENDSHIPS? PARTICULAR FRIENDSHIPS ARE FORBIDDEN, SINFUL. THEY VIOLATE RELIGIOUS LIFE. WE HAVE AN IDEAR WHAT KINDS OF THINGS YOU WERE UP TO, YOU KNOW. WELL, WHAT DO YOU HAVE TO SAY FOR YOURSELVES?"

With pursed lips and narrowed eyes, Mother Agatha frowns from one to the other of us, as if to say, I know all. Fear fixes me to the spot in front of her desk where I stand obviously guilty in her court of law, but something else begins to seep in and loosen the stranglehold of fear—anger, self-defense. I can't really make sense of anything, but my voice finds its own way out of the maelstrom gathering inside me.

"We . . . we didn't do anything . . . anything wrong, Mother."

"WHAT? WHAT DID YOU SAY?" she barks. "HOW DARE YOU LIE TO ME? DO YOU KNOW THAT YOUR VOCATION IS ON THE LINE? DO YOU KNOW THAT YOU ARE THIS CLOSE," and here she raises thumb and forefinger a quarter of an inch apart, "TO BEING SENT HOME? HOW DARE YOU, YOU BOLD ARTICLE? HOW DARE YOU LIE TO ME?!"

Her fury stuns and confuses me, making me question myself. Yes, I am guilty for breaking the Grand Silence, but no, I didn't do anything wrong. How can I make her see this; how can I defend myself, save my vocation, and win my life back?

Angela remains eerily mute, but Krista comes to my rescue. She clears her throat, and in her soft, high-pitched voice, she asks tentatively, "Mother, may I say something?"

"WELL?" she fires back.

Undaunted, Krista continues, and I can feel the fire heating up her wan cheeks, as it always does when she is embarrassed or fearful, and in this case both. "Well, what Sister means is that, all we did was talk to one another when we were feeling kinda down and homesick and a little overwhelmed by novitiate life. We . . . we would just go to the chapel and talk. Nothing more."

"SO YOU ADMIT YOU BROKE THE GRAND SILENCE?" Here her flat blue eyes examine Angela, then Krista, before coming to a halt on my face, causing me to shudder.

"Yes, Mother," I offer feebly.

"WHAT DO YOU HAVE TO SAY FOR YOURSELVES?"

"I'm sorry."

"I'm sorry."

"I'm sorry." Murmuring together, we sound like a dying chorus.

"TALKING? THAT'S WHAT YOU WERE DOING. TALKING?" she bellows. As she speaks, she rejects Krista's explanation by waving one hand, then the other, this way and that like a wand. Now she brings them down, folding them on the desktop in front of her, bringing her voice back down to a normal range, and trains her glare on me. "So I understand you're the ringleader. What did you talk about?" It feels more like a taunt than a question.

What did we talk about? Nothing. Everything. How can I explain? Then it occurs to me that it doesn't matter, that she doesn't *really* want to know, that she has already reached a verdict. Maybe it's hopelessness that fuels my courage.

"Mother Agatha, we were wrong to break the Grand Silence. But we didn't do anything harmful. We just talked about—I don't know, about our feelings. That's all." My defense turns into a plea. "You seem to be implying that we did something awful. I don't understand . . . what you think we did."

"HOW DARE YOU CHALLENGE ME?!" It comes out like a thunderclap, but I sense some uncertainty. I can't help but wonder where she got her information, what the informant or informants have told her, and whether she's operating on what they have said or her own suspicions. But my question remains unanswered. What in the world is she thinking we did? She wavers, as if deciding, her voice descending again. I wish she would keep it at one pitch. This up-and-down stuff is making me feel a little seasick.

"You are guilty of consorting with one another and breaking the Grand Silence." She pauses, her head cocked to the side now as if she's addressing someone outside the window. "And then there's this particular-friendship business." Her right hand goes up now to emphasize the point, and when she brings it down, her head turns back to us, but it's tilted slightly to the side. A long pause follows, and I am hoping that I'm the only one who hears my knees tapping against each other.

"I'm going to give you another chance," she snaps, but not as loudly as before. "So each of you wishes to remain in this community?"

Again a simultaneous "Yes, Mother," but it is more a prayer than an answer.

"You wish to take the vows of poverty, chastity, and obedience at the end of your novitiate, and you believe you have a vocation?" Without pausing for a response this time, she proceeds, making sure that the terror she has struck in our hearts this day will remain with us a long, long time. "All right then, you listen to me carefully. You are looking at another half-year in the novitiate to prove your worthiness. If you violate any rules or I get wind of any more of this particular-friendship business, you will be asked to leave immediately. Understand?"

I nod. Krista and Angela mutter, "Yes, Mother."

"Furthermore, you are not to speak of this matter to any of the others, nor are you to speak about it among yourselves, ever, not a word. Is that perfectly clear?" She looks at each one of us, getting the correct answer—a muffled and cowed "Yes, Mother"—in reply.

"Now, your superiors seem to think that you have the stuff for this life. You each have gifts, talents worth contributing to the community. But I don't care about that because I won't have this nonsense. I'll have obedience or nothing. You got that?" Not waiting for an answer, she snaps: "All right then, the three of you return to your duties and remember to keep your mouths shut, except with your novice mistress. I'll give Sister John a full report when she returns. That's all." She dismisses us with another wave of her hand, and I follow the others out a door that I hope never to walk through again.

All sorts of feelings are running together inside of me like bumper cars. The first is relief. I don't ever want to get this close to that kind of danger again. Shame and humiliation run a close second, having been reduced to the status of a criminal very nearly cast into exile. Then there's the indignation swelling into anger that I don't know where to direct. At Mother General and her brutal method? At a system that prizes the rule over the heart? True, we had broken the Grand Silence, but besides the fact that nearly every one does break it on occasion, what is the purpose of the rule but to help us be reflective and peaceful? And if we are in need of something else to return us to a state of reflection, such as companionship and an opportunity to discuss how we feel about what we're going though, shouldn't we be free to set the rule aside? Is there no place for the individual conscience in the vow of obedience? These unanswered questions disturb me. But there's something else even more disturbing, and that is the fact that someone, or ones, reported us, and that meant it had to be one of our own classmates. Who? Why? Does someone want to hurt us? Me? This move seems to have been carefully calculated to occur in Sister John's absence so that it could be reported directly to Mother General herself. This scenario is troublesome, and for the first time since my arrival in the convent, wariness and disquiet seep into my relations with my classmates—and into my vocation.

Over the next few days I move through my routine on automatic pilot, attending to duties, meals and communal prayer in a spiritless, detached way. I feel lean and listless. I look around me with an eye of suspicion. I avoid Krista and Angela altogether, sensing somehow that our special trio is altered, never to be the same.

Saturday afternoon and the day of Sister John's scheduled return finally arrive, and I hike back to the novitiate after spending a solitary morning of cleaning the ground floor of the motherhouse. I both anticipate and fear facing our novice mistress. I want to talk with her about what happened and I need her to understand our perspective, but I dread the prospect of disappointing and being reproached by her.

It's a chilly, gray day as I walk down the empty path, the last novice to make it back. When I round the roadway, I look up and in the direction of the back door of the house and notice Krista crouched on the frozen ground rearranging stones in our rock garden. Usually, of course, I'd call out, "What's up? Need any help?" or some such thing. But the last few days have sobered me considerably, or frightened me more like, so instead I'm inclined to ignore her and head into the novitiate. But rebellion rises up in me like a sudden, hot flame and before I can stop myself, I am standing over her. She doesn't look up right away, but she knows I'm there. Maybe she'll tell me to go away. I realize that maybe one of Mother Agatha's spies will see us, but I don't care. Krista is more important. She turns her head toward me and gives me a hint of a smile, a sad smile really, and asks, "You okay?"

I shrug and drop down beside her. "Trying to make sense of it all. You?"

"I'm good and angry," and her face, already flushed by the nippy air, turns another shade darker.

"Yeah, well. Not much we can do, is there? Have you talked to Angela? Is she all right?"

Krista shakes her head turning her moist eyes away from me. "I'm really worried about her. You know how fragile she is. This happening on top of her being sick all the time. I just don't think they even believe her. They think it's all in her head or something." Funny how we both feel so protective of Angela. I'd been thinking much the same thing. Why don't they get her to a doctor, or let her rest in the infirmary until she's fully recovered?

Then I realize that I am speaking with Krista and that, while we are obeying the letter of the law of Mother General's dictum, we are violating the spirit or intent. We are not talking about "it," but we are talking around "it." Crouching down, I start shifting the rocks along with her, careless of the original pattern, looking for another, I guess, to suit an altered perspective. A snowfall of silence settles over the ground for five, maybe ten minutes, when something tells me to look up. I see a shadow moving away from the large kitchen window at the back of the house. I look at Krista who has followed my eyes. "Joanne?" she asks. Then I realize she's not just talking about the shadowy figure in the window but Mother General's unnamed informant. I guess I have suspected the same.

"Do you think?" I realize she may be right. I share a dorm room with her and Laurie, and both have been behaving oddly, even for them—more distant and less and less friendly toward me.

"I can't imagine anyone else," she offers. "Can you?" In my mind, I thumb through the list of our classmates. No, not really. To tell the truth, I can't even imagine one or both of them reporting us. I feel such a sense of loss. My fine, perfect world has evaporated like yesterday's clouds, and something ugly has replaced it. Mistrust. Paranoia. Torn between guilt and indignation, I determine to put our case before Sister John and find a way to live with the rest. What else to do?

My hands are growing numb with cold because I forgot to put on my mittens, so I cup my hands and blow some warm air into them and stand up. "Come on, Krista.

We'd better go inside. They'll be putting supper together." I lend her a cold hand and help pull her upright. "I'm going to speak to John tonight. Tell her everything from start to finish."

Krista looks at me hopefully, and then drops her head as we walk in the direction of the house. Krista's arm reaches around and squeezes my shoulder. I feel the pressure beneath the padded wool, along with the weight of the vows we hope to take, as Krista leans into me and utters, "We can't let this come between us. We can't let it take us away from each other."

I love Krista for that.

Sighing deeply, I silently agree and swallow the tears I've held behind a dam of silence over the past few days. "Come on," I reach out for Krista's hand and tug her forward. "Race me into the house," and together we bolt like two girls in a schoolyard.

The kitchen, where I leave Krista, is a flurry of activity with Sister Gabriel directing the supper preparations in Sister John's place. Angela is not among them. I find her in the front parlor fooling around at the piano. She's looking thinner, and her normally olive complexion hides behind the constant flush of fever that's been plaguing her in recent weeks. "Hey, what are you working on?" I ask, trying to sound cheerful. "Need some help?"

She gives me her trademark half-smile, which is a good sign. "Sure," she says, only it comes out "shaw" since she cannot shake her New York accent no matter how much we tease her about it. "I've been working with some notes here," she offers. "I know what I want it to sound like, but per usual the lyrics are giving me trouble."

She slides down and I seat myself beside her on the piano stool so that I can study the notes propped up in front of her. Then Angela bangs out the chords to a bluesy folk song for our upcoming Christmas pageant, and I follow along while trying to find the words to fit the notes and the theme. We decide that it would be interesting to write the song from the point of view of the magi, and so I come up with some lyrics that seem to work:

> Something is coming our way / don't know what it is / but believe it will happen tonight / a search we must make / as we follow that star in the night / We've got to keep movin' on / Something great is coming / though some may not see / They will find their way/by the star that lies in their heart / Something great is coming.

I look over at Angela as we bring the first refrain to a dramatic conclusion. She's pleased. I love to see Angela this way—lost in her music and struggling to express herself—and then Bingo! It all finally comes together. We practice the lyrics with the notes over and over again until we are feeling comfortable with what we have, and even get a start on a second refrain when she pauses, tilts her head back and tosses me a big smile. "Thanks for helping me out," she says, as if that smile weren't sufficient. I return her smile with a fake punch to the shoulder and an offhanded, "Sure, any time. You know I love working on this stuff with you." I can tell that she's not thinking about what happened earlier this week. She has placed it on a shelf for the time being and run away with her music; and I hate to bring it up but I do anyway.

"Are you doing okay?" She knows I am not talking about her most recent illness, although that also weighs on my mind.

Staring straight ahead at the music, she gives me a half shrug, as if to say, "Yes, but no," which I fully understand.

"Krista and I have decided to be completely open with Sister John. I really think she will be more understanding; you know? She'll see that it's not as bad as it seems to be to . . . to . . . some people. What do you say? Want to go with us?"

Angela is quite scared. A nervous person anyway, she has been shaken to the core by our confrontation with Mother Agatha. Weakened considerably by her recent bouts with illness, she is especially fragile, and I don't want her to give up. I don't want to lose her. She is also mortified. I know because I know *her.* I can almost taste the shame bubbling inside her. It's a familiar taste. Our encounter with Mother General has sentenced us all to the shame pit, but I am determined to find the road to redemption for myself as well as my friends.

"Well," she finally concedes after a long sigh, "What can we lose?"

A blast of relief shoots through me, and I think that maybe we haven't lost Angela after all, and maybe the three of us will survive this terrifying ordeal. "Do you know what my dad would say in situation like this?" I ask with newfound confidence in my voice, knowing how fond Angela is of my dad, as I am of hers.

"No, what would Mike say?" she chirps.

I slap the air with my right arm and snap my fingers simultaneously, imitating my father and his understated enthusiasm when he is expressing a combination of confidence and encouragement: "*That's* the ticket." A wide grin spreads across Angela's face as she grasps my hand and places it against her warm forehead.

Later that night, following our group celebration of Sister John's homecoming, Krista, Angela, and I keep an already exhausted but energized Sister John up until nearly midnight to plead our case. Percolating with new ideas in the wake of the recent ecumenical changes that fueled her retreat of novitiate superiors, she has returned to us in a positive and decidedly more liberal frame of mind. Lucky for us. Unlike many of the more traditional sisters who resist altering long-held rules and customs, our novice mistress seems to embrace change, and we could not have caught her at a better time. We start at the beginning, describing the fateful summons to Mother General's office. Angela is characteristically reticent, allowing Krista and I to do most of the talking, with John listening intently, pausing here and there to ask for a detail or more clarification. Fully honest with her, we leave nothing out. We confess and explain the true nature of our late night meetings, and we defend ourselves against Mother Agatha's other incriminations and insinuations. We express genuine remorse, apologizing repeatedly for our actions. We also share how hurt we were by the betrayal of one or ones among us, as well as by their troubling, unclear allegations.

Sister John avoids taking sides, but she reinforces Mother's Agatha's point about the seriousness of our violation of the Grand Silence. Surprisingly, though, she does not chastise us. She reminds us that the novitiate is a training ground to challenge our resolve and confirm our worthiness for religious life. More than a test of obedience, the Grand Silence is an occasion to practice the vows that we hope to take at the culmination of our training period, and we have to expect to be closely scrutinized and evaluated. Our faults and mistakes provide us with an opportunity to demonstrate humility in accepting counsel and correction. Sister John explains all this quietly, patiently. She is perplexed by the fact that Mother Agatha acted so immediately and harshly in her absence, but she also does not yet know what information she acted on. And while it is well within Mother Agatha's power to order us to leave the community at any time, she assures us that it is not likely that she would do so without consulting with our immediate superior. She ends the session by urging us to examine our conscience and to pray for God's help in understanding the lessons of this experience so that they might make us holier and more humble servants of our Lord. After reciting a closing prayer and bidding us good night, she adds offhandedly, "And no more breaking the Grand Silence, Sisters." What a joker.

Relief and elation wash over me. This is how I *should* feel coming out of the confessional box each week but usually don't because it always seems as if there's something more I should be telling the priest even though I can't quite figure out what it is. When I recite my wrongdoings after the opening prayer, "Bless me, Father, for I have sinned. It's been a week since my last confession," I feel as if I'm making up stuff to satisfy him and the ritual: "I had an uncharitable thought about Sister Henrietta, Father"; or, "I felt envious of my classmate Deirdre." Afterwards, I don't feel cleansed or new. Not now. As a result of our talk with Sister John I feel reborn. The nightmare of the last days has dissipated, although it has left me with a sense of uneasiness, the way a bad dream casts a pall over the day. I want to find my way back to the pure promise of my religious vocation, yet I fear I cannot rid myself entirely of this lingering gloom. On the way back to my dorm room on the third floor, I pause at the landing to press my nose against the chilled windowpane and yearn to be one with the pure, night sky. Flakes of snow are just starting their steady dance downward, but it's hard to tell if the dancers are sturdy enough to swathe the earth entirely in a quilt of white.

# Part III

## Revolution (1967-1968)

# Autumn

A footpath leads away from the back part of the campus of Blessed Sacrament College, an all women's liberal arts college, into the adjacent woods. The wooded area comes as a pleasant surprise because the school is located near the northeastern edge of Philadelphia on City Line Avenue, a busy street along which the trolley runs on its way down into the netherworld of the humming city. I lose track of the pale autumn sun in the tree branches overhead as I follow the path into the thick part of the wood. The gold, rust, and red leaves writhe and crunch beneath my feet, and the trees shiver periodically, bowing to the pressure of a gentle wind and sending more leaves fluttering to the ground.

A short way in the path branches off in several previously explored directions. Today I take the one that leads to a small gurgling brook. A partially uprooted tree, too big and weary for life, has collapsed near the bank, affording me a secluded place to sit amid its split arthritic fingers. The ground is dry and comfortably softened by the colorful season's gift to the earth. A place to run away from the pressures of convent life and my college classes, it's also an ideal spot for reading and reflection. I've come prepared with my lunch of peanut-butter crackers and a carton of milk purchased from the school's cafeteria with my small weekly allowance. I swallow my meager lunch, eager to take advantage of the brief time I have to enjoy my special hideout. Pen and notepad in hand, I study my surroundings in search of images to capture and express the many sensations and longings I've been having of late.

I am an alien in the world of college and books and eighteen-to-twenty-two-year-old women dressed in everything but black. Each morning, I leave the motherhouse and walk down to the corner to catch the trolley to school for a day of expanding my mind, an experience which doesn't fit very well with the rest of my life. I return in the dark on the same trolley to the safety and duty of my narrow world.

I am changing. I can sense it. I am changing just as surely as the plants and trees acting out their death show on nature's glorious stage. Growth requires it.

I lean over the bank to examine myself in nature's mirror, but the brook's rippled surface only teases me with its shifting, uncertain reflections.

\*   \*   \*

It was quite a simple ceremony, really, that took place on 15 August 1967. Families and friends were not invited to this important community event signifying our break from the secular world and our formal initiation into religious life. Following the liturgy we stood in a line of twos in the center aisle of the chapel waiting for our turn to be summoned to the altar by a waiting Mother General and a small delegation of priests. Dressed in our Sunday-best black garb and holding a lighted candle, we prostrated ourselves before the church dignitaries before having our community name conferred upon us by Mother Agatha. We also accepted the four-by-two-inch black and silver cross to be worn on a chain around our necks. We were professing to be brides of Christ, after all, and the ceremony certified our acceptance and belonging in the Missionary Sisters of the Nazarene. We had worked so hard for it.

Over the past two years of trial and training, I had often fantasized about this day and how splendid it would be to realize my highest ambition by taking the solemn vows of poverty, chastity, and obedience, fully expecting to renew them every year until the taking of final vows seven years later. The vow of poverty was not that difficult for me, perhaps because I had grown up in a household with few material possessions and comforts, so we weren't afforded the opportunity to form attachments to things. The truth is that it didn't much bother me not to have money in my pocket, and I no longer had a desire to buy or accumulate "stuff." It was uncomfortable having to ask for my monthly supply of sanitary napkins, toothpaste, and other necessities, but such requests were an occasion to practice humility. And I was frankly glad not to worry any more about how I looked or which outfit to wear and whether I had shoes to match it. I did miss the casual comfort and fashionable look of my blue jeans, but my black granny shoes and the long simple black dress suited me fine. Not having to spend time laboring over these inconsequential things freed me to think about the things of the spirit. I wanted to get a jump-start on the afterlife. I didn't want to have to wait until the last minute of reckoning to prepare myself. My twelve years of Catholic schooling imprinted that indelible, urgent point on me, and two years of religious life sealed it.

Chastity was a little more troublesome than poverty for me. In my heart I couldn't deny having feelings of loneliness—not all the time but often enough—and a desire to be loved by just one person in a special way. I struggled with vague, undefined yearnings for love, affection, intimacy, but these were disembodied and disconnected because I could not allow myself to frame or put a face on them. At times, the unexpected disturbing sensations I experienced in Sister Anne Rose's presence confused me, and I didn't know what to do with them or how to confess them to the priest, and when I did stammer something about having "unchaste thoughts," he'd just urge me to "pray about it, Sister" before giving me two Rosaries as penance. So I took my questions and struggles up in prayer, imploring God for help and guidance to renounce these undefined yearnings that had no place in my life as a nun. By reaffirming my commitment to religious life, I secured myself and my longings with a strong will bolstered by the practices and austerities of convent life. I hoped that God's love and community life might fill the void left by unnamed and unfulfilled desires. Often they did, and I learned to rely on

God and prayer when they didn't. I was still growing accustomed to a life of denial and believed that any conflicts, with time and prayer, would be resolved. Our training taught us that if we gave ourselves to God through our superiors and the community, all our needs would be filled, all our longings satisfied. I trusted this lesson.

The visiting priest who led the weeklong retreat in preparation for our profession of vows echoed this view: Remember," he warned as he looked earnestly at the flock of nun-aspirants, "you will stand before the altar of God to become the brides of Christ. If you are worthy vessels, his love *only* will fill you up and prepare you to live a pure life of love and service to his people."

Obedience was the toughest of the vows for me. I often questioned a rule or the intentions of a superior, but the lessons exemplified in the life and writings of St. Theresa of the Little Flower and St. John of the Cross were most instructive on this point: by dying to the self, replacing my will with God's will, and making every act in my day, from cleaning the toilets to visiting the infirmed sisters, I could achieve blissful oneness with God. For me the greatest challenge was seeing God's will in the bullying demands of an irrational Sister Henrietta or recognizing God at work in Mother Agatha's tactics of intimidation. Poverty. Chastity. Obedience. St. John might very well say that love was the highest virtue, but he neglected to mention that the hardest of all the vows by which to achieve virtue was obedience.

The short profession ceremony by which we officially gained entrance into the community gave way to celebration, and throughout the day we were feted by the entire motherhouse. I received an array of congratulatory holy cards and small religious mementos, including a statue of St. Joseph, a small novena book of the Holy Spirit, and a new rosary from Angela, along with a small homemade card. On the front of it she drew a cross against a rainbow-colored background, and underneath it she wrote, "He who forgets himself for God's service may be sure that God will not forget him." On the back of the card was a personal message: "Dear Kathy, May the grace and peace of the Holy Spirit be with us forever. No prayer will please Heaven more than the prayer of the heart for charity. If you always give your heart to others for the love of God, you will be living for God alone. This is our life and let us continue to pray for each other and remain true friends. Congratulations and God love you always. I am offering one day for your special intentions. Love in the Trinity, Angela." Her message expressed my own most fervent belief. I cried when I read it.

My high school graduation had marked the high point of my young life up to this point, but it paled in comparison to this momentous occasion. With no clear goals and little sense of direction, I had sleepwalked my way through high school, and when it ended I felt more relief than accomplishment. So did my mother, who boasted of her intention to raise the American flag each time one of her seven children graduated after completing twelve tough years of Catholic-school education. On my profession day, I felt enormously proud and terribly humbled. I had wholeheartedly applied myself to this undertaking, which had required sacrifice, dedication, discipline, and hard work, and despite some stumbling along the way, with God's help and guidance I had finally made it.

Excitement filled the air, for Profession Day was equivalent to Christmas or Easter in the community. The motherhouse was awash with visiting sisters from the missions, and the profession ceremony was followed by a sumptuous noon-day feast of turkey, mashed potatoes, and creamed corn. It was one of those rare occasions when we didn't have to do a single chore because the second-year juniors volunteered to take over all our duties for the entire day.

I had a new name now too, Sister Kathleen Regina of Love, and I would never celebrate another birthday. Instead, I would celebrate my feast day on July 2 in honor of Mary and the visitation of the Archangel. Many of the senior sisters were stunned by the fact that Mother Agatha had given me the name of her devoted secretary who had died just a few months before. I had requested more unusual names: Adeodatus, which was the name of St. Augustine's illegitimate son and means "gift from God." Another was Jude, a name that I loved because Jude was the patron saint of hopeless cases. But failing to appreciate my romantic tendencies I suppose, Mother Agatha had seen fit to name me after a humble personage who had been revered within a small circle of sisters at the motherhouse. The honor was not lost on me, nor was the lesson in humility, as Sister Kathleen Regina's name symbolized a life of pure simplicity.

But the highlight of our profession came afterward when we were granted a week's leave from the motherhouse to be with our families. I had waited two long years for this day. When it finally arrived, I was like Odysseus returning home a stranger after having lived a new and very different life in a faraway land. We pulled up into the driveway in Dad's green 1959 Dodge. He was behind the wheel, of course, with my mom beside him, and I sat in the backseat as if I were still their child. It didn't take very long for me to realize that this was no longer the case and that it wasn't my home anymore. As I walked in the door, Thomas, the only one to throw caution and protocol aside, wrapped his arms around me. Gerry stood shyly and uncertainly behind him. The three girls, Maureen, Rosemary, and Anne Margaret, sat scrunched together and giggly on the sofa, as if they didn't know what to say or how to talk to their sister, the nun. I realized I no longer knew these people, and they didn't know exactly how to relate to me. And how, I wondered, did they all fit into this miniature house? Two intense and all-consuming years of community life seemed to have erased the sum of a short lifetime. The community had replaced my family, and I had somehow become more at home with a highly regulated life in institutional-sized rooms and buildings than I was with the clutter and familiarity of my family's house, which seemed like a disheveled dollhouse by comparison.

The TV console that took up half a wall seemed odd, too. Recognizing how many enjoyable hours Michael and I had spent watching Roz Russell corrupt her nephew in *Auntie Mame* on *The Late Show* and Katherine Hepburn trade quips with Cary Grant or Spencer Tracy on *The Late, Late Show* made me realize how drastically my habits had changed. Over the past two years I had lost track of movies, television, and popular music. The only TV we had seen had to do with the coverage of the Pole Paul VI's call for a Synod of Bishops in conjunction with the ecumenical changes extending from Vatican Council II. After obtaining permission from Mother General, G. I. summoned us to the community room where we gathered around the twelve-inch black-and-white television she had borrowed from the motherhouse janitor so that we could witness this historic development in the Catholic Church.

Every day that week my parents accompanied me to morning Mass at their parish church. I could tell how proud they were of their daughter, the nun, dressed in her new black habit. While my parents introduced me to the other parishioners, my younger siblings were pointing me out to their friends as if I were a show animal. None of my former high school friends came around to the house that week, though. After that first year and a few trips to the convent on Sunday-visiting day, they fell out of my life just as I had disappeared from theirs. Actually, I think I was the one who let go of them because I didn't know how to reconcile the old self that they represented with the new self that I was becoming. At first I was ecstatic to see Nancy, Anita, Pat, Donna, and Diane when they came to see me at the motherhouse, but the visits grew awkward. We no longer had much in common and we didn't know how to talk to one another. My best friends had become strangers. Rather, I had become a stranger to my best friends. Their concerns and pursuits now seemed trivial to me, while, in their eyes, I was no longer the same fun person. My high school friends occupied themselves with worldly concerns: the latest fashion or rock-and-roll craze, the salary that could buy the new car, the promising boyfriend, and the next vacation. Having lived in a community of sisters who were dedicated to God, self-sacrifice, and ministry, I no longer identified with such pursuits. I also knew that if I had been living on the outside I would be exactly like them and that frightened me. I had grown a world away from material interests, and I didn't want to regress. I was convinced that I was in the right place for the person I was striving to become. I so desired to be an unworldly person with a rich spiritual life. Separated by far more than distance and time, I drifted away from my former friends like a bottle out to sea, and a part of me was sad about that because I was certain that we would never find one another again.

During my one-week visit, my parents and I traveled to the Bronx to visit Angela's family. It was Angela's idea that I go in her absence to console her parents and brother, Angelo, and to be an emissary of her love. I did my best, of course, knowing that I was a poor replacement for their beloved daughter, who had been too ill to complete the novitiate and so prevented from professing her vows with the rest of her classmates. But Angela had not given up. As soon as she recovered, with Mother Agatha's permission, she planned to repeat the novitiate and take her vows the following year.

We were just a couple of months shy of profession when Angela was finally whisked from the infirmary and taken to a nearby hospital. We were not given an explanation for the relentless illness and high fevers that plagued our classmate, and we were discouraged from asking questions. Krista and I grumbled between ourselves about our friend's declining health and "their" reluctance, whoever "they" were, to provide her with the proper medical treatment in the early stages of the illness. Sickness was viewed as a weakness that must be resisted, denied and overcome through fortitude and prayer. But Angela's illness did not respond to spiritual prescriptions. Whatever was wrong with Angela just became more wrong. On profession morning when I saw Angela in her wheelchair, too weak even to walk, I had a momentary urge to lift her up, carry her to the altar and demand that she be permitted to take her vows along with the rest of us. God knows she had earned it. What kind of a rule would require her to repeat the entire year because she left the motherhouse grounds for several days' stay in a hospital? She was *sick*. She had a legitimate reason for violating the canonical rule. Why couldn't they see that and make an exception? She wasn't a schoolgirl to be left behind because she had failed to keep pace with her classmates. It just didn't make any sense to me. But my moment of insanity passed; how dare I question the holy rule and my superiors? Instead, I agreed to do as Angela requested, when she pleaded with me to go in her place to visit her family because "They love you, and it would mean so much to them. And to me. Please. Do this for me."

So I put on my best "Sister" face for Angela's family. I visited the garment factory where her mother worked and met many of her mom's coworkers, all of whom asked after "sweet little Angela." At her home I sat in her place on the organ bench next to Angelo, and together we sang as he played, just as he and Angela had done so many times before—their shared passion for music cinching an already close relationship. I consoled her doting dad and held his hand, just as I had seen her do so many times during visiting Sunday. I posed for the pictures he snapped: me and John at the organ, me on the front and back lawn of their brownstone, me next to the rose bush with an uninvited duck standing beside me, and me in front of a tree blooming with pink tubular flowers. I wanted so much to give them their daughter instead, her full cheeks and olive complexion restored to health as they had been on entrance day. But by necessity, I offered them myself as well as the assurance that next year they would be showering Angela herself with the same fuss and affection.

Shortly after returning from my home visit, I requested permission to see Angela. I knew I wouldn't get to see her much anymore since she would be a novice again and no longer my classmate, but I also felt certain that our bond would endure this temporary separation, and we would remain connected. Even our families were connected. It felt odd, though, having to ask for special permission to see someone with whom I had lived so closely over the previous two years. Since the day we had entered the community, we had eaten three meals a day at the same table, prayed and meditated together in chapel, slept under the same roof, wrote songs together, and sang side-by-side in our community's folk-singing group. Now it was as if we were orbiting the same sun but on different planets. She was like the school chum left behind a grade for poor performance, while I advanced, torn between guilt and satisfaction. I had never meant to leave her behind—then or later—and I will always regret it.

She was resting in the infirmary when I visited her. There were no traces of her normal complexion. Her skin, instead, looked sallow, and her round face had lost its healthy fullness. She lay in her bed wrapped in blankets, and she seemed alert and well, although the feverish eyes and glistening skin suggested otherwise. Her altered physical appearance, from a robust young woman to a frail one, alarmed me, but I dared not let her know that. Surely, she was being looked after properly now that the convent superiors were aware of the seriousness of her condition—wasn't she?

I was anxious to see her and give a full report on my visit with her family. Angela chuckled when I told her about how her mom dragged me through the factory introducing me to all her coworkers, and about the short fat Italian neighbor who kept kissing my hand and pleading with me in her broken English to "Pray for me, Sister. God bless you, Sister, so young, so beautiful. God bless. God bless." As I spoke, Angela reached over and clasped my hands, pulling me down on the bed beside her. Droplets of tears curled away from the corners of her eyes as she thanked me for spending time with her family. It was a little awkward at first, trying to regain the familiar ground of our friendship but mindful that we were not only separated by a class but also by this illness that loomed over her like a darkening sky. Positioned on the edge of the bed, I grew more comfortable. I ordered my own tears to wait as I tried to comfort and amuse her with bits and pieces of my visit to my home and to her own.

"I won't forget this," she declared, after I had given her a rundown of the entire day. "You don't know how much your going there meant to my family, to me. Not to be able to see them or them to see me for another whole year . . . ." Her throat tightened, and the words trailed away wistfully. I felt helpless and frustrated, but I couldn't let her know that. She looked so defeated and so sad. She needed bolstering.

"Hey, it was great. I had a fabulous time. They treated me like royalty. And I gotta tell you, your mom makes the most delicious spaghetti dinner in the world, bar none. I loved it. And you should've heard my dad praising your mom's cooking and griping to my mom: 'Why the hell can't you cook like this, Anne?'" With the exception of her infamous "cowboy stew," my mom's cooking was nothing to brag about, as Angela knew from our previous conversations. The nearest thing to Italian food that she served for supper was Chef Boyardi's ravioli in a can. Angela always got a kick out of hearing that.

She wiped the tears away from her face with the sleeve of her white nightgown and laughed. "Yeah, she's a great cook, isn't she? I sure miss her cooking. I think that's what I miss the most."

"The best," I echoed. Then we leafed through the pictures her father had taken, bound together in a little book with a cover that read "Our Photos." He had made a set for me, a set for her, and a set for each of our families, as if the photographs could freeze and certify our connection. In a way they did, but I wouldn't realize that until much later.

\*     \*     \*

I left my friend Krista behind in a different way. The community had seen fit to send some of us off to college and not others. We were not supposed to make a distinction between those of us who were to have the benefit of higher education and those of us who were not, but it was difficult not to see one as having an advantage over the other. We never had any idea who made those decisions or why. We had been given a battery of psychological and aptitude tests as part of our application process for admission to the community, and they may have figured in the determinations. As with most things though, we were just informed of the results. Krista, Noreen, Theresa, and a few others were assigned duties at the motherhouse, and it seemed to me that they were being shortchanged. While they faced the same old drudgery of manual labor day in and day out, the rest of us had graduated from motherhouse duties and moved on to college. I wondered if Krista would have to spend the rest of her religious life being missioned at the motherhouse with the likes of Sister Henrietta and Sister Peter. I certainly hoped not.

Our school days were long, and sometimes I didn't get to see Krista until the weekend. I missed her. I missed her easy laughter and the way she would lift me out of the doldrums by doing or saying something outrageous. Once when we were postulants, she, Angela, and I were walking down the hill on our way back to St. Gerard's House after a long night of extra duties. It was late, and we were tired and homesick. Suddenly, Krista blurted out, "So, you guys, ya wanna bust outta this joint and go visit our friends, or what?" I had visions of us sneaking out of our dorms in the dead of night for a pre-arranged rendezvous with one of our old friends. Angela just shook her head and rolled her eyes as if to say, "Is she for real?" but I broke out laughing. The absurdity of the prospect made me giddy with laughter, and before long they both joined me as we fantasized about "the great convent escape" that would take us to the edge of the grounds, over the wrought-iron fence, and into a waiting car that would signal us with three-flashes of its headlights. Pretty soon all three of us felt much better. Krista's contagious silliness always helped ease the tension. Besides missing Krista and Angela, I found college a bit intimidating. As a student in a nun's habit, I was constantly aware of being different from the others. We all stood out, of course, and because we were nuns our professors expected the highest possible performance from us. I had grown accustomed to working hard and completing chores to my superiors' satisfaction, but being a scholar in a nun's habit had catapulted me into a different league altogether. It called for academic rigor, an area in which I had not developed much confidence. My older brother was the natural brain; I was the natural athlete. What made the experience particularly disquieting was that the other lay students didn't know what to make of us "penguins," and we were instructed not to associate with them. We moved from psychology to history to biology to English classes in small black clumps, and between classes we worked on assignments in the quiet of the library. That's where I was when I met Brigitte.

I was sitting at a table by myself writing a critical analysis of an Emily Dickinson poem. A girl with long black straight hair and tawny skin sat down on the other side of the table, but I didn't pay too much attention to her until she poked at my book and blurted out, "Emily Dickinson? She's my favorite poet. Which one is this?" Then, with no compunction about intruding and no apparent need to ask my permission, she turned my book around and read the first couple of lines aloud, "'I measure every grief I meet with narrow probing eyes.' Hmmm," she muttered, "I don't know this one."

At first, I was taken aback by her directness, but something about the cultured quality of her speech and the steadiness of her earnest brown eyes intrigued me. Besides, we had something in common—Emily Dickinson. I was uneasy, though. I wasn't quite sure how to talk to a normal student, and I wondered if casual conversation would be construed by the authorities as "associating," which, of course, we were not permitted to do.

I decided that her comments deserved an honest and thoughtful response. "Well, actually, I'm just learning about her, and I like her poetry a lot. She's deep, and her images are so startling and powerful. You know?" She knew. I could tell by the way she nodded and smiled. Encouraged, I continued. "We just started studying the American poets for Sister Micina's English class, and she told me I could write my paper on her."

"Ah," she cooed, "Sister Micina." She was smiling broadly now. "Most of the students hate her because she's quite tough, and you have to work very hard to get a C or B, let alone an A. What do you think of her?"

This question came across as a challenge, or maybe a test. I was puzzled but not put off. "I don't know. I kind of like her, actually. She's demanding and a bit intimidating, but she's an excellent teacher; and she's read so many books. I keep a list of the ones she refers to in class thinking that someday I'll read all of them. I doubt that it's possible though."

I guess I passed the test because she nodded and leaned toward me confidingly. "Yes, I agree. She's by far the best teacher I've had at this school. Sister Placid is terrible," her face and voice soured at the name. "Have you had her yet?" I shook my head. "No? Very pedantic and elementary in her approach to teaching literature; and Mr. Lombardi . . . hah, what a pompous jerk he is." She raised her nose in the air, as if to emphasize his arrogance. I smiled uncertainly at her sharp observations and strong opinions about our illustrious professors, one of whom was a nun.

We talked for a few minutes more until the librarian nun behind the desk flashed us a warning look. This was the library, after all. The convent had no monopoly on silence.

If I was fascinated by Brigitte, she was equally mystified by me. Our library chat that day led to other brief meetings and then to intense, at times heated exchanges during walks around the campus. I soon learned that Sister Micina and Emily Dickinson were about the only things on which we could agree.

"Why are you becoming a nun?" Brigitte and a young woman my own age demanded to know during one of our sojourns along the wooded path adjacent to campus. The sun had heated up the chilly fall air, and we had decided to take advantage of the splendid day and leave our books and work behind in the library. Brigitte was wound up that day, as if she had decided that this was the day to throw down the gauntlet. I tried to explain my religious vocation to her, that I felt I was being called upon to make the supreme sacrifice of giving up my life to serve God and his people.

"That's all claptrap," she snapped dismissively, insisting that God would never want me to give up my young life to serve him, finally admitting that she wasn't even a Catholic. How could she understand? I also learned that she had grown up in Germany, which explained the unusual speech pattern that made her sound so sophisticated. It became increasingly clear that the cultural divide between us had to do with more than just my choice to be a nun, but that didn't stop us from trying to convert one another. More debates about Catholicism and theology and the meaning of life followed, and as exasperated as she made me, I came away from our discussions invigorated and stimulated. She was smart. She articulated her views confidently, and she forced me to question and to examine my vocation. A student in a Catholic school, she was no believer in Catholicism. At times shaken by her point of view and the differences between us, I fortified myself with faith. Certainly, I thought, one day I would have a new Catholic to show for my persistence. For the most part, I had known only Catholic schools and friends during my growing-up years. We always referred to the Protestant kids as "publics" and felt sorry for them because we knew they were all damned to hell. We were dissuaded from associating with them since they might pose a threat to our eternal souls, and I succeeded in avoiding "publics" until I met and dated first Bob and then Denny in high school. I discovered that Protestants weren't devils and that they were not too much different from me and the rest of my friends. Now that I was a nun, I was pretty much in the business of bringing people around to the faith, and so I decided that spending time with Brigitte could do no harm and might do some good. I gave up worrying about who we were and weren't supposed to mix with at the college, deciding that there was nothing wrong in sharing my religious convictions with a nonbeliever. Besides, the time we did have to spend together was precious little due to my rigid schedule.

As student nuns we carried a full course load and were expected to complete most of our schoolwork during the day. We cleaned up after supper and said evening prayers at the motherhouse, if we got home in time, and then completed our assorted duties at the juniorate house. We spent the better part of the weekend cleaning our quarters and pitching in at the motherhouse. Sister Vera Marie was the mistress of the juniorate, and she kept a watchful eye on the two classes of junior sisters, about forty-two sisters in all. I quickly learned that she also required watching.

Sister Vera Marie was, by far, the most intolerant of the three mistresses. She was downright menacing, and not just because of her imposing presence. Nearly six feet tall, she was broad shouldered and large boned, and whenever she corrected someone, she had this way of leaning into her, swallowing her space and making her feel very small. She had dark beads for eyes and a long horsy face with a tiny mouth that was not very attractive, especially when compared with Sister John's fine, balanced features and gentle, friendly eyes. It was her volatility that I most disliked because it made me uneasy and even caused me to doubt her sanity on occasion, and I was willing to exchange it for G. I.'s consistent severity any day of the week.

Sister Vera seemed intent on keeping me close by, maybe to keep an eye on me. That's how it felt anyway. None of us enjoyed sitting right next to her—or any of our superiors at the refectory table for that matter—because that meant we would be under closer scrutiny. Whenever Mother Agatha or her substitute at the head table rang the bell releasing us from the Grand Silence at table, it required us to engage in polite conversation with someone whose business it was to oversee and judge us. I had developed some good delaying tactics for reporting to table late under the previous two administrations, but

I dared not try them in the juniorate. Even when I was legitimately held up by duties, I trembled in fear as I explained my absence to Sister Vera, who presided at the head of the table like a distant queen, her eyes boring into me like a drill into a two-by-four. Very likely Mother Agatha had warned her about me and my novitiate debacle. Or maybe I had just grown a little paranoid, since I noticed that I was not the only one to merit her special attention. She liked to keep my second-year junior friend, Anne Rose, nearby as well, and Judy and Margaret too, but why that was the case was never clear to me because we were so different. Quiet and unassuming, Anne Rose, the "Good," seemed like the well-behaved model nun. Judith, the "Beautiful," was unexceptional except for her looks, which were exquisite. She could have been a model on the outside with her finely sculpted face, balanced features, and brown, highly polished Italian skin. Margaret, the "Brilliant," was the other "favorite" of Vera Marie. Bright and witty, she earned straight A's in all her college classes and spoke with the confidence and eloquence of a college English professor. Sister Vera's penchant for keeping the four of us close by mystified me.

There were times when Sister Vera Marie could be very funny, in a wry way, and even nice. On such good-humored days, she'd pat me on the back and ask me how my day had gone after a long day at school. And she laughed heartily at Sister Margaret's imitation of our psychology professor with the thick Polish accent. The brilliant but eccentric Dr. Patka admired Freud enormously and loved expostulating on his idol's theories of children's psycho-sexual development in his lectures, especially in a classroom nearly filled with self-conscious and embarrassed nuns. But she could turn from good-natured to ill-tempered as deftly and imperceptibly as a chameleon changes from brown to green, and for no apparent reason. Sometimes a sour mood might last for days, and I tried my best to tiptoe around it so as not to find myself the target of her caustic tongue or, worse, her chilly, silent treatment. Fully aware that the community was subsidizing my education, I labored conscientiously over my class work and performed reasonably well once I got over the hump of biology class. In the tenth grade, all I had learned from the experience of dissecting a frog was how to be nauseous. Science, and particularly animal dissection, was clearly not my strength, but I found myself enjoying my psychology class and thriving in English. But even though I reported to prayer and table on time and kept pace with my school work and motherhouse chores, I always had this vague feeling of guilt around Vera Marie, as if I were hiding something, and worse, that she knew about it.

Maybe my misgivings were connected to my relationship with Anne Rose and the special bond we shared. As classmates now, we slept in the same house and followed a similar routine, but our class schedules differed so we rarely took the same trolley to and from school. We chatted sometimes on our trek from the motherhouse to the juniorate in the evening, enjoyed occasional walks on the motherhouse grounds on a Saturday afternoon after our duties were completed, and had half an hour or so before benediction and supper. I basked in her presence during those precious times, and yet I felt agitated at the same time. Even though we guarded against exclusivity, I could not deny that there were undercurrents in our relationship, which I didn't understand or know how to address. Maybe that's why she was so skittish, at times warm and intimate, at others cool and distant. I was sure that no one in the world valued her gentle goodness as much as I did, and I couldn't believe that there was anything wrong with this. But at times I craved her company, and this craving gnawed at me and left me feeling ashamed and wracked with guilt. Conflicting feelings raged inside me: was it *wrong* to have these feelings? How could that be when our relationship seemed like a gift from God, intertwined as it assuredly was in our love for him? While strong, my own feelings seemed indecipherable to me, and I worried that they might be impure; but how, I wondered, could feelings or longings be impure when they were not expressed or explored? I considered confessing them to the priest, but I wasn't sure what to say.

"Bless me, Father, for I have sinned. It has been one week since my last confession."

"Yes, my child. What sins would you like to confess?"

"Well, Father, I have these feelings for one of my sisters."

"Yes, Sister. What kind of feelings exactly?"

And here's where I would get stuck and begin to stutter and sputter. It was as if I had a picture but no frame by which to make sense of it: I loved and admired her, and I yearned to be in her presence and felt frustrated when that was not possible. At times, I found that I was unable to stop myself from thinking about her, even during prayers, and this disturbed me. The love I felt for Angela and Krista and Eliza did not interfere with my spiritual practices in this way, and so as much as I could not fathom the nature of my own feelings, I sensed that there was something awry. I never knew if it was the same for her. I avoided her for days at a time, trying valiantly to erase her from my thoughts, and in the stillness of my bed at night I clutched my black rosary beads and prayed until the Hail Marys lulled me into peaceful slumber. I lost myself in my studies; I disciplined myself through meditation and prayer; I remained steadfast. But then a tender look or word or gesture from Anne Rose would melt my determination and throw me off course.

That's what happened the day she returned all excited and happy from teaching her Sunday-school kindergarten class in a neighboring parish. We were cleaning up after our noon meal when she invited me to come to the auditorium to see the children's art work. We stood in front of the long rectangular table on which she had arranged the cardboard-backed construction paper filled with colorful drawings. She was positively radiant as she boasted of the children's imaginative response to her lesson concerning Noah's Ark. "Look," she said eagerly, gesturing toward their depictions. "Aren't they wonderful? The little ones were listening so closely when I told them the story, and they took it all in. You can see their understanding of it in the details—the boat, the rain, the high water, the different animals."

"Yes," I agreed, as I praised the children's inventive designs and use of color. But to myself I thought, "It's you that's wonderful because of your dedication to God and the work you are doing with these little ones. The children's creations reflect your goodness and simplicity." I knew, then, what a special and pure-hearted nun she was. At the time I was feeling less certain about myself. What would the community do with me? How would they use me and *my* talents? What *were* my talents exactly? Totally inept at arts and crafts, I knew I could never teach kindergarteners about the Bible, and I was still very unclear about the "social work" performed by many of our sisters that were missioned in social service agencies scattered around New York, New England, and Pennsylvania. How did they know I had the capability for doing such work, and how would I develop the skills? And where would they send me? I knew I would learn all this soon, since I was scheduled to receive my first mission assignment the summer of my first year in the juniorate. The questions about what I would do, where I would live and with whom began to press in upon me as I looked to the future, beyond the juniorate and my four years of apprenticeship in the community.

So things had been building up: my troubling feelings for Ann Rose, the stress of being a nun in college with all the papers and exams, the prospect of living and working at a mission house instead of the motherhouse during the summer, the separation from both Angela and Krista, Vera Marie's hovering manner—all exacerbated by the exhaustion brought on by a recent illness that whittled away most of the thirty or so pounds I had added to my slender frame during the past two years with our starchy diet. I guess that's why I collapsed. I fainted, actually, as I later learned, right in the middle of doing table dishes in the refectory one evening after supper.

Vaguely aware that I was being half-carried, half-led out of the refectory like an unwieldy piece of luggage, I regained full consciousness only when we reached the infirmary. I was lying on a cot when Sister Stephen, the young nursing sister, propped up my head with one hand and placed something awful-smelling beneath my nose with the other one. My mouth felt funny. One of my front teeth had cracked as a result of the fall, I guessed correctly. In a chair across from the bed sat Sister Vera Marie, looking very sympathetic and concerned.

"Do you feel okay? Are you ready to sit up?" Sister Stephen asked in a gentle southern drawl. She had light blue eyes and fair skin, and the heel of her hand on my forehead felt cool and reassuring.

"Yes, I, uh, I think so, Sister. Thanks," I answered as I pulled my woozy body into an upright position.

She nodded gravely toward Vera Marie and then handed me a small cup with pills and a glass of water. "Here, take this. You'll feel a bit better, and they'll help you to sleep. Try and stay off the floor now, all right?" She gave me a modest smile and a pat on the head before disappearing out the door and leaving me alone with Vera Marie.

"Well, Sister, you gave us quite a scare. Are you feeling better now?" she asked solicitously.

"Yes, Sister, fine, well, a little lightheaded is all, and I think I chipped my tooth."

She pulled her chair closer to the bed to examine my mouth. "Yes," she offered offhandedly. "We'll have to see about that." But she was more interested in my state of mind than the injury to my tooth. "Do you remember what happened?" she pressed.

"I don't know. It's kind of foggy. I was drying the dishes at table, and then I felt like I was in a tunnel because everything echoed, and the walls were closing in, and then . . . I don't know what happened."

"You fainted. We carried you in here."

"Yes, Sister, I'm sorry, Sister . . . I . . . I feel so foolish. Nothing like that has ever happened to me before."

"No, no, Sister, nothing to be sorry for." Sister Vera Marie waved her hand in concert with a shake of her head, as if to wave away my discomfort before continuing. "We're concerned, of course, and just want you to be all right. Would you like to sit over here in the chair now?" I nodded, and she directed me from the infirmary bed to a chair nearer hers and the closed door. I found myself in the unenviable position of being alone with someone who seemed to smell death and was circling for the kill.

She picked up my hands, placed them between hers, facing me squarely, and spoke in the kindest of tones. It was disconcerting and way out of character for her. "Now, Sister, would you like to tell me all about it?"

Uncertain and perplexed, I shrugged my shoulders and looked straight into her eyes, which were less than a foot away from mine. "Gee, Sister. I don't remember anything else."

She closed her eyes for a second, shook her head twice, and then resumed. "No, Sister. I'm not referring to your fainting. I mean, in here," at which point she released my hands and tapped her chest. "What's going on in here? What's been bothering you lately?"

"Nothing, Sister, I mean, I don't think there's anything in particular, just school and trying to keep up, you know, but I'm doing better. It's taken me a while to adjust to the academic routine and get a handle on biology class, but gee, I don't know. Everything is fine, really." I was groping for specifics to satisfy her, which felt a bit like trying to catch a fish with my hands. I knew it, and she knew it. At the same time, I wondered what she had in mind. What did she want to know exactly? In my physically weakened state, I felt terribly vulnerable, and I suddenly had an image of myself as a helpless earthling being subjected to an alien probe.

"Sister, I think you're holding back," she said almost ruefully as her concerned face darkened just a shade, hinting at her disappointment. "Now, don't you think it would be best for you to open your heart to me?" She placed a heavy left hand on my shoulder and held my eyes. "You can trust me, you know. I am in a position to help you with your problems, but you have to trust me. I am genuinely interested in your well-being." Satisfied that she had touched the right chord in me, she eased the pressure just enough to remove her hand and gave me an eternity of several soundless minutes to come around.

At this point, I began to consider the possibility that she knew something about me I didn't and then immediately thought better of it; no, she doesn't know me. She wants to know me, and she wants to know me well. In the next brief, thunderous moments, I engaged in an internal debate: okay, this is your superior who speaks for the community and for God. She wants you to open up to her, to trust her completely, to share your fears and your confusion, your doubts and anxieties. Maybe this is the right thing to do; it may be exactly what you need. But what would I tell her? That at times I do not feel worthy of this life, that I fear I may not be good or pure enough, and that my feelings for Sister Anne Rose sometimes trouble me? And why does her concern feel threatening to me? Shouldn't I open my soul to her because I feel right in doing so and not because I am bullied into it? Is it a matter of obedience, and if so, does obedience require that I entrust my conscience, my innermost self, to this person with whom I do not feel at all safe?

"Well, then, Sister?" Her wan smile was betrayed by an impatient tone that made her words sound like "time is up."

The last thing I wanted to do was let her down. I dreaded seeing that long look of disappointment that always came over her face when she was displeased. But I sensed that surrender to her was dangerous, especially given my weakened state. What did she *want* from me? I couldn't make sense out of the doubts and confusion roiling inside of me, let alone figure out her unstated objectives.

I had to ease myself out of this dilemma. My mouth was growing drier from the medication, and the aftereffects of lightheadedness lingered like a leftover headache. I desperately wanted to escape from the confinement of that tiny room and breathe fresh air, but I collected my thoughts and tried to reassure her, "Sister, I'm fine, really, and there's nothing to tell you. I appreciate your concern. Really, I do. I just . . . don't know what else there is to say."

"No?" Vera Marie snapped back, giving herself away momentarily before promptly returning to her concerned manner. "I want you to know that I am available to you, at any time and for any reason. I want you to trust me, Sister. I am here to help you. Please remember that."

"Thank you, Sister. I do appreciate it, Sister, really I do. And I'm sorry for . . . for causing such a disturbance." I was trying to sound conciliatory to please her, but I was well aware that I was not pleasing her at all.

Her tone turned from neutral to cool. "Now you had best go to bed immediately. You may sleep in tomorrow until it's time for Mass. Shall we walk back to the juniorate together?"

"Sure, Sister." Suddenly I felt very sad for Vera Marie. I had let her down. She had wanted something from me and I hadn't given it to her.

I wasn't sure I could have without losing something essential of myself. When we reached the door to my new room, she expressed a brisk "good night" and left me to the silence.

In response to growing numbers of entrants in recent years, the community had constructed a brand new building to house the junior sisters. For the first time, each of us had her own room in the modern three-story building. Our second-floor bedrooms were furnished simply, with a single bed and a wooden cross on the wall above it, a sink, a desk and chair, and a chest of drawers. We hung our dress garb, school garb, and work garb in the tiny closet. The luxury of having my own room with a window that looked out at the woods to the east was not lost on me. One of seven children I had shared sleeping quarters, and even a bed, with my sisters long before I settled into a convent dormitory.

The entire evening had left me troubled, so I was grateful that I could escape to the privacy of my own room. I shut the door and disrobed in the dark, since the room was partially illuminated by the lights fixed to the outside of the building. By this time exhaustion had set in, hastened, no doubt, by the effects of the medication Sister Stephen had given me. I went through the motions of washing my face and brushing my teeth before pulling on my white convent-issued pajamas and collapsing into a bed of uneasy sleep.

Noises in the corridor—of doors opening and closing and of footsteps pattering into the bathroom a few doors down—blended in with my troubled slumber, until I seemed to awaken with a start. Was I dreaming? A patch of light from the hallway landed briefly on my eyes, before I was once again left with the silent black of the room. I sensed a presence and then heard a hushed voice. Anne Rose, soft and comforting, was saying, "Kathy, it's me. I had to see if you were all right." Slipping into the bed alongside me, she placed her hand on my forehead. "I was so worried," she whispered. "Are you all right? What happened?"

I felt trapped in the twilight between slumber and consciousness, and a pang of anxiety shot through me: Anne Rose, here? Now? Is she crazy? At the same time, her welcome concern for me felt like a gentle balm, especially after my collapse and Sister Vera Marie's unsettling interrogation. I mumbled groggily, "I'm okay." I was painfully self-conscious. Besides being fuzzy and out of it, I also became painfully aware of my broken front tooth.

"Shh. Don't worry. You rest now. I'll just stay with you awhile." Too spent to do anything else, I turned on my side away from Anne Rose and fell into a deep sleep that was interrupted by what felt like a hand on my skin beneath the pajama top. A physical sensation coursed through my body like a shock wave, immediately followed by fear that metamorphosed into guilt. Terrified that I would do the wrong thing, not knowing what I should do, wanting to explore the forbidden sensation and then not wanting to at all, I dared not move. A minute or so later, the hand was withdrawn. I sustained a frozen posture. When I awakened later, it was still dark, and I was utterly alone. How long had it been? Minutes? Hours? I had no way of telling. Had I been dreaming? Had Anne Rose actually come to my room and lain in my bed? Yes, I was almost certain she had. But had she touched me, or had I imagined it? What would happen now? The vague distress of the days and weeks before now solidified into misery.

After the early call for meditation the next morning, Sister Vera Marie tapped on my door and then opened it: "How are we doing?"

"Much better, Sister. Thank you."

"Good. You have my permission to sleep in. Can you catch Mass later at school?"

"Yes, Sister, I'm sure I can."

"Fine. See to it that you report to my office before you leave for school, so I may have a word with you." With that, she closed the door, and I leaned against it, listening to her heavy footsteps disappear down the hall toward the stairwell until my racing heart slowed down. Tears sprang to my eyes, and I offered a silent prayer, grateful that I wouldn't have to face her or anyone else right away.

Krista was the first person I saw. We ran into each other in the breezeway, the glass-enclosed corridor that connected our new juniorate building with the motherhouse, which meant no more treks up and down the hill in the cold. She had gone looking for me after the others had left for school or gone on with their motherhouse duties. Her pale blue eyes were wide with concern. "MY GOD," she said grabbing hold of my hand, "ARE YOU ALL RIGHT?" The hysterical sound of her voice echoed in the tunnel-like corridor and added to the eerie, exposed feeling in a space surrounded by windows for walls.

"Yeah, yeah. I'm fine. Really. Just a bit shaken up. But let's talk in the recreation room, okay?" She released my hand, and we walked back in the direction of the juniorate building, ducking into the first doorway on the left, which opened into a large community-recreation room. Closing the door behind us, Krista gave me a quick, comforting hug and then held on to my shoulders as she gazed steadfastly into my eyes. "Do I have to worry about the two of you now, Angela *and* you?"

I had to laugh, which, thankfully, relieved the tension. Krista started chuckling as well and then released my shoulders along with a volley of questions in a half-humorous tone, "What in the world is going on around here? What exactly happened to you? What did Vera Marie say?"

I leaned nervously against the wall behind the closed door, aware that someone might walk by or venture in at any time. Krista's eyes followed me, studying my face, and I knew she would not let me go without a full explanation. I sighed, groping for words to satisfy her as well as myself. "To tell you the truth, Krista, I don't know. I'm feeling a lot of stuff, you know? Tired. Confused. Overwhelmed. I don't know anymore if I'm in the right place, if I can do this." I waved my hand indicating the room, the building, the life. Her eyes understood. "I am trying so hard, but I don't know if I can do it; I don't know if I'm good enough. Vera Marie scares me. She's trying to get inside my head. You know what I mean? I don't think I want her there. I need to sort some things out—feelings and such I have but that I don't really understand—but not with her . . . ." My voice trailed away. Why didn't I confide in her about my troubling feelings for Ann Rose and the events of last night? I really wanted to talk to Krista; I longed to unburden myself, but my words were failing me and we didn't have much time to talk. And I was afraid, not so much of her judgment but of my own.

Krista took a deep breath and closed her eyes briefly. Then she leaned beside me against the wall after a quick peak out the door, probably to make sure that Sister Vera Marie was nowhere to be seen. "I know what you mean. Not about Vera Marie. She doesn't bother with me much, *thank God*, but the other part. I'm feeling a lot of the same things. It's not the same anymore is it? What's happened? What's happening to us?"

I don't know. I answered by shrugging my shoulders. I felt as if I were in a painting that I couldn't see. No perspective at all. Then a rush of panic swept over me as I thought about the third part of "us"—Angela. "What's up with Angela? Have you seen her? How is she?"

"Well, she's worried about *you* now, thank you very much," Krista whined. "Everybody saw you faint; it was awful. And it got back to her. I saw her this morning when I was cleaning the bathroom across from her room."

"Tell her I said hi, will you?" I asked earnestly. Being assigned to work at the motherhouse all day, Krista at least had the advantage of being able to sneak in and see Angela, who remained quarantined in her sick room. "Tell her I miss her. Tell her I'm fine. I'm just run down, and I'm under a lot of pressure at school and all." Aware that I had to get going to make the next trolley, I turned and glanced at the clock above the door. Both of us were aware that these stolen minutes and our conversation would have to be continued at a later time. We had duties to attend to and a schedule to keep.

By way of good-bye for now Krista gave me her feigned, stern look, emphasized by one raised eyebrow and a pointed finger in my face, "All right. I will. But no more fainting, you got that?"

"I promise."

"You'd better," she said in that familiar, uppity tone that I so loved to hear.

"I gotta go, or I'll miss English class," I offered resignedly.

"I know. Take care. God bless." That was Krista. Always saying God bless whenever we parted.

"Thanks," I said as I pulled away, opened the door, and headed in the opposite direction from Krista. Then, prompted by a pang of apprehension, I turned back and called out to her. "Krista. What about you? Will *you* be all right?"

A smile, a reassuring Krista smile, as spontaneous and genuine as my friend: "You know me. I'll be fine," she called back from the other end of the hallway. "I've requested to see my advisor, you know, Father Gallagher from Keene. He'll help me sort it all out."

"Good. That's good. I'm glad you have him to talk to." One more wave and we both disappeared through doors going in the opposite direction.

In the days that followed Anne Rose acted like her old self and betrayed no signs that anything indecorous had occurred. She expressed concern about my health, as did many of the others, but she didn't seek me out or speak to me privately. I was relieved, and disappointed. I was glad to be alone with myself as I mulled over the events of the night before and tried to sort out my conflicting feelings, keenly aware that Vera Marie was keeping a pair of wary eyes on me. I prayed for guidance. I prayed for help. I prayed for forgiveness.

*     *     *

I took a late trolley back to the motherhouse that evening after several hours of research in the library. The wind suddenly kicked up, and an unexpected chill swept across my back and neck as I trudged up the steep hill from the trolley stop to the gates of the motherhouse, warning me that winter lurked around a short corner. Dark was settling like a shade being slowly drawn. The evening was somber. Leaves that had presented such a colorful show in the weeks and even days before now looked ghastly. My colorful companions had fallen—dusty heroes that barely crunched beneath my shoes.

As I neared the main gate, I observed several cars returning the postulants to the motherhouse after their weekly visit to Riverside, the state home for the elderly who were often also infirmed, desolate, mentally unbalanced, and, in many instances, at the edge of death. I recalled how, as a postulant, I loathed those weekly visits. It took all of my willpower to battle the stench of human decay and abide the cloying and pleading of these dying and unwanted people because I felt so helpless. Yes, I prayed with them and listened to them; I consoled them and held their hands, all the while asking God for the strength to be with the terrifying sights and smells of dying and despair. I remembered one woman so clearly: in the prison of her wheelchair she sat parked in the hallway like a useless, abandoned car. Whenever she saw me, she cried out to me over and over again, "Sister, pray for me. Pray that God may help me." The postulants were chattering away as they piled out of the car. At least the outing provided them with a day free of motherhouse duties. I remembered that more enjoyable part of the routine as well. Despite the unsettling recollections of Riverside, from my present vantage point I looked back at the postulancy nostalgically and as a more innocent time. When the postulants spied me rounding into the driveway, my new younger sisters smiled and waved, as if eager for my recognition. They looked up to me, a junior sister. They aspired to be like me—I remembered that feeling—and the weight of their admiration at this moment felt like a heavy winter coat. "Hi, Sister," Susan offered as she came forward to greet me. She was perky and sweet, full of enthusiasm for this new life. "Welcome home. How was your day at school?"

"Good," I said. "Yours?"

She smiled. Past the smile, I saw the depressing, fetid hallways cluttered with wheelchairs holding the forsaken, forlorn and unwanted old people. "It was . . . well, you know. The same," she offered reluctantly.

"Yeah, I remember." I clapped an understanding hand on her shoulder. "Brrr . . . the air is changing, and it's starting to get a bit nippy, isn't it? We'd better get inside." She smiled that trusting postulant smile at me as I ushered her through the front door of the motherhouse, closing it with a quiet thud behind us.

# Part IV

## Flight

# Summer

"Hiya, Sister. Whatcha doin'?" a little girl called out in a singsong voice.

I turned around to face her, black soapsuds oozing from the fingers of my right hand sunk into the pores of the filthy sponge. "I'm washing these dirty old cars. What are you guys doing?"

I had been attacking the dried film of dust and road grime donated to the motherhouse cars by the Philadelphia streets, and I welcomed the interruption as an opportunity to catch my breath, take a swipe at the beads of sweat collecting on my nose and eyelids, and survey my handiwork. The small intruder had two short companions with her, one with blond pigtails held fast by matching blue barrettes and the other with a straight black ponytail jutting from just below the crown of her head with the help of a thrice-twisted rubber band. They eyed me shyly from behind their bold friend who had short reddish brown hair cut in the fashion of a pageboy and clusters of freckles climbing up her nose. Dressed for a hot, school-free day in their white sneakers, play shorts, and matching T-shirts, they looked decidedly more comfortable than I felt in my long black swishy garb.

"Nothing. We're bored. Do nuns drive?" she demanded as she blinked into the sun.

Her eyes followed my motions as I gave the sponge one final wring, tossed it to its drying place alongside the bucket, and picked up the bulging hose that was resting at the moment on the blistering pavement. I had to laugh at her naive question, but I collected myself and answered her serious query in like fashion. "Uh, huh, some do."

"Are they your cars?" she demanded to know, pointing to the five black Plymouths lined up like dutiful nuns in a pew. I aimed the hose and watched the now-bubbly, liquidated film slide down the cars and dissipate into the shiny asphalt, as I fielded her questions.

"No. They belong to the community."

"Oh," she mumbled, followed by a short pause and then two questions in quick succession. "What's a community?" And without pausing for an answer, "Are you almost finished?" Her two companions were squirming and didn't know what to make of me or their friend's inquisitiveness.

I decided she was just impatient and not disinterested, so I answered her question. "A community is an order of nuns, like the one I belong to, and, yup, almost finished. Want to help?"

She looked at her two friends who shrugged halfheartedly, and said, "Sure. What do we do?"

I gave each a piece of torn-up bath towel and showed them how to wipe the droplets of water from the car, wringing it out after a couple of wipes. As we worked, we chatted. I learned that the one who first addressed me was Karen, and the oldest at nine. Pigtail Patty was seven and the youngest of the three. Their friend Donna was eight and "not a Catholic," Karen offered apologetically. The other two had agreed to be friends with her anyway.

It was late morning on a bright summer Saturday. A penetrating sun already bore down on the black car tops as the insects buzzed steadily in the brush and trees alongside the parking lot behind the motherhouse. I had been enjoying the solitude of the quiet afternoon and the exercise of pure physical labor. My sleeves were rolled up, and I wore a pair of black Keds so as not to ruin my good black shoes. I realized I must be a sight to the children who surely expected nuns to be prim and formally clothed at all times, as I myself did as a youngster, but they didn't seem to notice or care. When we finished, I praised them for their good work and asked them to wait while I went to see if I could fetch them some kind of reward. I figured Sister Maureen should be good for a few pieces of candy for the neighborhood children, and now that I was a full-fledged sister, she had a little more regard for me than she had during my woeful postulant days.

They beamed when I returned with a handful of Hershey kisses and three lollipops, which they immediately tore into, carefully handing the discarded wrappings over to me. I stuffed them inside my deep pockets where I kept my tiny meditation book and faded black rosary-bead case. Having completed my chores, I was free until dinner at noon. Since the girls showed no signs of leaving, I decided to give them a tour of the convent grounds. We walked through the makeshift softball field, the girls oohing and aahing over the cluster of beautiful yellow flowers that were nothing more than dandelions, except to little kids and their uncritical eyes. They picked a few to take home to their moms, clutching them tightly in their hot little fists, and then we moved on.

We made our way past the postulant house and off the roadway onto the Bridle Path that led to a grotto at the edge of the motherhouse grounds containing the stone shrine of Saint Bernadette and Our Lady of Fatima. The Stations of the Cross were etched in oversized stone tablets that stood like sentinels alongside the path, with each one representing a different step in Jesus' march to Calvary. Whenever the weather allowed during the Lenten period, we were permitted to observe the Stations of the Cross in the outdoors and under the serene cover of trees screening the pathway. The path also doubled as a makeshift sledding hill in winter, and on snowy nights in the postulancy and novitiate we were sometimes granted permission to take out the beaten-up wooden sleds for an hour or two of fun. I remembered those child-happy days when we sped down the hill, two or three of us atop a sled, before overturning onto a snow bank. After scrambling to our feet and dusting off the accumulated snow from our second-hand navy pea coats, we trekked back up to the starting point for another run. But those days, like childhood, were long gone, and on this warm summer Saturday morning the grotto path was isolated except for the soulful coo of the mourning doves and the faint din of city traffic in the distance.

Karen did most of the talking as we walked, but after a while Donna loosened up as well. They wanted to know what life was like for me inside the convent, what I did exactly, and why I didn't have a husband or children of my own. When I tried to explain that I was married to God in a way, they looked puzzled at first and then decided that "it's probably okay to be married to God." At Karen's prompting, I started to explain the significance of the stone tablets, each depicting a different scene during Jesus' march to Calvary, when the youngest, Patty, reached up and took hold of my hand. Unlike the other two children who were more verbal and assertive, she remained quiet, content to listen.

They weren't too enthralled with my explanation of the Stations-of-the-Cross, so I decided on a different course of action. "So, do you girls like to sing songs?"

"I don't know," Donna answered. "YES," Karen said energetically. All I got from little Patty was a slight shrug.

"Aw, c'mon, you guys. Singing is fun. Now, who knows 'doe a deer, a female deer, re, a drop of golden sun'?" and then I put on my very best Maria voice and within minutes they chimed in as we held hands and skipped around the convent grounds. As I sang, I remembered all the songs in *The Sound of Music*, picturing Maria who sang so beautifully while combing the hills of Austria and teaching the Von Trapp children the rudiments of melody and harmony. My own little Von Trapp girls were attentive pupils who learned "Do, Re, Mi" in its entirety by the fourth time around, as well as "Edelweiss" and parts of "My Favorite Things." The girls seemed sad when I announced that it was nearly noon and time for dinner, so I promised to meet them again the next Saturday as I gave each a hug and turned to go. Little Patty tapped me on the arm, threw her arms around my waist and whispered, "Bye Sister," and then my three new friends stood there and waved as I raced back to the motherhouse, late for prayers before dinner just like Maria, and not for the last time.

\*　　\*　　\*

After nine months as a junior sister and one year of college, I finally received my first summer mission assignment to a relatively small house of three sisters in Greensburg, Pennsylvania. For the first time in my life I traveled by airplane. I was unused to being on my own and felt terribly self-conscious wearing a nun's habit away from the familiar grounds of the motherhouse and the college campus, even though our garbs had been updated and shortened to mid-calf in line with the recent ecumenical changes. A slight change in our costume helped but I still felt like I was on display.

At the Pittsburgh airport I was met by Sister Amelia, a pleasant sister in her late twenties, who drove me to the quaint brick house in a sleepy neighborhood. I was disappointed to learn that she and the other young sister, Sister Gregory, were leaving for vacation and another summer assignment the following day since that would leave me alone with the house superior, Sister Paul. Although cordial towards me, she wasn't as warm and welcoming as Sister Amelia. She was heavy-set and short, which gave her a dowdy appearance and made her age hard to determine, although I guessed it to be in her early sixties. She led me to an airy and pleasant second-floor bedroom, featuring two large windows with a view of the tall trees surrounding the large but modest house.

In my room that first night I cried myself to sleep. Away from the hustle and bustle of the motherhouse and the familiar company of my classmates, I felt terribly lonely. Deirdre, Celia, and Ann Rose were more fortunate because they were sent to larger missions with a nice mix of older and younger sisters. The rest of my classmates, who were scattered in towns and cities from the northeast to the south, were sent to smaller houses like my own where they got a good dose of isolated mission life.

Our routine at the mission was surprisingly flexible. Although we always met for Mass and evening prayers in the tiny room that served as a chapel and we sat down to breakfast and dinner together, we were free to meditate and say morning and afternoon prayers on our own. Our schedule revolved around the local social services office where Sister Paul was also in charge. Together we drove to the office each morning at 9:00 a.m. and left at 5:00 p.m., but I rarely saw her during the day because her administrative responsibilities took her to meetings away from the office. In addition to a slate of daily duties that involved letter-writing, filing, and assorted paper work, I received home-visit assignments from Sister Paul. The lay caseworker, Marion, was responsible for training me and Lucy, the secretary, kept me on task.

When Sister Paul was in the office, Marion and Lucy were polite and reserved. But in her absence they were fun and easy-going, and I really enjoyed their company. Under Marion's supervision I pored over the clients' records to prepare myself for the visit, and I learned to write up reports after a day in the field. We made several visits to a woman who was in prison for prostitution. I shuddered as I trailed Marion and a guard through thick steel doors that were slammed shut and locked behind us by another guard as we made our way to a cold and gloomy visiting room. Narrow and cramped and windowless, it held only a small table and three metal chairs. The thin dark-haired woman, outfitted in a drab prison jumpsuit, held fast to the nub of a cigarette between nicotine-stained fingers. She sobbed as she talked about her two little children, now in foster care, begging us to help her get them back upon her release. Another time we drove to the outskirts of town where a four-year-old girl with Down's syndrome lived in a home with eight other foster children in a dilapidated farmhouse. Every day brought a fresh encounter with lost, deprived, and abandoned people. I longed to be a good nun and help them, but I was finding out how limited we were in what we could do, and I had so little experience of the world and no wise counsel to offer. I decided just to listen, to hold their hands, and just be myself—to practice what St. John referred to as the greatest virtue—love. I became particularly attached to a tough-talking teenager who had been sentenced to the local facility for delinquent girls for skipping school and running away from home. She gave me the icy treatment at first, but after several visits she opened up and confided in me about how her step-father had sexually abused her. She didn't know what to make of me because of "that outfit" and the fact that I wasn't that much older than she was, so she kept demanding to know what I was doing "hanging out with a bunch of nuns" and when I was "comin' back" to see her. I especially disliked home visits to the poor because I saw the real face of poverty and what my own life might have been without a father who could work three jobs and a mother willing to devote her life for her children. In this depressed coal region, the majestic mountains and lush greenery belied the existence of so many destitute people living in ramshackle houses filled with desperate people and ill-clothed, hungry children. This, I now understood, was the bitter taste of life lived close to the bone. Being poor and deprived meant so much more than having second-hand furniture, or wearing your cousins' hand-me-downs, or accepting charity in the form of a food basket from the parish church.

My co-worker Marion and I fast became chums. We ate lunch in the office break-room together and chatted in the car to and from visits, discovering that we had more in common than age. She also came from a large family and had even considered entering the convent before deciding to become a social worker instead. Except for the perfunctory "how did your day go?" at the dinner table and our formal interactions during staff meetings at work, Sister Paul was content to ignore me. I was awfully glad Marion was curious about me and the choice that she did not make for herself because it made me feel less lonely. She pressed me for details about convent life and how I came to join. Only two years older but my superior in work experience, she treated me as if I were her "better," something that caused mixed feelings in me. I enjoyed the respect that came with wearing my nun's habit but felt the need to earn it on the basis of who I was and what I did rather than on the costume I wore.

I felt awkward when Marion invited me to a picnic lunch and then to the driving range to hit some golf balls on the occasional Saturday afternoon, but not wanting to turn her down I applied to Sister Paul for permission. Aloof anyway, she seemed disinterested in me apart from my duties at the office. I worried about her taciturnity but decided not to second-guess her when she gave her grudging approval. Despite Marion's painstaking lessons I never did learn to hit the golf ball very well, but the outings were fun and a pleasant diversion from what turned out to be a rather lonesome life at the mission house with Sister Paul as my only company. Separated from my classmates for the first time in nearly three years, I enjoyed finding a friend in my coworker. Life in the mission house became mechanical: I performed my duties in the household, observed the meditation and prayer schedule, and held my own in the office under Marion's competent supervision. I was negotiating my way through a difficult summer, keenly aware of some nagging concerns that I had brought with me from the motherhouse and would no doubt take back with me when my summer assignment ended. And I was still recovering from the shock, if not the surprise, of Krista's monumental decision.

Shortly before I left for Greensburg, Krista informed me that she was leaving the convent. I was thankful that in deciding to confide in me against Sister Vera Marie's instructions, she didn't just disappear along with the others who had fallen into the black hole of exile. She was crying uncontrollably when she delivered the news. We were sitting on the floor with our backs against the exterior wall of the empty priest's quarters on the first floor of the juniorate building. The nicest and best-furnished rooms of the building, this suite was only occupied by visiting priests over the holidays or during retreat week and it doubled as a refuge for us whenever we needed to avoid the eyes and ears of our superiors. I pressed my face against my knees that were secured by locked ankles to contain the torrent of feelings boiling inside. Krista sat with her arms crossed and her legs splayed out in front of her, suggesting a casualness that she couldn't possibly feel. It was late afternoon, and through the opening at the top of the corridor wall just beneath the ceiling we caught sight of the sun's ebbing light through the breezeway windows. We spoke in whispers so as not to be heard by any passersby.

"Are you sure?" I pleaded, lifting my head and trying to keep the panic out of my voice.

She came off sounding flippant, which is how Krista sounds when she's feeling insecure or uncertain. "As sure as I can be. I've talked it all over with Father Gallagher. He agrees that it's best. I'm just not happy."

"What about your family?" I was concerned with how they might take the news of her decision to leave the convent. In Catholic circles, "leaving" a religious order was tantamount to a crime and viewed as a shameful thing.

She smiled wanly and brushed away the tears, which finally slowed to a trickle, with the sleeve of her garb. "Oh, they love me any which way they can."

I had to smile at her peculiar expression. She had so many peculiar, endearing expressions. I didn't know how I could stay here without her, without having her nearby to joke around with, pat me on the back, and pick me up with one of her malapropisms. And what did that mean for our three musketeer pact? But it was clear that she had made her decision. I had sensed it in our discussions of late and yet I overlooked it. We saw each other so seldom after I was sent off to college that I didn't realize how she had been slipping away from me, little by little like a drowning person. I was too distracted to notice.

"But Krista," I argued with a final, desperate rallying call, "things are changing in here. It's going to get better, loosen up more. They can't continue to treat us like children. They have to give us more of a voice. You'll see. Change is a reality. They can only resist it for so long. It's just a matter of time. We just have to stick it out." Even as I said this, I wondered if I was trying to convince her or myself.

She placed her hand on her forehead momentarily, as if considering, then let it drop as she turned and looked at me with disenchanted eyes, "Oh, Kathy. We've tried. All the times we spoke out. We challenged things. What did it get us? Trouble, that's what. They don't want people who rock the boat. I just don't have the energy or desire anymore to do the rocking. I guess I don't want it enough."

She had capitulated. I couldn't blame her. She was also right. Apart from the single small battle we had won in the novitiate regarding public charity, we had little to show for our enthusiasm to do away with antiquated traditions that treated us like children. They wanted us to be sheep, not thinking responsible people. It seemed so crazy. Wouldn't the whole system work better if we had an open and active dialogue with our superiors, if there were a mechanism for questions and grievances, and if there were less emphasis on blind obedience? I had to wrestle with my humanity in my desire to live on a higher plain, but I was finding that I could no longer simply deny or negate it. The task of integrating my human nature with the all-consuming vows of poverty, chastity, and obedience was a tall order. Why couldn't they just help us with that instead of acting like hall monitors and despots? Why weren't there more Sister Johns who were open and understanding and fewer Sister Vera Maries and Mother Agathas? We had to make our superiors understand the need for change because their methods were pushing more and more young nuns out the door. But it was already too late for Krista.

I couldn't hold back my own tears any longer. They came in a rush like a fireplug suddenly opened. I turned and threw my arms around her, and we hugged like two little children lost in a wood, clinging to the only safety in sight—the arms of a friend.

"When are you leaving?" I almost choked on the words.

"Tomorrow."

I gulped. "That soon? Does Angela know?"

"No, I don't think I'll be able to see her. I have to ask you to do that."

"I'm going to miss you so much. Will you write?"

"Of course."

"I love you."

"I love you."

That was the last time I saw my beloved friend. I thought it had to be my most painful separation, but that was yet to come, as were the torturous revelations that followed.

*    *    *

I counted the days until my return to the familiarity of the motherhouse at the end of my summer mission assignment. Besides looking forward to being reunited with my classmates, I was anxious about Angela. If she could just make it through the summer without a relapse and another trip to the hospital, she could profess her vows and once again be my classmate. I missed Anne Rose terribly as well that summer, and we stayed in contact through occasional letters that, as I later learned, were being monitored by Sister Paul. She "reported" me to Mother General for consorting with the "lay workers"—referring, of course, to my coworker and supervisor, Marion—and for receiving letters and one phone call from Anne Rose who was missioned in Pensacola, Florida. I had no idea that my every move was being so closely scrutinized, and I later wondered why Sister Paul didn't just speak to me about her concerns before reporting me to Mother General.

Upon my return I was excited by the prospect of graduating to the level of a second-year junior sister, as this would mark the last leg of the trial period and I would become a full-fledged Nazarene, while Anne Rose, who was a year ahead of me, would be sent on her first yearly mission. The pending separation elicited feelings of both sadness and relief. My tangled emotions had yet to be sorted out, and I ached to be free of them for the sake of my vocation. That desire prompted me to confide in Sister Fiona, a senior sister who visited Greensburg during my summer mission assignment.

I first met Sister Fiona during a St. Patrick's Day celebration when she was visiting the motherhouse. A member of the order for seventeen years and the director of a social service agency, she had a lively sense of humor that complemented her professional demeanor. As I matured in religious life, I found myself seeking other role models besides Anne Rose who was too close to my own age and problematic for other reasons. G. I.? No. Vera Marie? Not a chance. Sister Fiona was a charming and accomplished senior sister and I liked her immediately. I was also flattered that she took an interest in me. I was finding that it was quite common for a senior sister to take on a fledgling sister as a protégé, although typically there was a prior connection, such as a shared hometown or parish. We were in the refectory enjoying the festivities the evening we met. Anne Rose had taught seven of us an Irish jig and under her expert direction—she was an accomplished Irish hoofer—we performed a synchronized version of it to entertain the community. Following our workmanlike routine, Sister Fiona, who was in her mid-thirties, tall with fair skin, a round dimpled face, and twinkling blue eyes, and looked "as Irish as Patty's pig"—as my mom would say—got up and did a more elaborate jig of her own. We all clapped and exhorted her as she performed the controlled and graceful movements of the Irish folk dance masterfully and with flair. When the festivities were winding down, I introduced myself and told her how much I had enjoyed her rendition of the jig. My compliment led to discussions about her experience with motherhouse life and her work in the missions. She seemed genuinely interested in me as well, asking about my family and what I was studying in my college classes. I was impressed when she told me she had earned both her bachelor's and master's degrees in social work while being a nun. Both a nun and a professional, she was also down-to-earth and fun-loving. She had a quick wit and a contagious smile, and her warm manner and affability stood in stark contrast to the rigid and unapproachable Vera Maries of the community. She was also obviously flourishing in religious life, and that gave me hope for myself. Although I didn't yet know her, I immediately trusted her. If I could get close to her, I thought, I might seek her guidance and counsel. She could help me find my way through this convent maze of unrealistic expectations and prohibitions. I needed a confidante as well as a mentor.

In the months following our first encounter, we corresponded. I reported motherhouse scuttlebutt, and she responded formally at first and then more and more freely, with increased enthusiasm and interest. I found a reliable and understanding sounding board in her, and she seemed to appreciate the detailed characterization of life inside the walls of the motherhouse from the perspective of the upstart insider who was bent on progress and change. The missioned senior sisters often felt isolated and cut off from developments and changes initiated at the motherhouse headquarters. They were not privy to news about the latest convent casualty—when someone left the order, for example—or how the new entrants were faring, or how the administration was incorporating ecumenical changes into the young sisters' formation. A small but growing American order that professed to keep step with the times so as not to lose touch with the poor and needy people with whom they worked still struggled with fear in letting go of long-held traditions. The lines of offense and defense were just beginning to form and the offense—the pro-change line—enjoyed the advantage of the dictums originating in Vatican Council II, but the defense—the old school—was formidable in its resistance.

When I received a card from Sister Fiona informing me of her intention to visit Greensburg on business, requiring a stay at my summer mission house, I was elated. I had battled homesickness during that entire summer, and the prospect of seeing and spending time with someone familiar promised welcome relief. A bit of anxiety crept in as well, since I intended to ask her to be my confidante and sponsor in the community. The practice was common, but it usually began when a senior sister shepherded a young woman into the community, acting as a kind of touchstone throughout the younger sister's formation period. The only senior sister I was familiar with upon entering the community was Sister Thomas, the convent recruiter. An attractive nun in her early thirties with a polite but stiff demeanor, Sister Thomas conducted herself with a cool, crisp, let's-get-down-to-business manner. Her voice sounded breathy when she spoke, oddly controlled and forced at the same time, and she wore a perpetual smile that looked artificial and reminded me of the wax lips we wore as kids on Halloween. Her sloping posture, with neck extended and chest thrust forward, accented the unmistakable sway in her walk and struck me as exaggeratedly feminine for a nun. I never felt very comfortable with her and I couldn't imagine looking to her as my community sponsor. I could handle firm—G. I.—and I could manage tough—Vera Marie—but I couldn't deal well at all with phony, and early on for some reason I pegged Sister Thomas as being inauthentic and untrustworthy. I steered clear of her despite the fact that she was the only nun I knew prior to entrance-day.

I decided to apply to Sister Fiona on the evening of her arrival at the mission house. I was determined to be completely open with her, confessing my growing uncertainty about my fitness for religious life and my qualms about my feelings for Anne Rose. During her visit I requested permission from Sister Paul to talk with her privately, and approval was granted. That evening we met in the second-floor sitting room. She sat in a straight-backed chair, alert and attentive. Almost ten feet away I sat cross-legged on the floor because I was nervous and needed to be child-comfortable. A lamp on the desk behind me provided the only dim light in the room, and I felt grateful not to be exposed, while in confessional mode, to the harsh glare of the overhead light. At first she appeared formal, even distant, but that was acceptable to me. Intending to reveal my innermost doubts and weaknesses to a professional who could be trusted, I was not looking to her for consolation. I needed firm guidance and I expected reproof.

I was prepared to disclose everything to her, no matter how personal and vulnerable it made me. I started by sharing my doubts about my vocation and the difficulty I was having with the vow of obedience. Then I informed her about the crucial incident that occurred in the novitiate when I was called to Mother Agatha's office to be reprimanded. I spared nothing, from my culpability to my anger at her tactics and the painful scars it had left on Krista, Angela, and me. I protested our innocence of any substantial wrongdoing in spite of Mother General's insinuations, and I expressed frustration at being denied an opportunity to defend myself or to face our unidentified accusers. I told her how betrayed I felt by the accusers who had to have been my own classmates, and how it had shaded my optimism toward community life. Then I got into the hard stuff about Anne Rose, disclosing to her my shameful infatuation with her and my desire to overcome it. A skilled social worker, she posed questions; she prodded me and guided me, but she never once betrayed a hint of judgment. I realized that I was exposing myself to her in the way that Sister Vera Marie had wanted me to do that evening in the infirmary after I fainted. I had resisted her because she was too unpredictable and dangerous. Fiona, by contrast, made me feel safe. I even related all the details of the night I fainted, including the unexpected visit from Anne Rose and the forbidden sensations it aroused.

After two interminable soul-searching hours, in which I exposed my innermost thoughts and faults, I collapsed into tears in a way I had not done since I was a child. Up to that point I had kept my emotions in check because I was eager to be mature and brave. But my entire body, finally succumbing to the terrible force of unleashed, long-restrained feelings, shuddered from the exhausting experience of advertising all my failings and tarnished ideals in the broad light of recognition for all the world to see. Well, for one person to see, but for me that night it felt like my imperfect young life was on public display.

I waited in dread for her verdict: would my revelations earn her contempt and send me into exile? Would she tell me what I most feared—that I was not fit for religious life and that I should leave the convent? After sobbing uncontrollably for several minutes, my elbows braced on my knees, my hands covering my face, I felt a reassuring hand on my head and another on my shoulder. She had moved her chair closer to the spot where I sat on the floor. I froze. "No, don't give me comfort. I want help. I don't want your comfort," I screamed inside but felt trapped and incapable of giving voice to the words. At that point I wanted advice, not comforting. I wanted a confessor not a friend, or so I thought. Then she spoke.

"What you're struggling with, we all struggle with," she said tenderly, almost regretfully. "There are no easy answers here, no simple roads in religious life. But you've taken an important first step in trying to face up to yourself and the things that trouble you. I'll do my best to help you," she assured me. "I'll speak to your superiors about establishing regular visits to help you work through some of these things that are troubling you."

Her comforting words flowed over me like clean rain, immediately dissipating the ominous cloud that had so long hung over me. We talked a bit more that evening. She probed me for more details on the showdown with Mother Agatha and the nature of my relationship with Anne Rose. When we finally said good night and good-bye, since she planned to drive back to Philadelphia early the next morning, she left me with a reassuring hug. I thanked her and went to bed, solaced by the prospect of forgiveness and renewal. I felt new again. I felt hopeful that I could honestly renew my vows and start over. That's how good it was to free myself of the demons that had gathered and threatened my spiritual well-being, my vocation, my life. It wouldn't be long before I found that my renewal was insupportable.

*     *     *

Several weeks later, I drove back to the motherhouse. I had never driven such a long distance by myself before, and the long dark tunnels through the mountains of Western Pennsylvania unnerved me a bit. I distracted myself by singing and familiarizing myself with some of the popular tunes on the radio. In Greensburg, Marion had turned me on to Simon and Garfunkel, much to Sister Peter's chagrin, but I was still woefully out of touch, and so I enjoyed listening to the popular songs on the radio, something we never got to do at the motherhouse. As a good-bye present, Marion had given me a couple of record albums, which were slowly melting on the shelf beneath the back window of the car. I wasn't sure I'd be allowed to keep them anyway.

I finally arrived home in the late afternoon after a six-hour drive. Despite my exhaustion from the drive, my eagerness to see familiar sights and faces revived my flagging spirits. Angela, I learned, had gotten through the summer without a relapse requiring a hospital visit, and so she was preparing to take her vows. Anne Rose had received her mission assignment to a small town in Western Pennsylvania, and we bid each other a long, tearful good-bye. For me it was like finally letting go, and it felt good. I knew she would always occupy a special place in my heart and would never be replaced, but my feelings for her were too unsettling. I had to be free of them. There was nothing else to be done about it. It had to be this way.

This annual time of sisters making their profession, the new postulants entering, and the junior sisters leaving for their missions was always an exciting one at the motherhouse, and it kept me distracted for a while. Soon thereafter, we received news that both Sister John in the novitiate and Sister Vera Marie in the juniorate were to be replaced, and we prepared ourselves for the change in command. Sister Vera Marie's replacement was Sister Thomas, the former vocation recruiter of whom I had always been so wary. As always though, we had no say in this or any other matter, nor were we given an explanation for the change. Certainly, Sister Vera Marie needed a different mission assignment. She was too volatile and quick-tempered, and that must have been apparent to others besides those of us who lived under her supervision. Some of my classmates and I found the prospect of living under her command for our final year of formation disconcerting: we had adjusted to Vera Marie, while Sister Thomas was very much of an unknown.

But others were delighted by the change. Once Sister Thomas was installed as our new "superior"—by now we had stopped using the term "mistress"—they fawned over her and followed her around as if she were the Pied Piper. I didn't get it. Supposedly, things were changing and we were being permitted to reexamine convent rules and policies and even make proposals, an opportunity we'd never had before. A few of us took it quite seriously. We studied some of the papers respecting religious life that came out of Vatican II to understand the guidelines better and determine how religious formation could be made more conducive to developing thinking, mature adults with a better grasp of our human as well as our spiritual nature. Denial of the self and death to the self might have worked well as spiritual strategies in the past or in a cloistered community, but ours was a modern community with a social-service mission that placed us squarely in the world. Many of us sensed that the insularity and lack of exposure to problems in the outside world had not prepared us well for that. Mission life did not in any way resemble the incubator of the motherhouse during our training. It required self-reflection, responsibility, and experience in handling freedom, not robotic behavior and blind obedience. How could we successfully manage these expectations when we were blatantly denied these opportunities for growth and development during our four years' training?

During our group sessions on these matters, many of my classmates waited to hear Sister Thomas' views before offering their own and risking her disapproval. I felt as if I had known my classmates quite well. During our three years of training, many had not hesitated to discuss or question certain policies, so I was aghast at their passive acquiescence to Thomas when we were finally given the very thing we had been clamoring for—the opportunity to speak out and bring about change. Clearly, they were more interested in pleasing our new superior, but not in the same "all right, we'll go along with this even though we don't understand or agree" manner they had with G. I. and Vera Marie. There was virtually no resistance, no criticism, certainly no challenge to Sister Thomas' authority, except from a few of us. She influenced many of my classmates' points of view, and they grew defensive of her no matter what she proposed. Ironically, given the opportunity for freedom they elected to align themselves with the familiar voice of authority. The same people I had come to know so well—Deirdre, Celia, Maria—had all fallen under the spell of her congeniality, and it was distressing to those of us who had escaped Sister Thomas' seductive power. Sure, the loosening of a few minor rules was a welcome gain. Instead of having to pray communally four times a day, now we were required to pray only three times a day as a group. But what about the harsh grand-silence rule, which was impossible to sustain in the mission field, or the rule that prohibited us from associating with lay college students? Shouldn't we be out there talking with young people, letting them know what we're about and finding out what's going on with them so that we can help them and serve God better?

For the first time I felt alienated from my own classmates, and the experience wasn't just like losing a sister or a brother but an entire family in a single plane crash. I had already left behind one family. My younger brothers and sisters had grown into strangers with friends and pursuits of their own, and my parents were remote figureheads leading a private life that did not include me. No longer was I their "sister" or "daughter," but "our sister, the nun" or "our daughter, the nun." Having immersed myself completely in this family of sisters that was community, I now dreaded and feared its loss. The prospect of such a loss was more than troubling and sad; it was tragic, and I took some solace in knowing that a few others who also walked out of step along with me suffered a similar disconnection. Together, we formed a small community of exiles within the walls of the motherhouse.

*   *   *

We sat on the large bed in the priest's quarters, me on one end, Monica in the middle, and Colleen on the other end. Colleen pulled out a cigarette and lit it. I almost fell off the bed. "Are you nuts?" My voice squeaked. "What are you doing?"

They both chortled, tickled at having disarmed me so. It was early evening during recreation period. The rules had relaxed some, and we were no longer monitored every single minute of the day. Freer to get into a little trouble, we appeared to be poised to do just that. Colleen passed the filtered Marlboro to Monica who took two long drags before offering it to me. I refused the first couple of rounds but then I gave in and took a puff. I had forgotten how harsh and bitter it felt as the smoke passed from my throat to my lungs, and a short coughing jag followed. We were adjusting to another name change as a result of a recent community ruling that decided we would now go by our given family names instead of the community name bestowed upon us on Profession Day. Suddenly, I was no longer Sister Kathleen Regina even though I would continue to celebrate the same feast day, and all the Johns, Peters, Pauls and Josephs were thrown out the convent window, along with the tradition of assuming a saint's—often a male saint's—name upon profession. I never understood why nuns were given male saints' names in the first place, although they clearly carried more weight than the female saints did. So here we sat, me (formerly Kathleen Regina), Colleen (formerly Michael Anne), and Monica (formerly Matthew). Well into our fourth year of training, we were hiding out in the priest's quarters smoking a cigarette. We were bold articles, indeed, as Mother Gabriel and Mother Agatha would have said. As I finished choking on the first puff of a cigarette I'd taken since the night before I entered the convent, they explained how they started smoking while on their summer mission. They had obviously been staying at a less strict house than my own.

While I was having a mild panic attack, they acted unconcerned. I whispered, "Do you think they can smell the smoke in the corridor?" Monica tilted her head and made a funny face while Colleen put her hands up in the air, as if to say, "Who cares?" We had been classmates for nearly four years, and while we got along well enough we had never been especially close. But now it seemed as if fate or circumstances or both had thrown us together in the same lifeboat. We formed an odd league. Colleen was brilliant in an absentminded professor kind of way. A straight-A student with a timorous personality and a penchant for avoiding trouble and reprimand, Colleen was the last person I expected to challenge the powers that be. She was lean and tall with a pinkish tint to her skin, and even the slightest embarrassment immediately caused her cheeks to flush crimson. I cringed whenever it happened because she looked so uncomfortable. Equally intelligent, Monica had poise, practical sense, and a sharp wit to support her impressive mind. She was short with brown-black eyes and a ruddy complexion that was slightly marred by the after-effects of adolescent acne. She wielded her quick tongue like a weapon, and I never wanted to be on the receiving end of it. Although flattered, I was a bit taken aback by their willingness to include me in their liaison, and I realized that it likely had more to do with our shared position on convent politics than with compatible personalities.

"I think Sister Thomas is a phony. A lot of the sisters in the field don't like her. They think she's a brownnoser. So says my sister, and she ought to know; she's been around for almost fifteen years." Monica was referring to Sister Patrice, her older sister and also a member of the community as well as a classmate of Fiona's, a fact that strengthened my newfound connection with Monica.

I jumped on Monica's observation, relieved that I wasn't the only one to feel so uneasy with Sister Thomas as our direct superior. "I'm so glad to hear someone else say it. She gives me the willies, and I don't trust her at all but I can't put my finger on what it is exactly. But why do the others like her so much? I don't get it. They're acting like wide-eyed kids around a movie star." I had expected it from Laurie and Joanne, but it really bothered me when Deirdre and Maria took such a liking to her. We had numerous discussions about it. They always defended her, insisting on how wonderful she was. Her appointment as our director served to deepen the lines of division within our class. In the early years, we were one for all and all for one. But a fissure had appeared in our class, originating in the incident in the novitiate when Krista, Angela, and I were reported to Mother Agatha. Then it had to do with trust. Now it also had to do with trust. Some of us just did not trust our new superior, while the others were falling all over themselves to please her. It seemed as if we were also taking sides in a battle—those of us who wanted to strengthen our own voice versus those who were happy to entrust theirs to this unknown quantity and representative of the convent administration. She may have been much younger than Sister John, but her wagon was still hitched to the old guard. Maybe it came back to obedience again. I had to confront the possibility that it was my problem after all, but if that was the case I was not alone. Colleen, Monica, and I accepted the fact that we were being branded as rebels. I guess we decided to fulfill their expectations.

Colleen took one last drag before snuffing out the butt in the lid of a glass jar and then offered her opinion. "It's because she's young and attractive. They think she's hip. They don't see what a snake she is." It seemed wrong to be talking about a fellow nun this way but awfully right at the same time.

"Yeah, and don't you just hate the way she talks?" Monica asked and then imitated its forced, breathy quality, "Now, Sisters, shall we go into prayers together?"

Her imitation sent us into muted hysterics, in the way that can only occur in sacred places, as we were ever alert to the shuffling and murmuring of people passing in the hallway.

"We'd better get going before we're missed," Monica warned.

"Yeah," I echoed. "I want to stop by Angela's room before it gets too late. Did you hear? She had to go to the infirmary today."

"Oh, no," Colleen cried, "not again." Monica had already heard. Their faces mirrored my own apprehension.

"Don't worry," Monica wrapped her arm around my neck to reassure me. "It's probably just a cold or flu or something. You know how susceptible she is." She and Colleen both understood how close we were, and how Krista's departure had affected both me and Angela. I appreciated their kindness and their support.

"You're probably right. Anyway, I'm going to stop by her room. Deirdre said that the infirmary nun ordered her to bed-rest for a couple of days."

We slid off the oversized bed, making sure to smooth out all the wrinkles on the white cotton spread. We didn't want anyone to know we'd been there, after all. After peeking out the doorway and seeing that it was clear, Colleen beckoned to us and we made our way to the stairway and up to the second floor. They headed in the direction of their rooms.

"Hey," Monica called out in a soft shout.

"What?"

"Don't forget. Patrice and Fiona will be here this weekend. Maybe they can get us outta this prison for a couple hours, huh?"

I laughed. "Dream on." It would be really nice to see both her sister and my friend, though, I thought. They were our pipelines to a saner world.

I darted up the stairs, made my way to Angela's room, and knocked on the half-opened door. "Hey, kiddo, how's it going?" I leaned my head and shoulders through the doorframe after Angela responded affirmatively to my knock. She was lying prone on her bed, and her face was a bit flushed. She seemed to perk up when she saw that it was me.

"Hey, stranger. Good to see you. I'm all right. Just a bit under the weather. Why don't you come all the way in? It's not time for night silence yet, is it?"

I laughed. "No. I just don't want to keep you up. You should be resting. What's going on, anyway?"

"I don't know." She sounded slightly exasperated. "They don't tell me much of anything. This is getting frustrating, you know? I thought I had recovered. They've done a bunch of tests and still don't seem to know why I come down with these fevers. I don't get too many explanations, and bed rest is about all they prescribe." She raised her eyebrows and frowned, a signal that she was finished talking about her health. I wanted to ply her with questions: What did her parents have to say? Shouldn't she be seen by another doctor or kept in a hospital until they figured out the problem or until she recovered fully? But I was also sensitive to the fact that she was frightened and didn't want to think about these things. Besides, we knew better than to question the judgment of our superiors, and appealing to our parents was out of the question now that we were full-fledged members of the order. Our parents no longer had a say in our lives. Actually, I wasn't even sure how much her parents knew about the state of her health, so I changed the subject.

"Mom and Dad and your brother all right?" I asked, solicitously.

She beamed. "Yeah. They're fine. Angelo's enrolled in music school and he's still playing the organ at the church. He's doing great. My folks are getting older, but they're in pretty good health. My mom wants to retire. I think it's a great idea. She's been working a long time. Yours?"

The trading of information about our families seemed to distract and calm her. "Great," I replied. "Good. Everybody's fine. My dad surprised me with a quick visit yesterday. He was on a truck route and stopped by to deliver about a hundred soft pretzels for us. I almost died when Sister Thomas told me that he showed up. Can you believe him?"

Angela was grinning and shaking her head. "Mike *is* a character."

"Yeah," I agreed, "and Anne should know." We both laughed. She knew my mom and dad well enough by now to appreciate their dynamics—my dad, reticent but full of surprises and my mom, a constant chatterer with a saying to fit any and every occasion. "Hey," I offered, "want me to get you a pretzel? They're in the downstairs kitchen."

"Sure. Sounds great."

"Right back," I assured her.

I half closed the door behind me and ran downstairs to our small kitchen where I grabbed a wonderfully large soft pretzel, the kind you could only buy on the streets of Philadelphia. As I came through the door at the top of the stairway and turned in the direction of Angela's room, I almost bumped into Sister Thomas. Our new juniorate director flashed me her "I'd like to have a word with you, Sister" look. I guess she had been stationed nearby Angela's room. Something about her stance and disingenuous smile warned me that she had been on the lookout for me.

"Where are you off to, Sister?" she demanded to know. She was well aware that my room was a hallway and a half away in the other direction.

"Just wanted to pop in to see Angela. Brought her one of the soft pretzels my dad dropped off to cheer her up."

She pursed her lips and glanced at her watch. "Well, Sister," she said, exaggerating the words so as to impress them upon me, "you realize it's ten minutes until the Grand Silence begins, and Sister Angela is quite ill and needs her rest. I think it would be best to forego a visit tonight, don't you? At least Sister Vera Marie's explosiveness was frank. Sister Thomas pretended to give you a choice when there really wasn't one at all. But I was not in a position to argue with her. "All right, Sister," I offered resignedly. I tried to make my voice sound indifferent: "Would you mind giving this to her?" With that, I handed her the pretzel, said good night, turned on my heels, and walked away.

I saw Sister Fiona that weekend. Now that she was officially installed as my community mentor, I was permitted to visit her periodically throughout the year and I confided in her about everything. She had become my friend as well as my counselor and she proved to be a good source of convent scuttlebutt. Through a friend of hers she had learned that, as Krista and I both suspected, it was Joanne and Laurie who had reported me, Krista, and Angela in the novitiate for breaking the Grand Silence, very likely in an effort to please convent authorities, through Sister Gertrude, a senior sister and friend from her hometown who took the matter up with Mother Agatha instead of waiting until Sister John returned from her retreat. By the time I learned the truth, I wasn't at all surprised. Nor was I surprised when Joanne and Laurie fast became two of Thomas' staunchest supporters, a development that did little to alleviate my mistrust of our new commander. Somehow it all felt so dirty. The discovery that two of our own "family" members had, indeed, conspired against us left me feeling betrayed and deeply distressed. Krista was gone now; Angela was alarmingly ill, and I was hanging on to the weakened threads of my vocation. In the days that followed a tight ring of secrecy solidified around Angela and her illness, and even Fiona with all her connections couldn't penetrate it. The new juniorate building housed two pay phones on the bottom floor that was open to visitors, and I made many a late-night collect call to Fiona, who listened sympathetically and tried to console me, especially after Angela's condition worsened and she was quarantined both day and night. I was not even permitted to see her by that time, which made me even more desperate. She was allowed no visitors with the sole exception of Sister Thomas who acted like a sentry patrolling up and down the hallway, making it virtually impossible to sneak into Angela's sickroom for a visit. I became very watchful, noting how she would enter Angela's room at night and not withdraw until a couple of hours later. At times she carried what appeared to be damp bedding out with her, probably from the perspiration caused by chronic fever. My growing concern over her condition and containment was aggravated by an overwhelming feeling of helplessness. The prospect that my friend might need me to do something, and that I didn't know it or couldn't respond, gnawed at me like a badly decayed tooth. My anxiety for her was constant and pervasive, yet any questions put to Thomas about Angela's condition always earned the same placid response that never told us anything: "Sister was better today" or "Sister had a difficult night." Of course, a name couldn't be affixed to her affliction because we weren't privy to such information. There were times when my desperation was so great that I had the urge to storm into my friend's room, knocking Sister Thomas over on the way, pick Angela up, and carry her out of the building. But go where and to do what? I was but an indentured servant by virtue of my vows. We were both trapped in a situation of our own making. Of course, I never attempted any such thing and my failure to act has haunted me ever since.

Guilt has many faces, and just as many functions. It may pass through you like a pang in the stomach that is readily dismissed, or it may attack and stay with you like a lingering virus. Such is the guilt I sometimes experienced when I behaved uncharitably or failed to live up to a vow. This guilt made me uncomfortable and desirous of reforming myself so as not to ever experience that dreadful feeling again. Then there were times when my guilt took on a different aspect and led to the recognition that there wasn't necessarily anything wrong with *me*. Perhaps it was the unreasonable circumstances that made me act, or not act, and my failure to do so caused me to feel guilt when I might have felt indignation. But then there is the monster guilt that is as menacing and all-consuming as Beowulf's Grendel. It results from the evil not recognized or dismissed, the step not taken, or the failure to act. This guilt does not have an end and can only hope for means of transformation—a catharsis of some sort to occur through therapy or penance or narrative healing. The monster metamorphoses into a dandelion; the dandelion changes into a weed and the seeds can at last be blown away.

My growing discontent with convent life had to do with more than my concern for Angela, although her illness and the circumstances around it played a major part. It was becoming clearer to me that I was simply ill suited to a life of blind obedience to a system that I questioned, and whose authorities I mistrusted. As I neared the end of my fourth year of training, I was becoming clearer about this unmistakable truth, which I shared with Sister Fiona, my sponsor and confidante and friend and the person I trusted most in the world. She listened and she cared and she knew me inside and out, and I was beginning to realize that my feelings about her were also getting all tangled up, just as they had been with Anne Rose. But I couldn't face the implications of my feelings and risk losing her at this juncture. Fiona was my savior. She would lead me into the light.

Revolt is a funny thing, at times overt and dramatic, at others silent and slowly seething. Mine was of the latter kind, begun and carried over from the previous year, and maybe longer for all I knew. Perhaps it was my limited mind that failed to reconcile the seeming contradiction of an order of nuns professing to love God and his people above all things, yet treating those inside its ranks with intolerance and, at times, inhumanity. The virtue of charity, which Jesus prized above all, took a backseat to obedience, from which flowed fear, rigidity, secretiveness, and paranoia. It was not, I decided, a healthy state in which to live. But it would take the full cycle of a year for my life-altering decision to become a conscious one.

In the interim I threw myself into my schoolwork, developed my association with Brigitte (who remains my friend, my dearest, oldest friend to this day), occasionally skipped Mass and breakfast, even when I didn't have an early class to attend, and ate my lunch by myself in the woods near the college campus to avoid my classmates. I was a rebel. Maybe I was preparing myself for the separation that seemed increasingly inevitable. Fear gripped me, and depression became my ready companion. My young life was inextricably wound together with this convent world, and while I couldn't entirely reconcile myself with it, I couldn't imagine leaving it. Where would I go? What would I do? How could I explain my decision to my parents? How could I face the shame they would surely feel, or my own for that matter? How could I think about leaving Angela behind? Leaving religious life was not a trifling matter from the perspective of those who are inside as well as outside. Nor was living it, and the rules for living it seemed more and more preposterous.

Colleen and Monica, traveling down the same road, were a step or two ahead of me, and their boldness fueled my own.

*       *       *

Christine approached me in the breezeway on the way to the postulants' quarters in the new building. They had finally leveled St. Gerard's, our old postulants' house. It was rumored that the fire department had declared it a hazard. I don't know about that, but I remembered never being able to get warm in that rickety building and fearing that the slap of a strong wind could blow it down. "Hey," she said. "Wait up. I want to talk with you about something."

She looked at me with that broad, innocent smile of hers. It went with the little girl demeanor that clashed with her razor sharp and skeptical mind. Although she was just a postulant, she liked to engage me in debates about theology, philosophy, and popular culture, the latter of which I admittedly knew very little. Associating with postulants was not encouraged, but it was difficult to prevent or monitor us as closely now that we all shared the same living space in the new building.

Christine's youthful earnestness amused me. One of the first things she told me was that I had to catch up and listen to the new albums of the "mature" Beatles. The group had a serious message to convey, she assured me. I figured she was probably right. Christine knew a whole lot more things than I did at eighteen. She came from the world of 1969, which bore little resemblance to the one I left in 1965. It was through her that I learned about a drug called "marijuana." I guessed people in my high school must have smoked it, but neither the word nor the weed ever came my way. Shortly after my departure from the convent, I was amused to learn that our juniorate mistress, Sister Thomas, had reported me, Colleen, and Monica to Mother General for smoking marijuana in the priest's quarters. (By that time I was already halfway out the door, as were Colleen and Monica, so they must have thought, why bother?) Sister Thomas couldn't be blamed for mistaking cigarette smoke for the scent of marijuana, but it was funny because at that time I had no idea what marijuana was. Christine straightened me out on that score, advising me to try it if I ever got the opportunity. I laughed. I figured Christine wouldn't last long in this convent world but I kept my thoughts to myself. She was curious, naive, and terribly frank. These qualities were not well suited to the game plan of convent life. I really liked her. So did my new friends, Colleen and Monica.

We paused outside the first-floor recreation room. No one was inside. I checked first to make sure. "Did you know that Ellen got permission to attend her dad's wedding?" A sly smile played around her lips. I wondered what scheme she was entertaining.

Ellen, Christine's classmate, had sort of latched on to my classmates, Monica and Colleen. I got to know her through them. She was full-blooded Irish, hearty, full of energy, and she strode around the corridors with an attitude tough enough to stop traffic, an attitude that did not match her angelic face. I had to wonder how long she would last as well. She was, after all, a free spirit.

"Yeah," Monica told me about her dad getting married. "Is she back yet from the wedding? What's going on?"

"Well," she said slowly as if to tantalize me, "she and I are planning a party after she gets back tonight, and we're inviting you, Colleen, and Monica. They've already agreed, and the plan is set."

"A party? What kind?" The palms of my hands started to feel clammy, but the idea sounded tempting. I was definitely interested. "What's the plan?"

The timing was perfect. Directors and delegates from throughout the community were meeting this week behind closed doors to elect a new mother general and decide on other major proposals and changes. Sister Fiona was one of them, and she had been so tied up in meetings that I barely got to see her. But so was Sister Thomas. It would have been a perfect time to sneak in and visit Angela, except that she was being closely monitored in the infirmary, reportedly having taken a turn for the worse.

When Ellen returned later that night, she didn't come empty-handed. She was Irish, after all, and had just left the Irish wedding of her father who had lost his first wife, Ellen's mother, to cancer. When we met outside Ellen's room, it was nearly ten o'clock and well after Night Silence. We didn't let that stop us though, emboldened as we were by our own rebelliousness and the postulants' brazenness. Ellen grinned as she produced a canvas laundry bag filled with beer. I lapsed into a stupor that lasted more than a minute, and when I regained consciousness, I saw the three of them beckoning me at the other end of the hall well on their way to the "party."

"C'mon," Monica called in a muted shout, her hand cupped around her mouth. I scooted down the hallway. We rounded the corner carefully, trying hard not to be too elated because we had to get around two more corners before we reached the back staircase that would take us outside and then to our destination—Camelot.

"Shh . . . Shh . . ." Colleen and I, the only ones with any sense at the moment, were cautioning the other three to settle down so as not to attract any attention. The corridors were quiet except for the occasional door closing or toilet flushing in one of the bathrooms positioned at the end of each of the four halls. Their snickering soon turned into contagious giggles that were hard to resist, especially at the sight of Ellen barely able to drag the heavy canvas bag along the floor. How much beer had she brought? As we neared the last corner, I poked my head around and caught sight of Carolyn and Nancy, two of our classmates, speaking in quiet tones in the middle of the hall. I jumped back and put my hands up, warning everybody, especially Ellen, to stop. They did, but not without emitting sounds of muffled hysteria. Carolyn and Nancy stopped talking, then resumed, and within a couple of minutes returned to their rooms.

Finally making it to the stairway, we bounded down the stairs like children just released from school for summer vacation, dragging the white bag filled with brew behind us. Within minutes we found the path that led to our secret place in the woods overlooking the trails of the neighboring park. The warm, soft air gathered around us like a light cape. We sat cross-legged on the hard earth in the middle of a grove of trees and laughed so much at the outrageousness of what we were doing that my side hurt. It took five minutes before we settled down. Ellen reached into the bag and pulled out a can of Budweiser for everybody, followed by a cigarette. She had thrown several packs into the bag. Her dad would never miss either the cigarettes or the beer, she assured us. Christine produced the matches, lighting each of our cigarettes in turn. I was once again starting to get used to the harshness of the nicotine in my throat and the elixir that came with inhaling it.

I tore off the metal ring and took a few swigs of beer. It tasted warm and sour, but that didn't stop me or any of the others from drinking it. I had tasted beer once before at a New Year's Eve party when I was seventeen. A bunch of midshipmen had crashed the party of mostly high school students, and they dared us to join them in a game of chug-a-lug. My competitiveness got the better of my good judgment and I went home sick and sorry that night. Never again, I vowed. The only other time I drank enough to get sick was with Denny after my senior prom. We had gone with a bunch of friends to the New Jersey shore where we rented a room for the night so that we could drink safely. I don't know what the other two couples did, but unaccustomed to alcohol, Denny and I both grew nauseous and fell asleep on the bed. Alcohol had not played a key role in my life, but on this particular night it felt dangerous, defiant, and terribly right.

I took a gulp of my second beer. We were busy entertaining ourselves by reliving this evening's daring escapade when I heard a rustling in the bushes behind me. I turned and started. It felt like my heart took a furlough when I saw a form coming toward me through the brush, and it didn't return to duty until I heard Ellen laugh and call out, "Joe, you made it. Come on. Meet my friends." As Ellen's older brother drew closer, I observed his features by the light of a spectacularly bright full moon. His flushed face betrayed his discomfort. He was with a bunch of young nuns in the woods, after all, and he must have felt a tad out of place. After a few minutes and three quick beers, he loosened up. He was cute and disarmingly shy, which added to his charm. Blond, blue-eyed and sporting a military crew cut, he talked about what life was like in the navy in response to my questions. He was thrilled to be stationed in sunny southern California, he told me, because it offered year-round warm weather, soothing palm trees, and plenty of surf for his favorite hobby. Tight-fitting blue jeans and a short-sleeved, button-down shirt emphasized his lean but muscular build on a six-foot-tall frame. Was he flirting? My God! Was I? After a while, I realized that it wasn't just the alcohol prompting my heart to beat a little faster. Irish charm just oozed from him, and I think I was not the only one to become infatuated that night. All the staunch barricades I had erected during my nun training seemed to be crumbling inside me, and this realization served as an unmistakable marker. Added to all the others that had accumulated over the past year or so, it was pointing me away from a life of poverty, chastity, and obedience. Not without tremendous sadness though. And regret.

Joe had brought a transistor radio along with him and after the excitement of our enterprise leveled off, we lapsed into quiet talk. In the background, we listened to the guttural sounds of Bob Dylan singing "the answer my friend is blowin' in the wind; the answer is blowin' in the wind." I looked around and wondered.

We were pretty tipsy when we headed back to the motherhouse, but my nerves stayed on red alert. Joe gave us each a hug and promised to see us on the outside. Colleen and Monica had both made their decision to leave the convent, so I tried to prepare myself to lose two more friends. Gloomy and eerily silent, the juniorate building waited for us as we approached and crept into the back door and up the stairs. Ellen was in the worst shape. Colleen and Monica kept her propped up as we steered her toward her room. We had to stop from time to time to stem the bouts of hysterical laughter but somehow managed to get both Ellen and Christine back to their rooms unscathed. I said good night to Colleen and Monica, deciding to take a chance that Fiona, who was here as one of the community delegates, might still be awake.

Stealthily, I made my way to her room and cautiously knocked on the door. She didn't look surprised when she opened it and promptly ushered me inside. The room was in shadows. It faced the inside of the open quadrangle and filtered light shone in from the outside lighting. I had caught her in the middle of preparing for bed, so she stood barefoot in the customary long slip and T-shirt. I had been drinking, of course, and unused to alcohol, I had become even more defenseless. But that didn't fully explain the rush of emotions and the ease with which I succumbed to them. I threw my arms around her neck and cried. I told her how frightened I was that I didn't seem to fit in anymore, but that I didn't know what I would do or where I would go. I confided my fear that there was something terribly, terribly wrong with Angela, and I didn't think they were taking good care of her. I told her how much I feared for Angela's well-being and how frustrated and helpless I felt to do anything about it. She had heard my litany of complaints before, but not the desperation. I was a waterfall gushing with emotion and pain. Tenderly, she led me toward the bed, lay down atop the bed covers and the propped-up pillows, and pulled me down beside her. After untold minutes of weeping, I fell asleep nestled in the crook of her arm. I felt safe and I decided not to feel guilty. Lately, guilt felt too much like a noose fastened around my neck. Somehow I needed to loosen it.

Another full cycle of a year had run its course, and I was no clearer about religious life and my vocation than I had been the summer before when I left for Greensburg. I understood only one thing: it was time for me to leave. Sister Gertrude, the senior sister who had reported us to Mother General on the word of our two classmates, had been elected mother general, and this turn of events did nothing to improve my hope for the future or alter my resolution. I didn't know if I would ever recover from the devastating feeling of failure borne of my decision, finally, to renounce my vows and leave the convent. I had committed my life to God. Now I was taking it back. I couldn't be or do what they wanted in the way they wanted, and I had to confront that reality. My failure left me with an abiding sense of shame, the full impact of which I wouldn't see until I looked into the disappointed faces of my parents. Irish Catholic parents lived and sacrificed for the reward of giving their children—the nun, the priest—to God and the church. Having children in religious life offered clear proof to the Catholic world that they had succeeded and accomplished their task on earth, a heavy burden for them as well as their sons and daughters. Since they had elected to be married and, therefore not chaste, thereby following a lesser route to heaven, offering a child to God was the best they could do to earn their heavenly reward and church approval.

I had to petition Sister Thomas for permission to seek a dispensation from my vows. Technically, we took temporary vows that had to be renewed each year, and even though the year was up I still needed to be released in the church's eyes. There were formalities involved that had to be followed. I approached Sister Thomas in the hallway outside her room.

"Sister, I need to talk with you," I announced. I had worked all morning to contain my emotions, determined not to betray my pain and humiliation.

She looked a little startled, probably because I rarely approached her or initiated discussion of any kind. "Certainly, Sister," she said, maintaining a serious demeanor that suited my tone. "Would you like to come down to my office?"

I gazed into the cool gray eyes that made me so uneasy. Did she sense how much I loathed her—she who had confiscated my friend and kept her in a room of inexplicable sickness surrounded by secrecy for the better part of a year? I maintained my calm. "No, Sister. That's not necessary. I can speak with you here." I paused for a moment, trying to keep my voice and courage from cracking and then resumed. I sounded far more controlled than I felt. "Sister, I would like to apply for a year's leave of absence." My request was a safety valve; I knew I would never come back.

Her face assumed an appropriately grim aspect but she didn't look terribly surprised. I needed her permission for everything, so she knew that Fiona had been counseling me via telephone and periodic visits. She knew that I had been struggling with my vocation.

Sister Thomas was very guarded, but I saw relief creep into the rigid lines of her face. She rarely gave herself away like this. Her true feelings were usually indecipherable, owing to the veneer that coated her persona. I was certain she disliked me because I refused to be seduced by her charm. She could not win me over and manipulate me, and on occasion, I sensed her frustration. She would have loved to stamp "not good enough" on my forehead and send me packing herself. But I had taken that pleasurable task away by acting first. She folded her hands and brought them up to her lips, looking downward while fishing for the correct response. She wasn't praying, as John or G. I. or even Vera Marie would have probably done. She was calculating. "Well, Sister, you know how serious a decision this is. Are you sure?" She was studying my eyes, which were fighting back tears. "Would you like to arrange a meeting with Mother Gertrude?"

Hah, I thought to myself. *Mother* Gertrude! I wanted to laugh and then thank her for introducing levity into the conversation. I wondered if she realized how absurd her suggestion was. After all, it was *Sister* Gertrude who had, reported me, Krista, and Angela to Mother Agatha for breaking the Grand Silence in the novitiate, having received the information from Laurie and Joanne. Why had she done it? Her actions had always puzzled me. She was a missioned sister with nothing to do with those of us in formation at the time, taking and acting on the word of two insecure novices with questionable motives.

My composure intact, I continued. "No, Sister. I don't see what good it would do to speak to Mother Gertrude. I've made my decision. I'm prepared to take the next step."

"Sister," she almost pleaded, "is there *nothing I* can do?"

I wondered if there was no end to her insincerity.

Clearly, she did not like me and wanted me to disappear. I had refused to play along. I challenged her in front of the group as well as in other more subtle ways, such as by thinking for myself and acting independently. Her passive-aggressive response had consisted of ignoring and alienating me. But she had also passed along the baseless charge that

Monica, Colleen, and I had been smoking marijuana to the convent's highest authority. Why didn't she just confront us about the smoking and learn the facts in advance of alerting Mother General? She was no doubt orchestrating my exit, something she would have relished had I not stolen the baton from her. It was painfully clear that fair hearing and justice were purely secular notions with no place inside these walls. My experience in the novitiate with Mother Agatha had effectively demonstrated that. Control through fear was both a means and an end, as it is in most authoritarian regimes. By invoking God and obedience, the convent authorities whittled away at our spirits and refashioned our minds—we were made to adapt to the system and there was no use challenging it. My growing awareness of this method bred a deep indignation in me because there was no higher justice to whom we could appeal. The convent administration cloned the church administration with its rigid lines of authority. After all, obedience to the pope and the bishop and the priest and the mother superior meant obedience to God. Sister Thomas was an adept commander in such an army.

Christine, three years younger and three classes behind me, read the convent signs better and sooner than I did. No less a dreamer and an idealist, no less dedicated to serving God and his people, she was, nevertheless, part of a rebellious generation that, one way and another, would challenge society and change the world. She left the community around the same time that Colleen, Monica, and Ellen did. I was the straggler who would catch up.

*    *    *

They say that extreme pain can cause the body to shut down. In a way, it's a form of self-protection. What your mind can't handle your body withholds. Emily Dickinson, a virtual recluse most of her life, wrote a poem about it. I wondered how she, who had so little experience of the world, could feel so deeply and describe suffering so well. It was as if her pen were a finger on the pulse of human suffering:

> After great pain a formal feeling comes—
> The Nerves sit ceremonious, like Tombs—
> The stiff Heart questions was it He, that bore,
> And Yesterday, or Centuries before?
>
> The Feet, mechanical, go round—
> Of Ground, or Air, or Ought—
> A Wooden way Regardless grown,
> A Quartz contentment, like a stone—
>
> This is the Hour of Lead—
> Remembered, if outlived,

> As freezing persons, recollect the Snow—
> First—Chill—then Stupor—then the letting go—

Some thirty years later, I still remember.

*　　*　　*

I walked through my last week of convent life benumbed. I couldn't see ahead of me, and once again, there was no looking back. Somewhere in that week, a senior sister drove me to the monsignor's office in downtown Philadelphia to sign my dispensation papers. The portly man with thinning gray hair and gold-rimmed bifocals sitting behind a splendid oak desk had probably gone through the ritual dozens of times, but it was a first for me. He wheezed and fidgeted while reading the report in front of him that had probably been prepared by Mother General. Then he sighed and looked up, sighed and looked up. I had no idea what the report said. It was *about* me; it wasn't *for* me, and that method typified what was most wrong with convent life—secretive and autocratic, it took the divide-and-conquer, control-through-fear-and-shame approach that had been so long effective in managing the rank and file. The monsignor kept asking me if I was sure that I was making the right decision and reminded me that my vows, even if temporary, were binding, and that a release from vows was a grave matter of dire consequence. I said little. I held my ground. I walked out of his office with the only paper I did get to see. It contained the bishop's signature and my signature, and it authorized my one-year leave of absence from the Missionary Sisters of the Nazarene. The leave, granted at my request, gave me an "out" or a way back "in," should I find myself unable to readjust to secular life. I was terribly frightened. I was not at all sure that I was doing the right thing. Since my entrance day, I had, of course, entertained doubts about my vocation, but I had never actually envisioned myself walking out the door and through the gates forever. My identity had been so drastically altered and reshaped that I was not at all confident that I would know who I was or how to live in a world without my garb and my "sister" identity that offered instant claim to worth and value. What would happen if I didn't make it on the outside? In a new and frightening light I remembered the disconsolate ex-novice I had left on the steps of the home for single women. What had happened to her? I shuddered to think.

Sister Thomas had warned me not to tell anyone of my departure, which was scheduled for 8:00 a.m., two days after my visit to the monsignor's office, when everybody was sure to be at breakfast. At least I wouldn't be leaving under the guilty shroud of darkness in the middle of the night. (A few things had changed for the better, after all.) I would leave, instead, in the broad light of day dressed in a borrowed skirt and blouse with no money and no clothes worth packing in the black trunk I was allowed to take home with me. Before leaving, I had decided to find a way to see Angela despite Sister Thomas's orders. I couldn't leave without saying good-bye to my dear friend. I skipped noon dinner the afternoon before my departure knowing that Sister Thomas was sure to be at table in the motherhouse. I was afraid of being caught but knew I couldn't leave without seeing her. I tapped on her door three times before a hoarse voice told me to open the door and come in. I hardly recognized her. Wrapped beneath several blankets, she leaned against three stacked pillows in a half-upright position. Her hands were folded around a small Bible, and a black rosary was coiled around her left hand. Her face looked puffy, almost bloated; the normally olive skin was blotched, and her brown eyes were glassy.

It had been weeks since I'd seen her, and I'd never seen her look this ill. I tried to act normally so as not to betray my shock and concern. I made my voice sound light and cheery as I walked toward the bed and sat on the straight-back chair positioned alongside the bed. "Hey, how's my buddy doing, huh? Mind if I sit down?"

A quizzical look darted through her eyes, and then she nodded slowly. It was then that I realized she didn't recognize me either. When she started talking, I felt less and less as if I ever knew her. She began waving the Bible at me, repeating random passages, mostly hell, fire, and brimstone stuff from the Old Testament that didn't make much sense. Who was this fearful, judgmental person who was lecturing me? She talked about God's just reward and how we needed to suffer for God here on earth. "The wicked will be punished," she exhorted. If I was distressed by her appearance, I was even more appalled by what I was hearing, for it did not sound at all like Angela. As she spoke, her eyes looked like red flames darting here and there. I sat there speechless, nodding my head, trying to listen and take in this new person whom I did not recognize. Suddenly, in a sparkling moment of clarity, a tender look of recognition appeared on her face. She dropped her Bible and reached for my hand (which I held as long as she permitted me) and cried out, "Kathy! It's you! Where've ya been? I've really missed you."

I tried to make the most of those fleeting moments of recognition, which receded like a wave, and then came back, receded, then returned, in that strange and final hour with my friend. While lucid, she recalled our friendship and closeness; the silly, crazy things we did with Krista; and the tough times we had been through together and the families that we so willingly shared. At one point she even pulled up her acoustic guitar from the far side of the bed, and as she strummed it, we reminisced about how we used to enjoy singing and writing songs together. The more versatile singer, she always sang harmony, while I sang melody. She started to strum an old Peter, Paul, and Mary favorite of ours, inviting me to sing along with her: "Turn around and you're three / Turn around and you're four / Turn around and you're a young girl / Going out of the door / Turn around / Turn around /Turn around and you're a young girl going out of the door." I wondered if she understood the ironic relevance of the lyrics that day. As she sang, her eyes glistened and her voice cracked. Then, without warning, she was gone. She returned to that strange place where she didn't know me and, no matter how much I tried, I couldn't reach her. I realized that any explanation about my leaving the convent was a pointless exercise and that I could not say good-bye to her as I had originally intended. Doing so would either mean nothing, or worse, it might terrify her.

\*     \*     \*

Emily Dickinson's poetry is pithy and portentous:

> Presentiment is that long Shadow on the Lawn
>
> Indicative that Suns go down
>
> The notice to the startled grass
>
> That darkness is about to pass.

The air hung heavy and hot. I sat on a lawn chair on the front porch of my parents' home watching the assorted firecrackers blaze a trail of short life against a cloudless night sky, two months after my departure from the convent. I had returned from a picnic outing with some friends at the boys' orphanage where I was working as a social worker, only to find no one at home, which was unusual. At the tail end of the long Fourth of July weekend, people were still celebrating. I had never much enjoyed the shock and crackle of fireworks, which insisted on reminding us of guns, smoke, and death, especially given the proliferation of TV images reflecting the war in Vietnam, so I distracted myself by studying the sky between flashes to see if I could still identify the Big and Little Dippers. I wasn't having much success when I heard the phone ring. I dashed to the front stoop, threw open the screen door, and made my way to the kitchen to pick up the phone on the third ring. It was Monica calling from her apartment in East Harlem to tell me that her sister, who was still a member of the community, had called to give her the news that Angela was dead.

I think I said "what?" three times, and "what do you mean?" several more. But no matter how much I stalled, resisting the truth, the answer was the same. I was beyond hearing or talking or thinking or feeling. Numbly, I hung up the phone and walked back outside. Years before my father had planted a pine tree, hoping it would beautify the front yard. I stood alongside that tree which had grown hugely tall with a muscular trunk, dwarfing our small house. My eyes followed the spindly branches that reached upward, bending toward the heavens. I raised my fist and shook it at those same heavens before my knees buckled and I dropped to the soft, moist grass, my tears joining the late-night dew.

Afterward, I wrote my own reply to Emily Dickinson's "Presentiment" poem:

Agony must be Presentiment fulfilled,

The long expansive shadow shrouding all the lawn

The folding Flower's darkling Fear

That the Sun's forever gone.

\*     \*     \*

I picked Colleen and Monica up at the train station and together we went to the funeral Mass at the motherhouse. We weren't exactly invited, but we didn't let that stop us. I was a sleepwalker following the cues of my friends who probably had no idea how disconnected I felt. Entering the motherhouse chapel through the outer front door instead of the inner doors was a strange experience. When two unfamiliar sisters directed us to a section of the chapel reserved for outsiders, it was made perfectly clear that we no longer belonged to this place that had been our home for nearly four years. Anger made a slight dent in my numbness when I saw a solicitous Sister Thomas, still the juniorate superior, leading Angela's bent and grieving mother to a pew alongside the coffin, where she was joined by her husband and surviving son. Other family members crowded into the pews around them but the better part of the chapel was filled with members of the community, some of whom had been our classmates and all of whom ignored us in our lay clothes. We were officially strangers.

Images blurred: two priests in black vestments, somber altar boys, sobbing relatives and friends, and a simple, closed coffin of dark wood in the center aisle containing the body of a friend long lost and never to be recovered. My own eyes did not cloud over until a slender, bound collection of Angela's songs, with the lyrics that I had contributed, were circulated among the congregation. I observed that my name was noticeably absent. Erased, like me. It was that easy.

Following the service I took a brazen, solitary walk on the motherhouse grounds. I strode down the hill and past the novitiate and across the softball field strewn with clusters of dandelion seeds to the bridle path that led to the grotto. I tried not to think. Thinking made my head hurt because there was so much I did not understand. I had already locked up my feelings in a chamber of my heart with a sign on the door that warned: Do Not Open! But I tried to find my way back to simpler, happier days when Angela, Krista, and I had trekked up and down the hill together and made our Three Musketeers pact. I realized that in different ways I had lost track of both of them despite my youthfully earnest intentions.

I made my way back under a darkening sky that shielded me from the July sun but failed to relieve the intensity of the muggy heat. To shorten the distance and come out on the other side of the motherhouse and the public parking lot, I cut across the dandelion field. I remembered how we had played softball in the summer on this field, and on snowy winter nights we plopped ourselves down on the white earth to form snow angels. Out of childhood habit, I scooped up a dandelion weed, holding it in front of me as I made a wish while blowing the seeds away.

Several weeks after Angela's funeral, I was surprised to receive an envelope that had been addressed to me and forwarded from the motherhouse. No explanation accompanied it, and I couldn't tell if it had been opened or not. Inside a five-dollar bill and two ones were enclosed in a card along with a separate note. The card pictured a little girl in a pink dress on a swing in the summertime and read, "Gee . . . wish you were here swingin' with me!" Signed "Love" three different times before each of the names written in an adult's script, the card was from Karen Schumaker, Patty Formica, and Donna Voigt. The poorly punctuated note looked to have been written by Karen herself:

> Dear Sister Kathleen: Hi How are you I am fine I miss you very much. we met 2 Sisters Sister Ann and Sister Pat. They are very nice but not as nice as you. when we go down to the Bridal path we sing a doe a deer and we start crying because we think of you. Gee I really miss you. I wish you where sitting next to me. Every night I pray that you will be back. write back. 8228 Craig Street Love Karen

Scrawled at the top of the note was a brief message from Karen's mother, informing me that the girls had taken up a collection for me and had been glad to do it.

My heart splintered. Unable to go back to that place in my memory, I packed the card away. I never wrote back.

# Part V

## Blowing the Dandelion
## Seeds Away (1974)

# Spring

On a balmy spring day in 1974 I kissed my nearly two-year-old baby good-bye and felt a pang as I handed her to her father, giving them both a long, warm embrace because it would have to last for two days. My husband was not an easy or a gentle man, but he wore his father role well, and I knew she'd be fine. It was the first time that I'd be away from her for more than an hour or two though, and this caused me some anxiety. I would miss my two-year-old firstborn who stretched me in different directions. Sonya was a lively, outgoing child who had led her shy mother into uncomfortable situations more than once. She thought nothing about leading me to the door of an unknown neighbor's house or chatting to strangers in the park, initiatives that I am still hard-pressed to take. Some of her courageous spirit must live in me, though. Years later, in middle age, I summoned the strength to walk away from a difficult and unfulfilling marriage, and I finally realized my true desires to be partnered with a woman, a *particular* woman. And so I made peace with the part of me that had loved Anne Rose and probably Fiona as well.

On one occasion, I even brought Sonya, nearly two years old, with me on a nostalgic visit to the motherhouse where I had lived as a young nun. I didn't know what possessed me to go there after nearly five years, but I was curious to see if it was as I remembered it. We walked tentatively through the front door into the foyer where the porter sat at the motherhouse switchboard. I remembered having been assigned to that duty myself once, along with almost every other duty that went around. I introduced myself as someone who used to live there. The young postulant gave me a very puzzled look and then seemed relieved when ol' Mother Michael came wheeling down the hall in our direction. I couldn't believe she was still alive and wheeling around the motherhouse! She recognized me at once and asked how and what I was doing. I told her I had married and was finishing college. Then I introduced her to Sonya who, sensing my distraction while conversing, had gone toddling down the hallway, drawn by some activity outside the chapel. I excused myself from Mother Michael and scooted down the hall in the direction of the inner sanctum to retrieve her, but only after she had made a point of introducing herself, in a manner of speaking, to several older sisters. I nodded politely to the sisters who commented on what a charming, darling child she was; scooped her up; and returned to Mother Michael who was watching the activity from her wheelchair parked just outside the switchboard room.

I positioned Sonya on my small hip with my arm secured around her, facing her outwardly, which was the position she preferred because it gave her the best view, and apologized to Mother Michael for the commotion she had caused. Reaching up, she grabbed hold of Sonya's tiny hand and shook it playfully. Then she looked at me and winked, a crafty smile playing around her lips as she said, "Well, it looks like someone's getting their comeuppance."

I smiled, remembering this visit, at Sonya and her dad, who waved at me as the Amtrak train pulled away, taking me to Manhattan for a visit with my friend and former classmate, Anne Rose. She had left the convent about two years after my own departure. I had seen her only once at a large reunion of ex-nuns. By this time, there were more of us outside the convent walls than inside, a phenomenon that had swept through most of the Catholic convents and monasteries during an era characterized by liberation and change. The two of us had talked briefly and shyly in Margaret's crowded living room as we tried to find our way around the strangeness of relating to each other as laypeople and catch up on each other's life. Afterward, we exchanged an occasional note or Christmas card expressing a desire to get together, but we had separate, demanding lives that left little room for old friends, especially old ex-nun friends. She was in New York working in the film industry and I was a busy mother finishing college, trying to figure out a way to pursue graduate work without money for school or child care. At the time, we were eking out a living from the grant money awarded to my husband, a graduate student of social work. When I received the invitation to visit her in New York for a weekend with the assurance that I needed nothing but to get myself there and back, I couldn't say no.

A weekend free of wife and mother responsibilities was one benefit, but more important was the opportunity to spend time with someone who knew and understood my past—*our* past. So often people asked me about the convent: Why did you enter? What made you leave? What was it like living inside a convent? Their questions exasperated me because I could not articulate the answers in a way that matched the profundity of the questions. If I did try to answer them in earnest, they looked befuddled and skeptical as if it were impossible for them to grasp my explanation. My unresolved feelings about Angela—the matter of her death, her lengthy sickness, and the way it was handled, the unnecessary and forced rupture in our relationship—fueled the frustration. I may have left the convent, but I never managed to leave behind this powerful feeling that there was something I had to do—to expose or redress wrongs that had been done. But who and what remained elusive and hard to pin down. I didn't expect that Anne Rose had any answers, but it would be comforting to spend time with someone who knew and understood what we both had lived through.

We didn't talk that weekend about the relationship we had left behind at the motherhouse. We had strayed into foreign, dangerous waters with our more-than-sisterly love, and we tacitly agreed not to uncover an experience that I had chalked up to adolescence, loneliness, and confusion. How she stored it, I didn't know.

On the first night of my visit she took me out for an Italian dinner at Mama Leone's. Then we caught a production of the long-running off-Broadway play, *The Fantastiks*, a delightful, upbeat musical that had been seen by everyone but me apparently, because Anne Rose laughed when I told her I'd never heard of it. By the time we returned to her Upper Westside apartment, we were both tired and decided to call it a night. She was gracious about giving over her single bedroom to me for my two nights' stay while she slept on a living-room sofa bed.

We enjoyed glorious weather on Saturday when we walked along the East River and later on Fifth Avenue across from the park. A bright sun warmed the clean spring air and promised that summer was not far behind. The trees looked fresh and green, a colorful contrast against a cloudless powder-blue sky. Even the New York pedestrians, normally rushed and short-tempered, seemed lively and carefree. This was the kind of day it was: warm not hot, fresh rather than sultry, blue not gray, mild instead of bitter. It made me feel young and new and alive. I was happy to spend this spring day with my old friend in Manhattan. Our daytime excursion ended splendidly with a visit to the Metropolitan Museum of Art, which is one of my favorite places even if it always does leave me in a reflective state. A visit there always found me seeking out the post-Impressionists, particularly Bastien-Lepage's *Joan of Arc*, a mammoth piece, in which Joan's transfixed eyes, gazing toward heaven under the guard of her angels, reflect a puzzled resignation to her calling, together with serenity. It always made me nostalgic about the lost possibilities of my religious life.

Up to this point we had talked only lightly of the people and activities in our respective lives, avoiding any matters of weight or consequence, and so we managed to find our way back to an easy familiarity even as we were searched for new common ground. And yet I also felt the urge to revisit our shared past. She made a light dinner that evening, and the combination of my reflectiveness carried over from the museum visit and our reestablished connection urged me to open up old wounds. For me, of course, that meant Angela. Sometime after she died, my father visited Angela's dad and learned that her illness and death were caused by a viral heart infection. But that information did little to resolve all the confusion and mysteriousness in the circumstances of her illness and the way it was handled.

Anne Rose had been away from the motherhouse during my last year in the convent, the same year that Angela died, so she was not familiar with the details of her confinement. Following dinner, we sat at the table and talked over sips of wine. As I related the course of events, recounting how Sister Thomas had isolated Angela and spent hours alone with her in Angela's room, keeping her classmates and me in particular from seeing her, Anne Rose grew quiet and grim. At first, I assumed that she was empathizing with the sadness I felt as I relived those days and the loss of my friend. My pain was laced with guilt, I explained, for not having done something to help Angela, and with frustration resulting from my overwhelming sense of powerlessness at the time. Anne Rose listened with rapt attention. Her grimness made me apprehensive, as I began to sense that there was something ominous behind the steel wall of her restraint. I stopped talking, placed my elbows on the dining room table, and folded my hands in front of my mouth, my thumbs locked beneath my chin. "What? What is it?" I asked fearfully.

She looked at me for a moment and rose from her chair, suggesting that we sit in the living room where we, rather *she*, would be more comfortable. I agreed. We sat side by side on the brown-and-cream-checkered couch that doubled as a hideaway bed. Her hands lay limp in her lap. I turned my body and faced her with one arm draped over the back of the couch, the other leaning on my knees that I had pulled up toward me, for safety, I think. I tried to relax and coaxed her to continue talking, assuring her that whatever it was she needed to disclose was safe with me.

Anne Rose started talking slowly and deliberately, as if she were in a confessional and determined to be honest at all costs. She explained how, to this point, only her confessor and psychiatrist knew about the events that occurred during her first-year mission that led to her departure from the convent and, subsequently, a nervous breakdown. As she described them, I almost tasted the tears that gradually swallowed up her eyes. She paused at intervals, unable to continue for moments and even minutes at a time, then she'd pick up the bloody trail of memories, determined to follow them back to the horrible, terrifying place they led. Her words struck me like gunshots to my head, my chest, my abdomen. They seared my flesh, tearing it open—but how much more painful for her who had suffered the betrayal, while I had only to listen to its reconstruction? I don't believe she ever intended to disclose this part of her past to me. It just happened. She did this for me, I think, for the sake of my having this important piece of information that both helped to explain things and left me in even more agony. I listened intently. I responded by nodding or shaking my head, occasionally shielding and wiping my own wet face in my hands, as though veiling the tears could help me to absorb the shock.

She reminded me that she had been missioned to a small house in a remote area of Western Pennsylvania. Her superior was Sister Gloria, a nun in her thirties who had exacted absolute fidelity and obedience from the youthful and inexperienced Sister Anne Rose. One of the things she required was Anne Rose's cooperation when she routinely visited her bedroom at night, taped her mouth, tied her to the bed, and molested her. Anne Rose's account of the torturous experience, in which a confused and inexperienced young nun bound by the staunch vow of obedience was exploited by her superior, took a bizarre twist: Sister Thomas, a friend and former classmate of Sister Gloria, was a regular visitor to the mission. Anne Rose went on to relate how Sister Thomas had participated with Gloria in the ritual molestation. It was the same Sister Thomas, of course, whom I had so mistrusted and under whose close care Angela had been placed for her last year or so of life. My mind shivered as it raced back and forth over the possibilities, but a combination of shock and fear prevented me from exploring them with Anne Rose.

I did not ask her how many times she—they—came uninvited to her room. I did not ask her to describe what specific acts they had performed. I had no frame of reference for such questions, and the mere outline of her account horrified me, stunned me, muted me. I was inexperienced in matters of sex, despite having been married for three years and given birth. Once in the first year or so of marriage, my husband took me to visit the family physician who assured me it was acceptable to do whatever my husband asked because sexual acts were natural and acceptable to God. I should follow the lead of my husband, he urged me, failing to understand that I was a product of a church in which asexuality was glorified in the person of Mary, Jesus' mother. I had learned my lessons well: sex was not acknowledged or taught or learned; therefore, it had no place in the life of a good Catholic girl. Suddenly, in marriage, I was being asked to unlearn the lessons of a lifetime. My introduction to the natural world of conjugal relations came hard. Following that, any introduction to unnatural or perverse acts seemed incomprehensible.

I did not ask questions, and so I failed to get the facts. But the images were as clear as the cross atop a church steeple: I saw tape, the color and strength of steel, pulled tightly across my friend's mouth, and a pair of hands helplessly bound to a headboard with segments of rough clothesline, while shadowy figures loomed over her sacred nakedness. These were images only. Possibilities. That's all I dared see. Anne Rose. Angela? Anne Rose. Angela?

My visit with Anne Rose ended on a somber note. Our relationship, as far as this life was concerned, had ended, despite periodic notes between us over the next thirteen years. What remained in its place was a connection through knowledge and pain that could not withstand the normal rules or limits of a friendship. Shared pain can sometimes be too heavy for the fragile bridge that connects two people. I knew too much about her and she was trying desperately to live without the pain, the humiliation, the shame, the brutal truth of her past, of which I was now aware. Our relationship may have gone in another direction under different circumstances, and I often wondered about those bends in the road that we failed to recognize or feared to take. Now it was much too late. We had both set a compass for certain, nonintersecting directions.

I had no reason not to believe Anne Rose, who has since rejoined another convent, a cloistered community this time so that she no longer has any contact with the world at all. But I have found no such exit, and her experience, which implicated Sister Thomas, confirmed my uneasiness and abiding distrust of her. It also identified and transcended my worst suspicions about her and her contact with my dear friend Angela. I was disarmed too, left with this information and no court of justice. Some day, I vowed, *I would tell the truth.*

But how could I be certain what the truth was exactly? And to whom would I tell it?

\*     \*     \*

# Epilogue

# Turning Forward

I sit here in the present examining two photographs. In the first one, two young women are wearing black calf-length overcoats and short less-than-stylish hairdos. They are standing so closely together that it's difficult to discern where the black form of the one ends and the other begins. It's a tiny picture, no more than two inches by two inches, and it is slightly yellowed and stained with age. Facial characteristics are indistinct, but it is clear that both nuns appear to be happy. The shorter one on the left is smiling broadly, and the other—taller by an inch or so—returns the camera's gaze with a bent, shy smile. These are certainly not the faces of children, but they share an expression of innocence and eagerness found only in the very young. The modified long dresses and short hairstyles tell me that this picture was taken in late 1968 or early 1969, after some of the Vatican changes had taken effect and altered the dress code in the Roman Catholic convent where we met and became friends, and where she died a few years later. She had barely made a dent in her twenties.

The second is a Polaroid picture that has been trimmed on either side so as to fit something, such as a plastic covering or a wallet. The two figures in this slightly larger and clearer photo are clad in full-length black dresses, an indication that the picture was taken a year or two before the previous one of me and Angela was taken. Anne Rose, the young nun on the right, wears the full habit, which signifies that she has graduated from the novitiate and taken her vows. She is a professed nun. The other is a novice. Although the figures do not blend into one another as they do in the first photo, each one extends an arm around the waist of the other, giving an impression of connectedness. They are smiling and squinting into the late afternoon sunlight while standing on a blanket of grass against a wooded area in the background. The trees, except for a lone pine, are sparsely covered, and the shrubbery appears faded and yellow: fall arranging itself to meet winter?

Fingering the thirty-some-year-old photographs, adding yet more thumbprints, I stare at the first picture of Angela and me, and then at the other picture of Anne Rose and me and wonder: whence those quixotic faces?

No matter how hard I concentrate, I cannot recall how the picture of Angela and me came to be taken in what I can clearly identify as the community room in the newly built juniorate house on the motherhouse grounds. It had to be one of those rare and short periods of time in the juniorate following Angela's recovery from her first bout with what proved to be her protracted and fatal illness. Was it on a visiting Sunday? It must have been because we appear to be dressed in our Sunday garb rather than in our workweek "swishies," and in those days, we did not have access to cameras, except on visiting Sundays and the occasional feast-day celebration.

I vaguely recall how the other photograph came to be taken. I was making my way along the gravel path from the novitiate to the motherhouse when I encountered Anne Rose who was with her family on the convent grounds one visiting Sunday. She was a junior sister, having successfully completed the trial-novitiate period, while I was still a novice and so not allowed to have visitors of my own. I waved hello to Anne Rose, who stood on the grass with her family members gathered awkwardly around her, and she summoned me to come over and meet her parents, two sisters, and brother. I remember noting how shy and handsome her younger brother looked, and how he shared his older sister's radiant smile. Out of place in the company of so many women, despite his father's imposing presence, he seemed relieved to have something to do when Anne Rose asked him to snap the photo of the two of us.

And that's what I have. A couple of pictures to go with the holy cards and notes I have saved, along with a Blessed Mother medal, a few written mementos, a tiny journal of my meditations, and a trunk full of memories. I cannot summon all the factual details around the occasion of the photographs themselves, but I can surmise them, for the world in which they were taken remains real and palpable. It lives with me, ever present, omnipresent like the childhood that has come and gone, leaving its indelible imprint on my spirit. I cannot place it. I cannot point to it. I know only what it *was*, is. It flickers within me like an eternal flame.

I now realize that Angela did not die because of something I did. My young dear friend died. I'm not sure why, or what caused it, or whether, with better care and vigilance, it may have been prevented. I do know that she was overworked and rundown by the convent routine, as we all were, but unlike most of the rest of us her body could not withstand the rigorous demands of convent labor and training. The circumstances around her illness and isolation were curious and enigmatic. Her ill health was too long ignored because of some misguided notion about the virtues of suffering and silence. I do know that by our third year, she was isolated and separated from her classmates for reasons unclear and unexplained to us, and this separation came to be—more than physical—emotional, spiritual, psychological, and perhaps all three. I cannot pinpoint exactly when or how she was altered. I only know that one day my dear, *particular* friend became a stranger. I lost her, the way one unwittingly loses a child, only to be left bewildered and wondering what I had done wrong and how the outcome might have been prevented or altered. For years afterwards guilt has hung from my heart like an iron anchor that rusts but does not weigh less with time.

No, I did not cause her death but during her long, mysterious illness, I sensed that something was terribly wrong. Neglect, maybe. Some kind of religious perversion or brainwashing, possibly. No, it's not what I *did* do; it's what I did *not* do: confront my superiors, appeal to an outside authority, and risk myself to help or protect my friend. But I was an insecure and frightened schoolgirl in the formidable house of the church.

Perhaps nothing would have come of it even if I had. Or, conceivably, I may have learned that there was a plausible explanation for all of my troubling suspicions about the way she was isolated and kept from her classmates, and the revelation of Anne Rose's molestation a few years after Angela's death would no longer haunt me. Or would it?

Anne Rose's account of her molestation by two senior sisters during her first mission muddles such a scenario raising, as it does, the specter of another horror with a name and a picture of the nun who was responsible for Angela's well-being. I could never quite absorb the implications of the fact that the same person who was authorized and sanctioned by the community to supervise the physical and spiritual well-being of the naive and vulnerable junior sisters was one of Anne Rose's alleged molesters.

So many times I have asked myself: was Anne Rose telling me the truth? Again and again I have arrived at the same conclusion. Why would she have contrived such a story, especially when there was nothing to be gained from it nearly four years after our departure from the community? And I never knew her to speak a mistruth. Yes, she was foolishly naive, as was I. And yes, I loved her, as she, I believe, loved me. On several occasions I proclaimed my love for her, and she did the same, but we lacked worldly experience and we had no other way of understanding and framing this love but as an extension of God's love for us and our love for him. We were nuns, after all, dedicated to living a chaste life in the service of God. In our passionless beds at night we felt yearnings, but these were temptations to be reported to the priest in the confessional, not feelings to be acted upon. At least, not for us. In our relations we never got beyond soulful looks, tender handclasps and touching, and warm but controlled hugs. I had no words other than spiritual love to characterize the cauldron of unexpressed emotions within me, and although they troubled me at times—because wasn't all love from God and, therefore, pure and good?—I chalked up the need to *express* love to temptation that threatened my chaste and obedient life. We learned to seal our emotions and inclinations with the cement of discipline and prayer and labor. And silence, of course. But natural things often find a way of seeking the light and sprouting through cracks. Perhaps some, in the process, become deformed.

One night in the juniorate, shortly before Anne Rose's departure to her first mission and after the fainting episode when I awoke to her in my bed, I came unnervingly close to naming this "temptation." It was prompted, I suppose, by a painful awareness that Anne Rose and I might be forever separated once she was gone from the motherhouse, and I was sent on my own first mission the following year. Oh, we might bump into each other at Christmas or Easter at the motherhouse from time to time, but we would never again share the same house, the same duties, the same concerns, the same community life together. In her infinite wisdom Mother Superior surely realized that ours was a friendship to be monitored, and I guess it was.

That evening, tortured by an unidentifiable desire, I crept from my room around midnight or so and found myself tapping wistfully on her door. It was as if she had been waiting for me when she wordlessly ushered me into her dimly lit room. Night Silence was in force, but that is not what prevented me from speaking. There was another person directing my body, someone—me but not me—who wouldn't permit me to express myself in any other way. I found my way to the window, where I proceeded to remove my black robe and white pajamas until I was naked, revealed to myself and her in this room as I had never been in my adult life, exposed for the first time as a sexual being. I leaned against the heating unit beneath the window, with my head and body half-turned to the window, staring out at the black world between the white blind slats. I was transfixed by the torrent of incomprehensible emotions coursing through me, silencing me, like the rush of a powerful waterfall. I have no idea what Anne Rose was feeling or thinking, as she, too, never spoke. And though I sensed her glancing at me from time to time from the chair at her desk where she sat with a book in front of what must have been blind eyes, she made no gesture of approval or disapproval. I couldn't think what I wanted from me or from her. I certainly couldn't act. At last, after maybe twenty minutes or so, maybe more—I had no way of knowing as time did not exist—my other self ordered me to gather up my bedclothes and put them back on. Then I stumbled out the door and back to my own room where I fell across the bed and wept as a child does, with quick, breathy sobs and complete abandon, fully aware that I had fallen, like Adam and Eve.

After that episode I was relieved by Anne Rose's departure for her first mission and the space that it gave me, which is why we lost contact over that next year and I heard nothing of her ordeal at the hands of her new superior. After a complete confession to God, if not to the priest, I felt freed from the paralysis and confusion caused by the storm of my feelings for Anne Rose. I returned to the purity of my religious vocation with renewed dedication and zeal. For a time, anyway, I successfully disregarded and avoided the cracks in my newly patched vocation.

Anne Rose, I imagine, responded to this event and to her own humanity much as I did, with denial and repression. I do not know that for a fact since we never discussed what *didn't* happen that night in her room. But I am certain that we were cut from the same pious and artless cloth and ached to be pure, virtuous, and committed nuns in the service of God. How ironic that, despite the intensity of our desire and the strength of our efforts, we both ended up abandoning our shared religious vocation. Fully cognizant, though, of the force of her commitment to her religious vocation, I was not really surprised when, several years later, she called to tell me of her decision to reenter a cloistered community somewhere in the Midwest. We exchanged notes maybe two or three times after that, until the heavy curtain of the grandest of all grand silences finally sealed her from the world and effectively terminated our friendship.

The implications of Anne Rose's revelation about being molested rekindled my angst over Angela's loss and my failure to help her. At the time, I craved justice, and maybe even revenge. I wanted someone to pay, to suffer, to answer for the terrible wrongs that had been committed in God's house. But who was to blame? Except for a single individual with a face and a name, the enemy was invisible, unlocatable and lost inside the convent jungle. And where was the evidence? In the convent the imprints of fallen nun aspirants lay everywhere, like memories along dustless corridors and sparkling floors—dead soldiers left behind on a bloodless battlefield—palpable but invisible. In the face of missing bodies, crimes could not be proven. Besides, after four years of learning and practicing silence, I was mute. So I tried to braid the strands of my fractured life and waited for my paralyzed vocal chords to heal. Telling my story, finally, has healed my vocal chords.

And now? Time folds like the sand with the current of ocean waters, down and back, appearing, disappearing, reappearing. It does not go away and it never comes back, slipping, as it does, forever and back on to itself. I am different. I am the same. I forget. I remember. I cannot see the sand that slides beneath the folds because I am the sand. I cannot see the picture in which I stand, but I know that the truth, some truth, is in the picture.

And now? Justice, anger, and revenge sit on my palm like the seeds on a dandelion weed. Justice, I see, is an unreliable changeling that is not to be expected in this world, and while anger serves the purpose of propelling us forward, it eventually strangles the soul. As for its handmaiden, revenge—it is a pointless poison. With a mighty puff, I blow and watch their seeds flutter and fly on the wind's breath.

Made in the USA
Lexington, KY
07 November 2010